Attention is directed to the penalties attaching to any infraction of the Official Secrets Acts

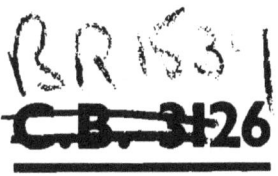

BRITISH MUNITIONS

RECOGNITION AND DISPOSAL

(For Bomb Safety Officers)

1944

The Naval & Military Press Ltd

UNEXPLODED BOMB DISPOSAL DEPT.,
ADMIRALTY.

U.B. 294/43.

Published by

The Naval & Military Press Ltd
Unit 5 Riverside, Brambleside,
Bellbrook Industrial Estate,
Uckfield, East Sussex,
TN22 1QQ England

Tel: +44 (0) 1825 749494
Fax: +44 (0) 1825 765701

www.naval-military-press.com
www.nmarchive.com

The Library & Archives Department at the Royal Armouries Museum, Leeds, specialises in the history and development of armour and weapons from earliest times to the present day. Material relating to the development of artillery and modern fortifications is held at the Royal Armouries Museum, Fort Nelson.

For further information contact:
Royal Armouries Museum, Library, Armouries Drive, Leeds, West Yorkshire LS10 1LT
Royal Armouries, Library, Fort Nelson, Down End Road, Fareham PO17 6AN

Or visit the Museum's website at
www.armouries.org.uk

PUBLISHERS NOTE:

This reprint of the original working copy taken from the MOD Pattern Room Library contains many tip-in amendments and hand written corrections. In order to accommodate these, some pages have been intentionally duplicated and the handwritten amendments have been left unedited.

In reprinting in facsimile from the original, any imperfections are inevitably reproduced and the quality may fall short of modern type and cartographic standards.

AMENDMENTS

AUTHORITY	Amendment No.	Inserted by	Date
DUBD. technique. cancelled CAFO-P.1641/44.)	No. 1.	Barlo.	9 May 1944.
P.575/44.	No. 2.	"	22.2.45.
P.6/45.	No. 3	"	2-3-45.

ADMIRALTY, S.W.1.
January, 1944.

The accompanying book, "British Munitions—Recognition and Disposal," having been approved by My Lords Commissioners of the Admiralty, is hereby promulgated for information and guidance.

By Command of Their Lordships.

H. V. Markham

BRITISH MUNITIONS

INTRODUCTION

1. In the British Isles, unexploded British bombs will normally be dealt with by the R.A.F. The circumstances, where action by Naval parties will be required, are set out in current A.F.O.s.

2. Overseas, the disposal of British bombs is primarily a function of the R.A.F., but occasions will arise where action by Naval parties will be essential, in order that danger to Naval personnel and material and to objects of Naval importance may be prevented. Any bombs that can be left without interference with Naval objectives or operations should be left. Bombs which can be detonated *in situ* should be so dealt with; and normally this should be the method of disposal resorted to. Bombs, which by reason of their position present a danger to Naval operations, should be dealt with as set out in the accompanying directions; but where the nature of the fuze, or fuzes, cannot be ascertained or determined, work must proceed, on the assumption that the bomb may fire on movement or through delay action; the advisability of detonating such bombs *in situ* should therefore be borne well in mind.

3. In enemy territory, detonation *in situ*, where the effects of detonation will not adversely affect operations should be the general rule.

BRITISH MUNITIONS

Part I　　　　　　　　　Recognition

Part II　　　　..　　　Rendering Safe and Disposal, etc.

Notes

(*a*) Diagrams and photographs are situated at the end of the relevant chapter.

(*b*) After recognising a munition from Part I, do not touch that munition until the relevant section in Part II has been read.

(*c*) A distinction is drawn between a fuze and a pistol in British bombs.

A *pistol* is used in combination with a separate detonator. There is no explosive included in the pistol itself.

A *fuze* has its own cap and magazine as an integral part of the fuze.

(*d*) There is not a diagram or photograph of each munition; therefore if a munition is recognised as similar, but not identical, to a given diagram or photograph, always refer to the text on the munition shown and see whether there is another related munition, *e.g.*, the G.P. 250 lb., Mark IV, is not shown, but it is the same shape as a G.P. 500 lb., Mark IV, although smaller.

PART I

RECOGNITION

Chapter	Pages
I.—H.E. Bombs and their Fuzes or Pistols	1
II.—Incendiaries and Pyrotechnics	19
III.—Depth Charges Dropped from Aircraft	34
IV.—Aircraft-laid Mines	35
V.—Rocket Devices	36
VI.—Miscellaneous Devices	38

CHAPTER I

H.E. BOMBS AND THEIR FUZES OR PISTOLS

N.B.—Diagrams 1–3 and Figures 1–31 are at the end of the chapter.

Section	Page
1.—Notes on Bomb Racks	1
2.—Notes on Carrying Small Bombs	2
3.—Anti-personnel Bombs	3
4.—General Purpose Bombs	4
5.—Semi Armour-piercing Bombs	6
6.—Armour-piercing Bombs	7
7.—Anti-submarine Bombs	8
8.—High Capacity Bombs	9
9.—Medium Capacity Bombs	10
10.—Anti-tank Bombs	11
11.—Fuzes used in H.E. Bombs	12
12.—Pistols used in H.E. Bombs	14
13.—Miscellaneous : (a) 6 lb. Infantry Training Bomb	18
(b) 250lb "B" Bomb.	18.
(c) 6 lb Training Bomb H.E.	18A.

CHAPTER I

SECTION 1.—NOTES ON BOMB RACKS

The bombs are held by electrically controlled release slips. Fuzes are armed in two stages, firstly by the removal of a safety pin by the armourer and secondly, by the withdrawal of safety forks by wires, called fuze-setting control links, which pass from the safety forks to electrically controlled fuzing boxes. To drop a bomb " safe," the end of the link in the fuzing box is released so that the safety fork is not withdrawn from the fuze or pistol when the bomb drops, but drops with the bomb.

Part I, Chapter I

SECTION 2.—NOTES ON CARRYING SMALL BOMBS

(a) 250-lb. Small Bomb Container

These are rectangular metal boxes without bottoms. They are suspended in the normal bomb racks and are used for carrying small bombs and pyrotechnics. The bombs are held in by drop bars which have special release slips. The bombs are dropped by releasing the bars. They can only be dropped safe by jettisoning the whole container. There are adjustable bulkheads which are positioned in the container according to the requirement of the bombs that are being carried.

(b) Light Series Carriers

These are carried by the normal bomb racks and themselves carry four bombs. Each bomb is held in a small rack.

~~(c) Clusters~~

~~In the near future small bombs will be carried in clusters which will open in mid air.~~

Cluster Projectiles

1. Cluster projectiles are used, as an alternative to the small bomb container, for the carrying and dropping of incendiary bombs.

2. They are also used for carrying and dropping of reconnaissance flares of various types.

3. The following types have received official nomenclature :—

   (a) Cluster projectile aircraft, 18-in., 270-lb., No. 1, Mark I, carrying 7 by 4·5-in. reconnaissance flares.

   (b) Cluster projectile aircraft, 12-in., 140-lb., No. 2, Mark I, carrying 4 by 4·5-in. reconnaissance flares.

   (c) Cluster projectile aircraft, 18-in., 400-lb., No. 3, Mark I, carrying 4 by 7-in. hooded flares.

   (d) Cluster projectile aircraft, 500-lb., No. 4, Mark I, carrying 14-lb. by 30-lb. " J " incendiary bombs. Fuzed tail fuze, No. 867, Mark I (see Section 11).

   (e) Cluster projectile aircraft, 500-lb., No. 14, Mark I, carrying 106 by 4-lb. incendiary bombs.

   (f) Cluster projectile aircraft, 750-lb., No. 15, Mark I, carrying 158 by 4-lb. incendiary bombs.

   After (f) add :—

   (g) Cluster, Projectile, Aircraft, 500 lb., No. 7, Mark V, carrying 56 8 lb., " F," Mark II, Bombs.

   (h) Cluster, Projectile, Aircraft, 500 lb., No. 6, Mark I, Smoke.

(T. 06720/44.—C.A.F.O. P.6/45.)

CONFIDENTIAL

C.B.3126 - Amendment No.1   March 1944

British Cluster Projectile A/C)
500 lb. No.14 Mark I Incendiary) see figs. 19 and 20

General

1. The Cluster Projectile Aircraft 500 lb. No.14 Mark I Incendiary, will shortly be introduced into **service**.

2. It is designed to replace the Small Bomb Container as a means of carrying 4 lb. Incendiary Bombs.

Description

1. The Cluster Projectile (2) measuring 67" long by 14" in diameter and weighing approximately 450 lb. when filled, contains 106 - 4 lb. Incendiary Bombs arranged in 2 faggots of 53 bombs, arranged nose to tail, with all safety plungers facing inwards.

2. The bombs are retained in position by the front and rear end plates (20) and (18), the top and bottom beams (3) and (13), four wooden slats (7) and four tensioning straps (5).

3. Lateral pins (22) on the retaining bar (1) engage with and hold in position the tabs (19) of the tensioning straps (5).

4. A shear wire (4) near the nose end of the retaining bar (1) acts as a safety device.

5. To the rear end of the retaining bar (1) is secured the pivoted lever (16) the opposite end of which engages the piston (8) in the fuze adapter (9).

6. The fuze adapter is fixed to the channel plate (11) which in turn is fastened to the rear end plate (18).

7. A nut (10) welded to the centre of the rear end plate (18) receives the tail tie rod (14) to which is secured the tail unit (12) by a tensioning nut.

8. ...

8. The tail unit No.42 Mark I measuring 21" long by 14" in diameter is located by the two dowel pins (17) and is provided with two inspection windows (15) to ensure correct alignment of the arming forks when air armed fuzes are used.

> NOTE: At present the cluster projectile is fuzed with a No.42 Mk.IV fuze (see Chap. II Section 11) and one of the inspection windows is removed to allow the fuzing link to be attached to the fuze setting control link.

9. A suspension lug (23) and rear fairing (6) is fitted to the top beam (3) and a nose fairing (24) is secured to the front-end plate (20).

10. Holes (21) on the top beam are provided for fixing American suspension lugs when the cluster is carried on American type aircraft.

Action

1. On release from the aircraft the Cluster Projectile falls in a normal manner until the fuze functions.

2. The explosion in the magazine forces the piston (8) forward in its housing to cause a rocking movement of the pivoted lever (16).

3. The sudden movement of the pivoted lever exerts a pull on the retaining bar (1) to break the shear wire (4) and to disengage the lateral pins (22) from the tabs (19) of the tensioning straps (5).

4. The straps thus released fly outwards, to release the bombs which function normally on impact.

British Cluster Projectile A/C 750 lb. No.15 Mark I

General

1. The Cluster Projectile Aircraft No.15 Mark I Incendiary will shortly be introduced into service.

2. It is designed to replace the Small Bomb Container as a means of carrying 4 lb. Incendiary Bombs.

Description ...

Description

1. The Cluster Projectile, measuring 67" long by 17.3" in diameter and weighing 650 lb. approximately when filled, contains 158 x 4 lb. Incendiary Bombs, arranged in 2 faggots of 79 bombs each

2. In all details other than the tail unit it is identical with the Cluster Projectile 500 lb. No.14 Mark I Incendiary described on page 2a.

3. It is fitted with a tail unit No.43 Mark I, measuring 21" long by 17.3" in diameter.

Action

The action is identical with that described on page 2a for the 500 lb. No.14 Mark I Cluster Projectile.

British Cluster Projectile A/C 18" 270 lb. No.1 Mark I) see figs. 21 and 22.

General

1. The Cluster Projectile A/C 18" 270 lb. No.1 Mark I will shortly be introduced into service.

2. The cluster holds 7 x 4.5" reconnaissance flares.

Description

1. The Cluster Projectile A/C 18" No.1 Mark I is a cylindrical container measuring 62¾" overall, 18" in diameter and weighs approximately 260 lb. when filled.

2. It consists of the nose unit (9) recessed to receive the noses of 7 x 4.5" recco flares and the fuze adapter (5) from which radiate six flash tubes (6) to the igniters (3) and three flash channels (11) leading to the explosive pellets in the piston housing (12).

3. The nose unit is secured to the panel locating plate (10) and the tail plate (4) by the T-section suspension bar (1) and the clamping bars (2).

4. The clamping bars (2) consist of a bar to which is welded two panels.

5. The clamping bars (2) locate the panels (8) and are secured through the panel locating plate (10) to the tail plate (4) and to the nose unit (9) by spring washers and nuts.

6. The nuts securing the clamping bars to the piston housings (12) are further secured by split pins.

7. The tail tie rod (13) is screwed into the tail plate (4) and the tail unit (7) fastened to it by a spring washer and nut.

8. The 7 x 4.5" recco flares from which the suspension lug and domed caps have been removed are located by the recesses in the nose unit (9) and panel locating plate (10).

9. The flares are fuzed with special igniters (3) consisting of the body and dome portion of the No.42 fuze without the percussion cap and striker mechanism and sealed with primed cambric.

10. A No.42, 848, 849 or 860 Mk.II nose fuze is screwed into the fuze adapter (5).

Action

1. On release from the aircraft the cluster falls normally until the fuze functions.

2. When the fuze functions the flash from the magazine passes through the flash tubes (6) to ignite the igniters (3) in the nose of each flare and through the flash channels (5) to explode the gunpowder pellets in the piston housings (12).

3. The explosion of the pellets forces the pistons out of their housings (12) causing the clamping bars (2) to swing outwards, thereby releasing the nose unit, panels and initiated flares.

4. The flares then function in the normal manner.

British ...

British Cluster Projectile A/C 500 lb.)
No. 4 Mark I Incendiary 'J'   ) see figs. 23 and 24).

General

1. The Cluster Projectile aircraft 500 lb. No.4 Mark I Incendiary 'J' will shortly be introduced into service.

2. It is designed to replace the Small Bomb Container as a means of carrying 30 lb. 'J' type incendiary bombs.

Description

1. The Cluster Projectile, hexagonal in shape, measures 69" long by 15" in diameter and weighs, when filled, 477 lb. approx.

2. It contains 14-30 lb. 'J' Incendiary bombs in two faggots of 7 bombs each, the bombs being placed nose to nose and arranged in superimposed rows of 2, 3 and 2, in each faggot.

3. The bombs are retained in position by the front and rear end plates (1) and (12), the top and bottom beams (7), the side fairings (13), tensioning straps (9) and the retaining bar (5).

4. The front and rear end plates (1) and (12) secure the spring loaded covers of the bomb parasheet containers.

5. Lateral pins (8) on the retaining bar (5) engage with and hold in position the tabs (3) of the tensioning straps (9).

6. A shear wire near the rear end plate acts as a safety device for the retaining bar.

7. To the rear end of the retaining bar (5) is secured the pivoted lever (17) the lower end of which engages with the piston (18) in the fuze adapter (11).

8. The fuze adapter is fixed to the channel plate (20) which, in turn, is fastened to the rear end plate (12).

9. A nut (19) welded to the centre of the rear end plate (12) receives the tail tie rod (16) to which the tail unit is secured by a tension nut.

10. ...

10. The tail unit No.44 Mark I, measuring 25.75 in. long by 15 in. in diameter, is located by the two dowel pins (13) and is provided with two inspection windows (21) to ensure correct alignment of the arming forks.

11. A suspension lug (6) is fitted to the top beam (7) and tapped holes (10) are also provided for the fitment of American lugs where necessary.

12. A nose fairing is secured to the front end plate (1) and fairings are fitted to the top beam, the fairing adjoining the rear end plate (7) being slotted (14) to receive the fuzing lanyard of the fuze.

13. The cluster is fuzed with a No.867 Mark I tail fuze and the fuze setting control link is connected directly to the fuzing lanyard of the fuze (22) and to the safety wire (23) of the tail unit.

NOTE: The part of the transit casing (24) shown is not a part of the cluster projectile.

Action

1. On release from the aircraft, the fuze setting control link withdraws the safety wire from the tail unit and at the same time, breaks the shear wire of the fuze by means of the fuzing lanyard.

2. The cluster falls normally until the fuze functions.

3. The explosion in the magazine forces the piston (18) forward in its housing to cause a rocking movement of the pivoted lever (17).

4. The sudden movement of the pivoted lever exerts a pull on the retaining bar (5) to break its shear wire and disengage the lateral pins (8) from the tabs (3) of the tensioning straps (9).

5. The straps, thus released, fly outwards, to release the 14 bombs which on impact function normally.

SECTION 3.—ANTI-PERSONNEL BOMBS

20-lb. F. (fragmentation).
20-lb. F. with parachute.
40-lb. G.P.
40-lb. G.P. with parachute.

1. **20-lb. F.** (*See* Diagram No. 2 (includes dimensions).)

Fuzing.—No. 34 nose pistol, or ⎫
No. 38 nose pistol, or ⎬ *See* Section 118/12 for details of the pistols.
No. 45 nose pistol. ⎭ — N° 873 nose fuse.

Colour and Markings.—Bomb body and tail are yellow.

There is a ½-in. red band round the body, ½-in. from the nose, indicating the bomb is filled H.E., and a 1-in. green band 4 in. from the nose, indicating the type of explosive used. The filling is indicated by stencil markings on the green band, e.g., T.N.T. or R.D.X./T.N.T. is stencilled on the band in black.

Other markings are stencilled on the bomb in black, such as lot number, etc.

General Remarks.—The tail is secured by a central bolt and is a cylinder held by fins to the tail cone.
The bombs are usually carried in small bomb containers, 12 per container.
Some bombs have no suspension lug.

20-lb. F. with Parachute

Fuzing.—No. 33 nose pistol.

Colouring and Markings.—As for 20-lb. F.

General Remarks.—The bomb is like the ordinary 20-lb. F., but is adapted in the same way as the 40-lb. G.P. with a parachute attachment (*see* later).

3. **40-lb. G.P.** (*See* Diagram 2. " 8 lb. F. (Fragmentation) ".)

Fuzing.—No. 34 nose pistol, or ⎫
No. 38 nose pistol, or ⎬ *See* Section 115/12 for details of the pistols.
No. 45 nose pistol. ⎭ — N° 873 Nose fuse.

Colour and Markings.—The bomb and tail are painted dark green.

There is a ½-in. red band 1-in. from the nose, indicating that it is filled H.E., and a 1-in. light green band round the maximum diameter with black stencilling to indicate the type of filling.

Other markings, such as lot number, etc., are stencilled in black on the bomb.

General Remarks.—The tail is similar to the 20-lb. F.

The bombs are carried six in a small bomb container, together with two packing pieces. Often the packing pieces are left out and eight bombs are carried per container.

Some types have no suspension lug.

5. *8 lb. F.* (see Figure 27 (includes dimensions)).

Fuzing.—880, 881 or 883 Tail Fuze (*see* Section 11). Difficult to distinguish the above types visually.

Colour and Markings.—Green with a red band round the body.

General Remarks.—The bombs are carried in a cluster, projectile No. 7, Mark I, which contains 56 bombs.

On release from the cluster, air pressure removes the closing plate of the bomb and this in turn pulls out the parachute. The parachute opens and the arming cord (attached to two of the parachute cords) pulls out the fuze safety-pin. The fuze arms on impact with the ground.

40-lb. G.P., but the central parachute is held in by a .. The lid is attached to the wn the outside of the bomb ens it arms the pistol. This by full lines.

Notes.—(a) The closing plate attached to the parachute by a thin cord keeps the parachute in position while the bomb is in the cluster.

(b) The safety bolt and long steel pin shown in the diagram will never be found in position. They are safe in transporting before the bombs are fitted into the cluster.

(c) Once the safety-pin is removed from the fuzes it is impossible to replace it.

(*T. 06720/44.—C.A.F.O. P.6/45.*)

SECTION 3.—ANTI-PERSONNEL BOMBS

20-lb. F. (fragmentation).
20-lb. F. with parachute.
40-lb. G.P.
40-lb. G.P. with parachute.

20-lb. F. (*See* Diagram No. 2 (includes dimensions).)

Fuzing.—No. 34 nose pistol, or ⎫
No. 38 nose pistol, or ⎬ *See* Section 12 for details of the pistols.
No. 45 nose pistol. ⎭ — N° 873 nose fuse.

Colour and Markings.—Bomb body and tail are yellow.

There is a ½-in. red band round the body, ½-in. from the nose, indicating the bomb is filled H.E., and a 1-in. green band 4 in. from the nose, indicating the type of explosive used. The filling is indicated by stencil markings on the green band, *e.g.*, T.N.T. or R.D.X./T.N.T. is stencilled on the band in black.

Other markings are stencilled on the bomb in black, such as lot number, etc,

General Remarks.—The tail is secured by a central bolt and is a cylinder held by fins to the tail cone.

The bombs are usually carried in small bomb containers, 12 per container.

Some bombs have no suspension lug.

20-lb. F. with Parachute

Fuzing.—No. 33 nose pistol.

Colouring and Markings.—As for 20-lb. F.

General Remarks.—The bomb is like the ordinary 20-lb. F., but is adapted in the same way as the 40-lb. G.P. with a parachute attachment (*see* later).

40-lb. G.P. (*See* Diagram 2. " 8 lb. F. (Fragmentation) ".

Fuzing.—No. 34 nose pistol, or ⎫
No. 38 nose pistol, or ⎬ *See* Section 12 for details of the pistols.
No. 45 nose pistol. ⎭ — N° 873 Nose fuse.

Colour and Markings.—The bomb and tail are painted dark green.

There is a ½-in. red band 1-in. from the nose, indicating that it is filled H.E., and a 1-in. light green band round the maximum diameter with black stencilling to indicate the type of filling.

Other markings, such as lot number, etc., are stencilled in black on the bomb.

General Remarks.—The tail is similar to the 20-lb. F.

The bombs are carried six in a small bomb container, together with two packing pieces. Often the packing pieces are left out and eight bombs are carried per container.

Some types have no suspension lug.

40-lb. G.P. with Parachute (*see* Diagram 2)

Fuzing.—No. 33 nose pistol (*see* Section 12).

Colour and Markings.—As for 40-lb. G.P.

General Remarks.—As can be seen in the diagram the bomb is like the ordinary 40-lb. G.P., but the central part of the tail has been enlarged into a cylinder which takes the parachute. The parachute is held in by a lid which overlaps this central cylinder and just fits in the outer cylinder of the tail. The lid is attached to the parachute and acts as a pilot chute to draw out the main parachute. A wire runs down the outside of the bomb from the arming pin of the pistol to the parachute so that when the parachute opens it arms the pistol. This wire is held to the side of the bomb by three strips of tape shown in the diagram by full lines.

SECTION 4.—GENERAL PURPOSE BOMBS

40-lb. G.P. (*see* Section 3).
G.P. 250 lb. and 500 lb., Mark III.
G.P. 250 lb., Mark IV (Fig. 1).
G.P. 500 lb., Mark IV (Diagram 1).
G.P. 250 lb. and 500 lb., Mark V.
G.P. 1,000 lb., Marks I and II (Diagram 1).
G.P. 1,000 lb., Marks III and IV.
G.P. 1,900 lb., Mark I (Diagram 1).
G.P. 4,000 lb., Marks I and II (Diagram 1).

American An-M-type bombs.

General Notes on G.P. Bombs

1. *Colour and Markings.*—The bombs and tails are painted dark green. There is a ½-in. red band 1 in. from the nose to indicate that the filling is H.E. and a 1-in. light green band round, or just forward of, the maximum diameter on which, or just below which, is stencilled in black the type of filling in three places round the bomb.

2. Other details are stencilled in black on the bomb, such as maker's monogram, date, etc.

3. If a No. 37 or 17 pistol is used the arming vanes in the tail are red.

4. *Description.*—The bombs are streamlined and heavy cased (C.W. ratio about 30 per cent.). They are used for general bombardment. They can be fuzed nose and tail, and have exploder pockets at either end, with the exception of the G.P. 250 lb. and 500 lb., Marks III and V, which have a central tube going right through the length of the bomb. The exploder pockets screw into the bombs and are themselves threaded to take the pistol or fuze. The priming pellets are held in position by the detonator adaptor and are usually left in the bomb. The central tube type of bombs have separate exploders.

5. *Fuzing.*—There are three schemes for fuzing G.P. bombs, with the exception of the G.P. 250 and 500 lb., Marks III and V, which will be dealt with separately. The schemes are:—

   (a) No. 28 tail pistol alone or with a No. 27 nose pistol.
   (b) No. 30 tail pistol alone or with a No. 42 or No. 44 nose pistol.
   (c) ~~No. 37, Mark III or IV long delay and anti-withdrawal tail pistol and No. 845, Mark II, anti-handling fuze.~~ *No. 845, Mk II anti-handling fuze. Note. This fuze is obsolete.*

   N.B.—Arming vanes for the No. 37, Marks III or IV pistols, are always red.

6. *Notes.*—If a tail pistol is used by itself the nose has a screw bung in position. For details of fuzes and pistols, *see* Sections 11 and 12.

7. *Tails.*—In general, the tail has a cylindrical tail vane of the same diameter as the bomb. This is held to a central cone by vane supports. The cone is secured to the bomb.

8. There are different types of tail which can be used for the same bomb. These will be indicated in the notes on the bombs given below. When a clip-on tail is referred to it means the tail is held in position by four spring clips. In the later types the clips are held down by rotating retaining strips. To remove a clip-on tail two adjacent clips should be released at the same time. Other tails are held on by four wing bolts. These are used in the bigger bombs and can be recognised by the holes in the tail cone which give access to the bolts.

9. Usually the difference between tails which can be used on the same bomb lies in the length of the tail vane. Originally the vanes were long, but short vanes have been introduced. Some are to facilitate the stowage of bombs in given racks and others so that the bombs may be carried externally in fast aircraft.

10. The tail pistols or fuzes are screwed in the base of the bomb and are armed by rods which pass up the centre of the tail cone and are attached to arming vanes, of which there are normally four. When short tail vanes are used for external stowage, then the number of arming vanes is reduced to two.

C.A.F.O. P.575/44

Add new page 5a.

5a

28. *Some American AN-M series bombs used in British Aircraft* :—

　　AN-M 44 and 65　..　1,000 lb. bombs.
　　AN-M 43 and 64　..　500 lb. bombs.
　　AN-M 57　..　..　250 lb. bomb.

Details are as given in C.B. 3131, except that the tail units are in two cases of the drum type secured by the usual American type locking ring.

　　1,000 lb.—Tail unit No. 55, Mark I, measures 18·5 in. by 18·8 in.
　　500 lb.—Tail unit No. 54, Mark I, measures 14 in. by 14·2 in.
　　250 lb.—Normal American tail unit.

29. Tail fuzes are those normal to American bombs, but the British No. 52, Mark I, nose pistol (*see* Section 12) with a special exploder adapter, is used in the nose.

(*U.B. 294/43.—C.A.F.O. P.575/44.*)

(*Previous amendment No. 1.—C.A.F.O. P.464/44.*)

G.P. 250 lb. and 500 lb., Mark III

11. For size and shape *see* the Mark IV's, from which they differ in having a central tube instead of exploder pockets. They are fuzed with a No. 19 nose pistol and a No. 22 tail pistol, and the exploders are fitted into the central tube.

12. These bombs are obsolescent.

N.B.—Unlike the Mark V bombs, the central tube extends to the point of the tail cone.

G.P. 250 lb., Mark IV

13. Similar to the G.P. 500 lb. (*see* Diagram 1). It differs only in size.

Dimensions.—Length, 4 ft. 8 in. Diameter, 10·2 in.

14. The bomb is suspended horizontally by a lug. The tail is always of the long clip-on variety.

15. The nose bung used when there is no nose pistol or fuze, is an eye bolt.

G.P. 500 lb., Mark IV (*see* Diagram 1)

16. The bomb is suspended horizontally by a lug.

17. The tail is either long (as in diagram) or short like the M.C. 1,000 lb. in the diagram. In the latter case it would not have the holes in the tail cone as it is a clip-on tail.

G.P. 250 lb., Mark V, and G.P. 500 lb., Mark V

18. The bombs are externally the same as the Mark IV, but have a central tube instead of the exploder pockets at either end. It is used by the Fleet Air Arm only. The fuzing is in the tail. The nose is closed with a bung which has a cross cut in it and not a ring as in the Mark IV bombs. The pistol used is the No. 17 long delay and anti-withdrawal (*see* Section 12). The exploders are put in when the bomb is fuzed.

N.B.—The arming vanes are red.

G.P. 1,000 lb.

19. Marks I and II are fuzed nose and tail.

20. Marks III and IV are fuzed tail only, and have a bung welded into the nose. The bung is shaped to give a pointed nose.

21. The bombs can be carried in 2,000-lb. bomb racks which use a locating lug and support the bombs by two straps going under the bomb bodies. Alternatively, the ordinary racks can be used.

22. The tails are of either the long or short type, held on by four wing bolts to the bomb base.

G.P. 1,900 lb., Mark I (*see* Diagram 1)

23. The bomb can be suspended by a lug or in a 2,000-lb. bomb rack with two straps passing under the bomb.

24. There is a shallow groove cut out of the bomb round the circumference at the suspension lug.

25. The tail is always of the long variety, with four wing bolts.

G.P. 4,000 lb. (*see* Diagram 1)

26. The two additional lugs are used for hoisting the bomb into the aircraft.

27. The tail is always as shown in the diagram.

Part I, Chapter I

SECTION 5.—SEMI ARMOUR-PIERCING BOMBS

S.A.P. 250 lb. and 500 lb., Marks III, IV and V (*see* Diagram 2, which includes dimensions).

General Notes on S.A.P. Bombs

1. *Colour and Markings.*—The bombs are painted dark green, with a ½-in. white band next to a ½-in. red band round the nose (the white band nearer the nose) and a light-green band round or near the maximum diameter of the bomb. The white/red band indicates an S.A.P. bomb filled H.E. and the green band has the type of filling stencilled on or close to it. Other markings, such as lot number, etc., are stencilled on the bomb, in black.

2. *Description.*—The bombs are fairly thick walled (C.W. ratio is rather less than 20 per cent.). They have pointed noses and are fuzed in the tail only. The different marks are the same size for given weights.

N.B.—S.A.P. bombs are smaller than G.P. bombs of the same weight.

Fuzing.—For details of fuzes and pistols, *see* Sections 11 and 12.

Mark III has a No. 30 tail fuze, and the locking ring has a left-hand thread.

Mark IV has a No. 30 tail fuze, and the locking ring has a left-hand thread.

Mark V has a No. 28 or No. 30 tail pistol.

3. *Tails.*—The tails indicate the major differences between the different marks of bomb. They all have fairly long cylindrical vanes attached to the tail cone by vane supports.

4. The Mark III bomb has a tail which is short in the conical part, and is held on by a large locking ring which threads on to the base of the bomb and presses down on the top of the tail cone. A No. 30 fuze protrudes 3 or 4 inches out of the base of the bomb and carries its own arming vanes (*see* Section 11).

5. The Mark IV bomb tail is similar to the Mark III, but instead of being held on by a locking ring it is a clip-on tail (*see* Diagram 2—500 lb. S.A.P., Mark IV).

6. The Mark V bomb tail is similar to the normal G.P. bomb clip-on tail. The main difference is that the tail cone is smaller than that of the G.P. bomb tail. The vanes are part of the tail unit and arm the fuze by means of a rod through the centre of the cone.

" 7. In order that the S.A.P. 500 lb. bombs may be carried in American aircraft two steel bands with suspension lugs can be fitted."

SECTION 6.—ARMOUR-PIERCING BOMBS

A.P. 2,000 lb., Marks I, II (III and IV not yet in use) (*see* Diagram 2)

(An A.P. 1,600 lb. is used by the Fleet Air Arm. This is an American bomb and is described in the book on American bombs.)

1. *Colour and Marking.*—The bombs are painted dark green, except for the nose, which is painted light green up to the shoulder. Also round the nose in the position of the dotted lines on the diagram are three bands, two white with a red one between them. The red and white bands indicate that the bomb is A.P. filled H.E. and the light-green nose indicates the filling of Shellite.

2. *Description.*—The bomb is thick walled (C.W. ratio of less than 10 per cent.). The body has actually a slight taper from the shoulder to the base. They are fuzed in the tail only.

3. *Fuzing.*—Marks I and II have a No. 37 fuze in the tail.
Marks III and IV will be fuzed with a pistol detonator combination.

Tails

4. *Mark I Bomb.*—The tail has a long cylindrical vane as shown in the diagram. It has a large hole in the tail cone through which the No. 37 fuze protrudes. The No. 37 fuze carries its own arming vanes (*see* Section 11).

5. The tail is held on by six screws as indicated in the diagram.

6. *Mark II Bomb.*—The tail is similar to the Mark I, but it is secured to the bomb by four wing bolts, as in the G.P. 1,000-lb. bomb's tail.

7. *Marks III and IV Bomb.*—These bombs are not in service yet, but they will have tails similar to the G.P. 1,000-lb., *i.e.*, vanes incorporated in the tail.

Part I, Chapter I

SECTION 7.—ANTI-SUBMARINE BOMBS

A.S. 100 lb., Marks III and IV, & VI ..
A.S. 250 lb., Marks III and IV .. ..
A.S. 500 lb., Marks III and IV .. .. ⎫ See Diagram 2.
A.S. 600 lb., Mark I .. .. ⎭
A.S. 35 lb. .. .. See Diagram 3.

1. Dimensions

	100 lb.	250 lb.	500 lb.	600 lb.	
Mark III ..	3 ft. 6 in. 9 in.	4 ft. 11·5 in. 11·2 in.	6 ft. 4½ in. 14·3 in.	—	Overall length. Diameter.
Mark IV ..	3 ft. 5 in. 8 in.	4 ft. 9½ in. 11·4 in.	6 ft. 0 in. 14·3 in.	—	Overall length. Diameter.
Mark I ..	—	—	—	4 ft. 8½ in. 1 ft. 5·4 in.	Overall length. Diameter.

2. Colouring and Markings

Similar to that of the G.P. bombs (Section 4).

3. Mark III Bombs

Description.—The bombs are thin cased. A ballistic cap screws on to the nose of the bomb. The cap has square cut shoulders which reduce the chance of the bomb bouncing on striking the water. C.W. ratio is about 60 per cent. except for the 100-lb. bomb, which is about 50 per cent.

Fuzing.—No. 32 nose fuze (see Section 11).

Tail.—A cylindrical vane is attached by vane supports to a dome, which is itself secured to the bomb by a central bolt.

4. Mark IV Bombs.

Description.—These bombs have a flattened nose to prevent ricochets when they strike the water. C.W. ratio is about 60–65 per cent., except for the 100-lb. bomb which is about 50 per cent.

Fuzing.—No. 30 tail pistol (see Section 12).

Tail.—Similar to the ordinary G.P. clip-on tail (see Section 4). The cone is smaller than those of the G.P. bombs, but rather longer than those of the S.A.P. bombs. The comparison is between bombs of similar size, not weight. The vanes are incorporated in the tail and arm the pistol by means of a rod passing down the centre of the cone.

5. A.S. 600 lb., Mark I

Description.—The bomb has the characteristic shape shown in the diagram. There are three suspension lugs, the central one is for use in British aircraft and the other two for use in U.S. aircraft. The nose is concave (this is shown diagrammatically in the Diagram 2—an elevation would show a straight line at the nose). There is a domed ballistic cap made of sheet metal clipped over the concave section of the nose (shown by a dotted line in the diagram). This is to improve the ballistics of the bomb until impact with the water when this cap collapses.

Fuzing.—No. 862 hydrostatic tail fuze (see Section 11).

Tail.—A short cylindrical vane is attached to a central cone by vane supports. It is a clip-on type of tail. There is a hole in the top of the cone to allow water to enter. Also there is a hole for an arming wire in the cone face.

6. A.S. 35 lb., Mark I/A (See Diagram 3)

7. *A.S., 100 lb., Mark VI.*—This bomb is similar to the 100 lb., A.S., Mark IV, but differs from it in that :—

(a) A spoiler is fitted to the nose to prevent ricochet and improve underwater trajectory.

(b) The tail unit is secured by three bolts.

Fuzing.—895A, Mark I, Tail Fuze (see Section 11).

(T. 06720/44.—C.A.F.O. P.6/45.)

SECTION 8.—HIGH CAPACITY BOMBS

H.C. 2,000 lb., Marks II and III (Mark I is obsolescent).
H.C. 4,000 lb., Marks III and IV.
H.C. 8,000 lb., Marks I and II (*see* Diagram 1).

General Notes on H.C. Bombs

1. *Colour and Markings.*—The bombs are painted dark green except a ½-in. red band within a few inches of the shoulder at the nose of the bomb, and a 2-in. light green band about half-way between the suspension lug and the nose. The red band indicates that it is filled H.E., and the light-green band has the type of filling stencilled on or near it.

2. *Description.*—The bombs are cylindrcial and light cased (C.W. ratio is about 75 per cent.). The nose is domed outwards.

In addition to the suspension lug, there are two hoisting lugs on the 4,000-lb. bomb and four hoisting lugs on the 8,000-lb. bomb.

There is usually a short cylindrical " spoiler " round the nose which extends forward a few inches like a rim.

3. *Fuzing.*—The fuzing is in the nose only and in all the later marks there are three nose pistols :—

Three No. 27 nose pistols, or
Three No. 42 nose pistols, or
~~Three No. 44 nose pistols.~~

N.B.—The central pistol has an exploder which runs the full length of the bomb. The other two have short exploders.

Paragraph 4. *Add* new sub-paragraph: " *H.C. 12,000 lb.* Similar to H.C. 000 lb., Mark II, but made in three sections. It has a drum and cone type tail. otal length, 17 ft. 6 in. Diameter, 40 in."

(*U.B. 294/43.—C.A.F.O. P.575/44.*)

conical. The bomb is now obsolescent.

H.C. 2,000 lb., Marks II and III, as shown in the diagram has two bands running round the bomb, one near the nose, the other near the tail. These are only used during transport to protect the bomb.

H.C. 8,000 lb., Mark II, differs from the Mark I in that it is made in two parts which are both bolted to a ring girder. The suspension lug is part of this girder.

Part I, Chapter I

SECTION 7.—ANTI-SUBMARINE BOMBS

A.S. 100 lb., Marks III and IV, & VI ⎫
A.S. 250 lb., Marks III and IV ⎬ See Diagram 2.
A.S. 500 lb., Marks III and IV ⎪
A.S. 600 lb., Mark I ⎭
A.S. 35 lb. .. .. See Diagram 3.

1. Dimensions

	100 lb.	250 lb.	500 lb.	600 lb.	
Mark III	3 ft. 6 in. 9 in.	4 ft. 11·5 in. 11·2 in.	6 ft. 4½ in. 14·3 in.	— —	Overall length. Diameter.
Mark IV	3 ft. 5 in. 8 in.	4 ft. 9½ in. 11·4 in.	6 ft. 0 in. 14·3 in.	— —	Overall length. Diameter.
Mark I	— —	— —	— —	4 ft. 8½ in. 1 ft. 5·4 in.	Overall length. Diameter.

2. Colouring and Markings

Similar to that of the G.P. bombs (Section 4).

3. Mark III Bombs

Description.—The bombs are square cut shoulders which reduce 60 per cent. except for the 100-lb.

Fuzing.—No. 32 nose fuze (*see* Section 11).

Tail.—A cylindrical vane is attached by vane supports to a dome, which is itself secured to the bomb by a central bolt.

4. Mark IV Bombs.—*Description.*—These bombs have a flattened nose to prevent ricochets when they strike the water. C.W. ratio is about 60–65 per cent., except for the 100-lb. bomb which is about 50 per cent.

Fuzing.—No. 30 tail pistol (*see* Section 12).

Tail.—Similar to the ordinary G.P. clip-on tail (*see* Section 4). The cone is smaller than those of the G.P. bombs, but rather longer than those of the S.A.P. bombs. The comparison is between bombs of similar size, *not* weight. The vanes are incorporated in the tail and arm the pistol by means of a rod passing down the centre of the cone.

5. A.S. 600 lb., Mark I

Description.—The bomb has the characteristic shape shown in the diagram. There are three suspension lugs, the central one is for use in British aircraft and the other two for use in U.S. aircraft. The nose is concave (this is shown diagrammatically in the Diagram 2—an elevation would show a straight line at the nose). There is a domed ballistic cap made of sheet metal clipped over the concave section of the nose (shown by a dotted line in the diagram). This is to improve the ballistics of the bomb until impact with the water when this cap collapses.

Fuzing.—No. 862 hydrostatic tail fuze (*see* Section 11).

Tail.—A short cylindrical vane is attached to a central cone by vane supports. It is a clip-on type of tail. There is a hole in the top of the cone to allow water to enter. Also there is a hole for an arming wire in the cone face.

6. A.S. 35 lb., Mark I/A (See Diagram 3)

This bomb is identical with the " Unicorn." (*See* Chapter 6, Section 2.)

N.B.—The fuze differs from that used in the " Unicorn." The two fuzes are also described in the above Section 2 of Chapter 6.

Part I, Chapter I

SECTION 8.—HIGH CAPACITY BOMBS

H.C. 2,000 lb., Marks II and III (Mark I is obsolescent).
H.C. 4,000 lb., Marks III and IV.
H.C. 8,000 lb., Marks I and II (*see* Diagram 1).

General Notes on H.C. Bombs

1. *Colour and Markings.*—The bombs are painted dark green except a ½-in. red band within a few inches of the shoulder at the nose of the bomb, and a 2-in. light green band about half-way between the suspension lug and the nose. The red band indicates that it is filled H.E., and the light-green band has the type of filling stencilled on or near it.

2. *Description.*—The bombs are cylindrcial and light cased (C.W. ratio is about 75 per cent.). The nose is domed outwards.

In addition to the suspension lug, there are two hoisting lugs on the 4,000-lb. bomb and four hoisting lugs on the 8,000-lb. bomb.

There is usually a short cylindrical " spoiler " round the nose which extends forward a few inches like a rim.

3. *Fuzing.*—The fuzing is in the nose only and in all the later marks there are three nose pistols :—

Three No. 27 nose pistols, or
Three No. 42 nose pistols, or
~~Three No. 44 nose pistols.~~

N.B.—The central pistol has an exploder which runs the full length of the bomb. The other two have short exploders.

4. *Tails.*—The tails are metal cylinders bolted to the rear of the bomb.

2,000 lb., Mark I, has only one nose fuze and a parachute tail attachment. The nose is conical. The bomb is now obsolescent.

H.C. 2,000 lb., Marks II and III, as shown in the diagram has two bands running round the bomb, one near the nose, the other near the tail. These are only used during transport to protect the bomb.

H.C. 8,000 lb., Mark II, differs from the Mark I in that it is made in two parts which are both bolted to a ring girder. The suspension lug is part of this girder.

(C 51447)

Part I, Chapter I

SECTION 9.—MEDIUM CAPACITY BOMBS

M.C. 250 lb., Marks I–IV (4 ft. 8 in. long, 10·2 in. diameter).
M.C. 500 lb., Marks I–IV (*see* Diagram 1 and Fig. 2).
M.C. 1,000 lb., Mark I (*see* Diagram 1).
M.C. 4,000 lb., Mark I (9 ft. long, 30 in. diameter).

1. *Colour and Markings.*—These are the same as for G.P. bombs (*see* Section 4).

2. *Description.*—These bombs are intended to replace G.P. bombs. They differ from the G.P. bombs in having no streamlining (*i.e.*, they have a cylindrical central section), and in having a higher charge weight ratio (about 50 per cent.).

3. They have the usual single suspension lug for carrying the bombs in British aircraft but, in addition, they have two lugs 14 in. apart, one near the nose and the other near the tail; these are used for carrying the bombs in U.S. aircraft. The additional lugs are on the opposite side of the bomb from the single lug.

Fuzing.—As for G.P. bombs (*see* Section 4).

Tails.—*See* Section 4 (Tails for G.P. Bombs).

M.C. 250 lb. have long clip-on tails.

M.C. 500 lb. have long or short clip-on tails.

M.C. 1,000 lb. and 4,000 lb. have short tails with four wing bolts.

SECTION 10.—ANTI-TANK BOMBS

9 lb. Anti-tank, Marks I and II. (*See* Diagram 2.)

1. *Colour and Marking.*—The bombs are painted dark green and have a ½-in. red band round the nose.

2. *Description.*—There is a cavity in the nose of the bomb and the bombs have a slight taper towards the nose so that one bomb can be placed in the tail of another. The nose cavity is just large enough to go over the tail fuze. The bombs are always dropped in pairs and the second bomb has a retarding plate fitted across the rear of the tail so that it draws the bomb out of the tail of the first bomb. The second bomb also has a metal cylinder and plate which fit in the tail. The cylinder covers the fuze and the plate draws the cylinder off the fuze when the bombs are dropped, because of the rush of air. The cylinder and plate drop clear of the bomb.

3. *Fuzing.*—No. 847 tail fuze (*see* Section 11).

4. *Tail.*—The tail is part of the bomb.

Part I, Chapter I

SECTION 11.—FUZES USED IN H.E. BOMBS

(*See* note on title page indicating the difference between a fuze and a pistol.)

No. 30 tail fuze (Fig. 3).
No. 37 tail fuze (similar to Fig. 3).
No. 32 nose fuze (Fig. 4).
No. 845 nose fuze (anti-disturbance) (Fig. 6). *obsolete*
No. 880, tail fuze.
No. 885, barometric fuze.
No. 895A, Mark I, hydrostatic tail fuze.
No. 896, Mark I, barometric fuze.

No. 30 Tail Fuze (Fig. 3)

1. *Bombs in which used.*—S.A.P., Marks III and IV.

   Body Construction.—Brass.

   Implements Ammunition.—No. 111 for Mark III bomb locking ring. No. 134 for Mark IV bomb locking ring. (*See* Part II, Appendix).

2. *General Details.*—The vanes are secured after the tail is in position by the vane securing pin.

   The safety pillar is removed and placed in the pilot's cockpit when the bomb is finally in the carrier. A safety clip, which fits over the neck just beneath the vanes and has a rod protruding between the vanes, now prevents the fuze from arming. This clip is attached to the fuze setting control link (arming wire). When a bomb has been dropped and this safety clip is missing, it is impossible to tell whether the fuze is armed or not.

   The fuze is fired by 2 strikers moving forward against the resistance of a creep spring. It has 1/10th sec. delay.

   The whipcord becket shown in the figure is present until the fuze is put in a bomb. It is then removed, together with a wire and lead seal which prevent the safety pillar from being removed. These are shown in position on a No. 32 fuze in Fig. 4.

No. 37 Tail Fuze

3. *Bomb in which used.*—A.P. 2,000 lb., Marks I and II.

   This fuze is the same as the No. 30 tail fuze, except that it is about 8¼ in. longer. The additional length is in the fuze body above the locking ring shoulder.

No. 32 Nose Fuze (*see* Fig. 4)

4. *Bomb in which used.*—A.S., Mark III.

   Body Construction.—Brass.

   Implements Ammunition.—No. 89 for locking ring. No. 126 for delay setting. (*See* Part II, Appendix.)

5. *General Details.*—The arming vanes attachment and the external safety devices are exactly the same as for the No. 30 tail fuze. Therefore, the relevant part of the description for the No. 30 fuze should be read. There is an additional external setting on the No. 32 fuze. On the diagram on the side of the fuze is a screw cap marked " Replace firmly after setting." An implement ammunition No. 126 (*see* Part II, Appendix) fits over the exposed spindle. An arrow on the head then points to the delay for which the fuze is set. When this arrow points to " Bridge " the fuze is safe.

6. In Diagram 2 the fuze is shown in the bomb. The ballistic cap covers the fuze up to the shoulder, so that the delay setting can only be uncovered by removing the ballistic cap. The ballistic cap screws on the bomb nose and is secured with a grub screw. The arming vanes have to be detached before the ballistic cap can be removed.

7. The fuze screws into the bomb and is fixed in position by the locking ring.

8. The fuze fires with a delay by an inertia pellet moving against the resistance of a creep spring and a striker. If some hard object is struck, the shoulders, which are specially weakened, collapse and the fuze fires instantaneously.

No. 845 Anti-handling Nose Fuze (*see* Fig. 6).

9. *Bombs in which used.*—G.P. and M.C., together with a long delay tail fuzing.

   Body Construction.—A zinc alloy (dull grey).

   Implement Ammunition.—No. 104 (*see* Part II, Appendix).

10. *General Details.*—The fuze contains a battery and mercury switch which fires the fuze if it is moved after impact with the ground. The fuze must have armed before impact.

C.A.F.O. P.575/44

Add new page 13a.

13a

27. No. 873 Nose Fuze, Mark I (*see* Fig. 26). C.A.F.O. P. Series Diagram 74/44.
28. Bombs in which used : 20 lb. F. and 40 lb. G.P.
29. Description : The principle is the same as the No. 45 Nose Pistol. There is an additional safety device. The detonator and C.E. pellet are incorporated in the fuze, the detonator being in a spring-loaded shutter which is kept out of line with the striker until the safety cap and vanes unscrew. The "stud" shown in the diagram is pushed out as soon as the "lever" is free.
30. *No. 880, Tail Fuze.*
31. *Bombs in which used.*—8 lb. F.
32. *General Details.*—The No. 880 is a long delay fuze, the delay being obtained by the length of time taken for a spring-loaded striker to shear through a lead wire.

The delay varies between 0 and 6 hours at 50° F., though the length of delay is approximately doubled for every 15° F. fall in temperature.

On release from the cluster the safety-pin is pulled out from the fuze by the opening of the parachute, and the force of impact causes the fuze to arm.

33. *No. 885, Mark I, Tail Fuze.*—The fuze is similar in appearance to the No. 867, Mark I, Fuze. It is used in the cluster, H.E., 500 lb., No. 17, Mark II.

34. *No. 895, "A," Mark I, Tail Fuze (see* Figure 28).—Bombs in which used : It is a hydrostatically armed fuze used in the 100 lb., A.S., Mark VI, and it is designed to function at a depth varying between 14 and 22 ft.

35. *Description.*—(i) The fuze consists of the following main components :—
   (a) The fuze body (12).
   (b) Safety plunger (8).
   (c) Lock sleeve (10).
   (d) Spring-loaded striker (11).
   (e) Moving sleeve (13).
   (f) Three water entry holes fitted with anti-countermining valves (6).
   (g) Rubber bellows (14).
   (h) Rotary type detonator holder (7).
   (i) Magazine (16).

36. *Action.*—(i) On release from the aircraft, the safety-pin (1) is withdrawn to release the safety plunger (8).

(ii) When the bomb is submerged, water enters the fuze through the water entry holes (6), and as the bomb sinks, the pressure of the water causes the bellows (14) to expand.

(iii) The water entry holes (6) are covered by spring-loaded valves to prevent countermining.

(iv) The expansion of the bellows causes the moving sleeve (13) to move up and compress the striker spring (3) and, at the same time, the safety plunger is forced up by the head of the striker (11).

(v) As the moving sleeve rises, a projection on the end of the rod (15) which forms part of the sleeve and which engages with the rotary detonator holder (7) causes the latter to rotate until the detonator is positioned under the striker.

(vi) When the bomb reaches a depth of approximately 18 ft., the striker retaining balls (5) are forced into the groove (4) and the striker, under the influence of the striker spring, impinges upon the detonator.

(vii) Should the bomb impact tail first, the lock sleeve (10) sets forward overcoming the spring (2) to force the safety locking balls (9) into the striker channel, thus preventing the striker from rising and arming accidentally.

37. *No. 896, Mark I.*—(i) The No. 896, Mark I fuze is similar to the No. 860, Mark II (used in T.I. bomb (Chapter 2, Section II)) except that a delay unit has been introduced between the cap and the magazine.

(ii) The fuze is designated either A.2, A.3 or A 4, the figure in each case indicating the length of delay in seconds.

(*T. 06720/44.—C.A.F.O. P.6/45.*)

Part I, Chapter 1

SECTION 11.—FUZES USED IN H.E. BOMBS

(*See* note on title page indicating the difference between a fuze and a pistol.)

No. 30 tail fuze (Fig. 3).
No. 37 tail fuze (similar to Fig. 3).
No. 32 nose fuze (Fig. 4).
No. 845 nose fuze (anti-disturbance) (Fig. 6). *obsolete*
No. 847 tail fuze (Fig. 5).
No. 862 hydrostatic tail fuze (Fig. 7).
No. 867 barometric tail fuze.

No. 30 Tail Fuze (Fig. 3)

1. *Bombs in which used.*—S.A.P., Marks III and IV.

Body Construction.—Brass.

Implements Ammunition.—No. 111 for Mark III bomb locking ring. No. 134 for Mark IV bomb locking ring. (See Part II, Appendix).

2. *General Details.*—The vanes are secured after the tail is in position by the vane securing pin.

The safety pillar is removed and placed in the pilot's cockpit when the bomb is finally in the carrier. A safety clip, which fits over the neck just beneath the vanes and has a rod protruding between the vanes, now prevents the fuze from arming. This clip is attached to the fuze setting control link (arming wire). When a bomb has been dropped and this safety clip is missing, it is impossible to tell whether the fuze is armed or not.

The fuze is fired by 2 strikers moving forward against the resistance of a creep spring. It has 1/10th sec. delay.

The whipcord becket shown in the figure is present until the fuze is put in a bomb. It is then removed, together with a wire and lead seal which prevent the safety pillar from being removed. These are shown in position on a No. 32 fuze in Fig. 4.

No. 37 Tail Fuze

3. *Bomb in which used.*—A.P. 2,000 lb., Marks I and II.

This fuze is the same as the No. 30 tail fuze, except that it is about 8¼ in. longer. The additional length is in the fuze body above the locking ring shoulder.

No. 32 Nose Fuze (*see* Fig. 4)

4. *Bomb in which used.*—A.S., Mark III.

Body Construction.—Brass.

Implements Ammunition.—No. 89 for locking ring. No. 126 for delay setting. (See Part II, Appendix.)

5. *General Details.*—The arming vanes attachment and the external safety devices are exactly the same as for the No. 30 tail fuze. Therefore, the relevant part of the description for the No. 30 fuze should be read. There is an additional external setting on the No. 32 fuze. On the diagram on the side of the fuze is a screw cap marked " Replace firmly after setting." An implement ammunition No. 126 (*see* Part II, Appendix) fits over the exposed spindle. An arrow on the head then points to the delay for which the fuze is set. When this arrow points to " Bridge " the fuze is safe.

6. In Diagram 2 the fuze is shown in the bomb. The ballistic cap covers the fuze up to the shoulder, so that the delay setting can only be uncovered by removing the ballistic cap. The ballistic cap screws on the bomb nose and is secured with a grub screw. The arming vanes have to be detached before the ballistic cap can be removed.

7. The fuze screws into the bomb and is fixed in position by the locking ring.

8. The fuze fires with a delay by an inertia pellet moving against the resistance of a creep spring and a striker. If some hard object is struck, the shoulders, which are specially weakened, collapse and the fuze fires instantaneously.

No. 845 Anti-handling Nose Fuze (*see* Fig. 6).

9. *Bombs in which used.*—G.P. and M.C., together with a long delay tail fuzing.

Body Construction.—A zinc alloy (dull grey).

Implement Ammunition.—No. 104 (*see* Part II, Appendix).

10. *General Details.*—The fuze contains a battery and mercury switch which fires the fuze if it is moved after impact with the ground. The fuze must have armed before impact.

C.A.F.O. P.575/44

Add new page 13a.

13a

27. No. 873 Nose Fuze, Mark I (*see* Fig. 26). C.A.F.O. P. Series Diagram 74/44.
28. Bombs in which used : 20 lb. F. and 40 lb. G.P.

29. Description : The principle is the same as the No. 45 Nose Pistol. There is an additional safety device. The detonator and C.E. pellet are incorporated in the fuze, the detonator being in a spring-loaded shutter which is kept out of line with the striker until the safety cap and vanes unscrew. The " stud " shown in the diagram is pushed out as soon as the " lever " is free.

(*U.B. 294/43.—C.A.F.O. P.575/44.*)

1. Fig. 6 is a rough diagram which indicates the shape, but not the exact dimensions. There is no other r pistol with this domed shape. When in the bomb all that is visible is the part above the threads.

2. There are two arming vanes only. A horseshoe-shaped clip fits under the base of the arming spindle ushes two legs attached to the vanes into a groove which runs across the fuze head. There is a spring the vanes which is pushing them upwards. When the horseshoe clip comes away as the bomb leaves rcraft, the vanes are pushed up by the spring, the legs come out of the groove and the vanes can rotate.

3. There is a weak section of the arming spindle so that the vanes and upper part of the spindle usually away on impact. Often the whole fuze head shears off at the end of the threads.

4. The fuze has to be used in conjunction with a D.38 detonator (*see* Fig. 8); there is only a flash r and detonator train in the fuze.

5. The fuze screws into a normal exploder pocket (*see* Fig. 8 for the pocket).

17 Tail Fuze (*see* Fig. 5)

6. *Bomb in which used.*—9 lb. anti-tank.

Body.—Painted black and primer painted yellow.

No key required.

7. *General Details.*—The arming tape is held in position by a rubber band until the bombs are fuzed. bombs are dropped in pairs. The arming tape of the front bomb is held in position by the nose of the d (*see* Section 10). The tape of the second bomb is held in position by a cylinder and plate. On release he aircraft, the cylinder falls away and the bombs separate. The tape then unwinds and withdraws the pin. The fuze fires by a striker moving forward against the resistance of a creep spring.

Hydrostatic Tail Fuze (*see* Fig. 7)

Bomb in which used.—A.S. 600 lb.

Body Construction.—Steel.

Implements Ammunition.—Nos. 208 and 209 (*see* Part II, Appendix).

. *General Details.*—The diagram gives the general appearance of the fuze and not the exact dimensions. ze itself screws into the base of the bomb. Around the fuze and attached to the bomb by a locking key No. 209) is the anti-countermining chamber which shuts if there is any sudden increase of pressure, reventing the bomb being fired by momentary increases of pressure such as explosions will produce.

. The fuze fires at a depth of 20–24 ft.

. The fuze setting control link (arming wire) comes through holes in the tail and anti-countermining er, and passes through the safety shutter in the side of the fuze. This shutter is moved inwards into the ous position by water pressure. The shutter is safe when it is flush with the end of the cylinder which ted in the diagram, *i.e.*, the cylinder through which the safety wire finally passes.

. The cover plate on top of the anti-countermining chamber can be removed by the No. 208 key. This it possible to see whether the arming wire is in position.

.B.—The safety shutter only requires a depth of a few feet to place it in the dangerous position. The r returns to the safe position on removal of the fuze from the water. There is a possibility that after long sion, the shutter would remain in the armed position even after removal of the fuze from water.

. 867 Barometric Tail Fuze, Mark I

. *General.*—The fuze tail No. 867, Mark I, is normally used with the Cluster Aircraft, 500 lb., No. 4,

. *Description.*—(i) Internally the fuze is identical in construction with the No. 860, Mark II, used in get illumination bomb. (*See* Chapter 2, Section 11.)

) Externally the fuze differs only in the appearance of the arming mechanism.

i) The arming vanes are replaced by a cylindrical nut screwed to the outer end of the arming screw.

) A fixed bar is passed through the nut to engage with the arming forks of the tail unit.

During transit a metal cap covers the arming mechanism.

. *Action.*—(i) On release from the aircraft the fuzing lanyard breaks a shear wire to release the spring-safety pin and clear the flash channel.

At the same time the arming vanes rotate to withdraw the arming screw, thus arming the fuze.

) Subsequently the action of a fuze is the same as the No. 860, Mark II.

Part I, Chapter I

SECTION 12.—PISTOLS USED IN H.E. BOMBS

(*See* note on pistols and fuzes on the title page.)

No. 19 Nose Pistol.
No. 22 Tail Pistol.
No. 27 Nose Pistol.
No. 28 Tail Pistol.
No. 47.   Long Delay Side Pistol.
No. 53 and 53a.   Long Delay Tail Pistol.
No. 54.   Tail Pistol.

No. 34 Nose Pistol.
No. 37 Long Delay Tail Pistol.
No. 38 Nose Pistol.
No. 42 Nose Pistol.

(*T 06720/44.—C.A.F.O. P.6/45.*)

1. *General Notes on Pistols.*—On the left of Fig. 8 is shown the shape of a normal detonator used with pistols. On the right is shown an exploder pocket with a pistol detonator combination in position. The pocket, pellets and detonator are in section, the pistol in elevation. There are four holes in the top of the pocket to take a pin spanner.

There are two distinct types of pistols :—

Those which have a pointed needle striker and pierce the detonator (capsule type—1 in. of the detonator shank end is painted green), and those which have a blunt striker with an anvil type detonator (detonator shank is unpainted). The latter are less dangerous when the bombs are dropped and found unexploded.

2. Detonators have a colour band round the head to indicate the time of the delay.

3. Most pistols have a spring clip as shown in Figs. 11 and 12. These clips fit round the pistol and have dints which fit into small cavities in the pistol. There is a leg about ¼-in. long projecting below the clip. When the pistol is screwed into the bomb exploder pocket (*see* Fig. 8), the leg engages in one of the holes on top of the pocket. This prevents the clip from moving round with the pistol and gives a ratchet effect, *i.e.*, sufficient force has to be used to push the dints of the clip out of the cavities. This device prevents the pistol from working loose while in the aircraft and yet leaves the pistol only hand tight in the bomb, so that it can be removed easily.

Paragraph 3.   At the end *add* " The exploder pocket is locked in the bomb by a grub screw through the flange. The screw lies midway between two spanner pin holes and close to the outer edge of the flange.   It is about one-eighth inch in diameter."

Body.—Brass.

Vanes, Cap, and Pressure Plates.—Steel.

Safety Devices and Action.—(*a*) Safety fork and safety pin. The pin is put through the ends of the fork and prevents it being pulled off. It is only removed when the bomb is loaded in the aircraft. The pin must be replaced if the bomb is ever unloaded. The fork passes under the safety plate.

(*b*) Safety cap and vanes. These thread onto the threaded spindle in the centre of the pressure plate. The pressure plate, striker and threaded spindle are all one piece.

(*c*) The striker cannot move onto the detonator until impact, because of a shear wire.

(*d*) The fork is withdrawn by the fuze setting control link (arming wire) as the bomb leaves the aircraft. The cap and vanes screw off and fall away in mid-air.

Note.—The shank of the pistol will be inside the bomb so that only the part above the threads is visible.

5. **No. 22 Tail Pistol**—used in G.P., Mark III, bombs only.   (*See* Fig. 10)

Body.—Brass.

Striker and Spindle.—Steel.

Safety Devices and Action.—(*a*) A safety pin passes right through the pistol and striker spindle. This is not removed until the bomb is loaded in the aircraft. It must be replaced if the bomb is ever unloaded.

(*b*) A transit clip is placed between the vanes and pistol shoulder during transit to prevent the vanes screwing off.

(*c*) The safety clip is always placed in position when the transit clip is removed. It clips onto the top of the pistol and has a rod which stands up and prevents the vanes from rotating.

(*d*) The safety vanes prevent the striker moving downwards.

(e) The safety clip comes away when the bomb leaves the aircraft, the vanes then screw off in mid-air. The striker is held away from the detonator by a creep spring until impact.

Notes.—If a red ring on the striker spindle is not visible, it means that the striker is in a dangerous position relative to the detonator.

The pistol screws into the base of the bomb, which being a G.P., Mark III, has a central tube coming right to the top of the tail cone.

The whole of the shank of the pistol is within the bomb.

6. **No. 27 Nose Pistol** (*see* Fig. 11)

Bombs in which used.—G.P., M.C. and H.C.

Body.—Brass.

Vanes, Cap and Pressure Plate.—Steel.

Safety Devices and Action.—The same as for the No. 19 nose pistol.
 (a) The striker is blunt and has an anvil type detonator.
 (b) Figs. 1 and 2 show unarmed No. 27 nose pistols in bombs.
 (c) The pistol is put in the bomb hand tight. The spring locking clip prevents it from working loose.

7. **No. 28 Tail Pistol** (*See* Fig. 14 and also Fig. 12)

Note.—This pistol is the same as the No. 30 except that it has an anvil type detonator with a blunt striker whereas the No. 30 has a capsule detonator with a needle striker. Externally the No. 30 has a green band round the pistol (Fig. 12) and the No. 27 has no band.

Fig. 12 shows a side view of these pistols and Fig. 14 shows the view from above.

Bombs in which used.—G.P. and M.C.

Body.—Brass (some were made of plastic, but they are obsolete).

Safety Devices and Action.—(a) The safety vanes are part of the tail units used with these pistols. They are connected by a rod down the centre of the tail cone to the pistol. This rod ends with a fork which is the same size as the arming fork of the pistol, so that when it turns, it turns the arming fork also. The arming fork is screwed onto the upper end of the striker. When the fork screws off it leaves the striker free to go forward on impact. There is a creep spring between the striker and the detonator. The vanes are prevented from rotating until the bomb leaves the plane by a safety clip like the one in Fig. 10. This safety clip is attached to the fuze setting control link (arming wire).

(b) During transit a safety plate fits into the pistol, preventing the fork from turning, and a safety cap clips over the head of the pistol, preventing the safety plate from falling out. These are not removed until the tail is fitted on the bomb just prior to loading it in the aircraft.

N.B.—The pistol is unarmed when the fork is below the top of the pistol and the striker spindle is about level with the ends of the fork. Fig. 12 shows the pistol partially armed.

Figs. 1 and 2 show No. 30 tail pistols in position in bombs.

8. **No. 30 Tail Pistol** (*See* No. 28 tail pistol)

9. **No. 33 Nose Pistol** (*See* Fig. 18)

Bombs in which used.—20 lb. F. with parachute ; 40 lb. G.P. with parachute (*see* Section 3).

Body.—Brass.

Safety Cap and Pressure Plate.—Steel.

Safety Devices and Action.—(a) The wire mentioned in Section 3 which runs from the parachute down the bomb side ends in a pin which is fitted in the hole next to the safety pin hole. When the bomb is placed in the plane the safety pin is removed (and must be replaced if the bomb is unloaded). On leaving the aircraft, the parachute opens and pulls out the arming pin ; the spring safety clip then flies out taking the wedges from under the pressure plate. The safety cap is pushed off by a spring. The pistol in this state is identical with the armed No. 34 nose pistol (*see* Fig. 15 and below) except that it has a very thin shear washer instead of a shear wire.

10. **No. 34 Nose Pistol** (*See* Fig. 15)

Bombs in which used.—20 lb. F. ; 40 lb. G.P.

Body.—Brass.

Safety Cap and Pressure Plate.—Steel.

Part I, Chapter I

SECTION 12.—PISTOLS USED IN H.E. BOMBS

(*See* note on pistols and fuzes on the title page.)

No. 19 Nose Pistol.	No. 34 Nose Pistol.
No. 22 Tail Pistol.	No. 37 Long Delay Tail Pistol.
No. 27 Nose Pistol.	No. 38 Nose Pistol.
No. 28 Tail Pistol.	No. 42 Nose Pistol.
No. 30 Tail Pistol.	No. 44 Nose Pistol.
No. 33 Nose Pistol.	No. 45 Nose Pistol.
	No. 17 Long Delay Tail Pistol.

No. 52 MkI. NP. (handwritten)

1. *General Notes on Pistols.*—On the left of Fig. 8 is shown the shape of a normal detonator used with pistols. On the right is shown an exploder pocket with a pistol detonator combination in position. The pocket, pellets and detonator are in section, the pistol in elevation. There are four holes in the top of the pocket to take a pin spanner.

There are two distinct types of pistols :—

Those which have a pointed needle striker and pierce the detonator (capsule type—1 in. of the detonator shank end is painted green), and those which have a blunt striker with an anvil type detonator (detonator shank is unpainted). The latter are less dangerous when the bombs are dropped and found unexploded.

2. Detonators have a colour band round the head to indicate the time of the delay.

3. Most pistols have a spring clip as shown in Figs. 11 and 12. These clips fit round the pistol and have dints which fit into small cavities in the pistol. There is a leg about $\frac{1}{4}$-in. long projecting below the clip. When the pistol is screwed into the bomb exploder pocket (*see* Fig. 8), the leg engages in one of the holes on top of the pocket. This prevents the clip from moving round with the pistol and gives a ratchet effect, *i.e.*, sufficient force has to be used to push the dints of the clip out of the cavities. This device prevents the pistol from working loose while in the aircraft and yet leaves the pistol only hand tight in the bomb, so that it can be removed easily.

19 Nose Pistol (*see* Fig. 9)

in which used.—G.P., Mark III, only.

Body.—Brass.

Vanes, Cap, and Pressure Plates.—Steel.

Safety Devices and Action.—(*a*) Safety fork and safety pin. The pin is put through the ends of the fork and prevents it being pulled off. It is only removed when the bomb is loaded in the aircraft. The pin must be replaced if the bomb is ever unloaded. The fork passes under the safety plate.

(*b*) Safety cap and vanes. These thread onto the threaded spindle in the centre of the pressure plate. The pressure plate, striker and threaded spindle are all one piece.

(*c*) The striker cannot move onto the detonator until impact, because of a shear wire.

(*d*) The fork is withdrawn by the fuze setting control link (arming wire) as the bomb leaves the aircraft. The cap and vanes screw off and fall away in mid-air.

Note.—The shank of the pistol will be inside the bomb so that only the part above the threads is visible.

5. **No. 22 Tail Pistol**—used in **G.P., Mark III**, bombs only. (*See* Fig. 10)

Body.—Brass.

Striker and Spindle.—Steel.

Safety Devices and Action.—(*a*) A safety pin passes right through the pistol and striker spindle. This is not removed until the bomb is loaded in the aircraft. It must be replaced if the bomb is ever unloaded.

(*b*) A transit clip is placed between the vanes and pistol shoulder during transit to prevent the vanes screwing off.

(*c*) The safety clip is always placed in position when the transit clip is removed. It clips onto the top of the pistol and has a rod which stands up and prevents the vanes from rotating.

(*d*) The safety vanes prevent the striker moving downwards.

Part I, Chapter I

Safety Devices and Action.—(a) The safety fork passes through the safety cap and under the pressure plate, and is removed when the bomb is put in a carrier. If a small bomb container is used then the pin and the fork are both removed when the bombs are loaded. They must be replaced if the bombs have to be unloaded at any time.

(b) When the bombs leave the aircraft, if they are carrier borne, the safety fork is removed by the fuze setting control link, and the safety cap, which has a spring underneath, is pushed off. If the bombs are carried in a small bomb container then the caps fly off as soon as the bombs leave the container.

(c) The striker is rigidly attached to the pressure plate and on impact a wire is sheared and the blunt striker is driven on to the detonator.

Note.—There is a spring locking clip which prevents the pistol from unscrewing although it is only in hand tight.

11. No. 37 Long Delay Tail Pistol (*N.B.*—Red arming vanes.) (*See* Fig. 13)

Bombs in which used.—G.P. or M.C.

Body.—Brass.

Period of Delay.—(Approximate only, as the temperature has considerable effect on the delay) 6 hours to 144 hours.

Anti-withdrawal Device.—This pistol must *never* be unscrewed as this causes immediate detonation of the bomb.

Note.—The pistol is the same externally as the No. 28 tail pistol, but it has a V-shaped groove round the body, as can be seen in Fig. 3.

Safety Devices and Action.—(a) The system of arming is similar to the No. 28 tail pistol. The vanes in the tail unit are, however, painted *red* when this pistol is used. Also, an instructional tag is always wired on to the pistol (the wire running in the V groove). When the tail is fitted this tag is removed from the pistol and attached to the safety clip. If a bomb has to be unloaded this tag must be returned to the pistol immediately the tail is removed.

(b) The arming fork, instead of screwing off the striker, is attached to the spindle and on being turned by the vanes screws the spindle into the pistol. This breaks a capsule of acetone and causes the fuze to function.

12. No. 38 Nose Pistol (Fig. 16)

Bombs in which used.—20 lb. F. ; 40 lb. G.P.

Body.—Mazac (zinc alloy).

Cap, Vanes and Pressure Plate.—Steel.

Safety Device and Action.—(a) The safety cap and vanes screw on to the pressure plate. A safety pin prevents the cap unscrewing until the bombs are in the aircraft. When the bombs are loaded in a small bomb container, the pins are removed (the pins must be replaced before the bombs are unloaded if they are brought back).

(b) A pair of wedges, held together by spring steel, fit under the pressure plate and jump away when the safety cap unscrews.

(c) The pressure plate and blunt striker are driven in on impact, shearing a wire which is threaded right through the pistol body.

(d) In older marks there are no wedges and the safety pin itself passes under the pressure plate and right through the other side of the safety cap.

Note.—A spring locking clip is fitted.

13. No. 42 Nose Pistol (*See* No. 27 Nose Pistol)

This pistol is exactly the same as the No. 27 nose pistol, except that it has a needle striker and therefore uses a capsule detonator.

Externally the only difference is that the No. 42 pistol has its vanes painted green.

14. No. 44 Nose Pistol (*See* Fig. 17)

Bombs in which used.—G.P., M.C.,

Body.—Brass.

Safety Cap and Vanes.—Steel.

Note.—The pistol screws into the bomb and is held tight by a locking ring.

C.A.F.O. P.6/45

Add new page 17a

17a

18. *No. 47 Long Delay Side Pistol* (*see* Fig. 31).

The 47 long-delay pistol is being fitted, on a limited scale, to the *side* fuze pockets of certain large British bombs.

Description and Operation
  (i) The pistol is of the chemically operated (acetone/celluloid) type with a maximum designed delay of half-hour. As with other pistols of this type, the actual delay in any particular case may vary between wide limits, but a 47 pistol is most unlikely to function after three hours have elapsed since the bomb fell.
  (ii) The pistol differs from the 37 chiefly in the method by which the arming screw is rotated, and in the fact that *no anti-withdrawal device is fitted.* A normal detonator is fitted below the pistol.
  (iii) A drum, on which a length of copper arming wire is wound, is attached to the arming screw. The outer end of the copper wire is attached to the plane.
  (iv) As the bomb falls away from the aircraft the drum is rotated by the pull on the arming wire and the arming screw is screwed into the body, where it breaks a glass solvent vessel in the same way as in the 37 pistol.
  (The glass vessel may, however, be expected to be broken on impact even though the arming screw has not rotated, and the pistol should always be regarded as being in the armed condition if found in an unexploded bomb.)

19. *No. 53 and No. 53a Long Delay Tail Pistols*

1. Similar to the 37 pistol but the V-shaped groove is painted white. There is no anti-withdrawal device.

2. The delay periods are No. 53 pistol—30 minutes, and No. 53a pistol—60 minutes.

3. Bomber Command paint the arming vanes white but the practice is not general.

20. *No. 54 Mark I Tail Pistol* (*see* Fig. 29)

Bombs in which used.—It can be used in any bomb which is normally fuzed No. 30. tail pistol.

Body.—Brass.

General Details

1. The pistol, bomb, tail, D.A., No. 54, Mark I, is an " all-ways " pistol, and is used with a sensitive type detonator.

2. Unlike the No. 30 pistol there is no green cannelure to indicate the presence of a sensitive type pistol-detonator combination.

3. The pistol is similar in external appearance to the No. 28 Mark III pistol, except that the diameter of the body has been increased to $2\frac{1}{2}$ in.

4. The arming fork is screw threaded through the retaining plate (5) and heavy inertia ring (6) into the head of the steel spring-loaded striker (2).

5. The retaining plate (5) which locates the inertia ring (6) is retained in position by three grub screws (1).

6. The head of the striker (2), which is enlarged and chamfered, receives the arming fork and also forms a seating for the inertia ring.

7. The striker is located by the striker guide (4) and is prevented from rotation by the guide pin (3) engaging in a slot in the head of the striker.

8. The pistol is secured to the bomb by a multi-tabbed locking washer.

9. On release from the aircraft, approximately 14 revolutions of the arming vanes are sufficient to arm the pistol.

10. On impact in the normal manner the striker sets forward to overcome the creep spring and function the detonator.

11. Should the bomb impact at an angle, the displacement of the heavy inertia ring depresses the striker to function the detonator.

(*T. 06720/44.—C.A.F.O. P.6/45.*)

Page 17.

Safety devices and action. Delete "(a) The safety cap ... the aircraft" and *substitute* "The safety cap and vanes are held in position by a safety pin. This is withdrawn when the bomb is stowed in the aircraft and the safety wire has been threaded through the cap and locking ring. The fuzing wire is withdrawn when the bomb leaves the aircraft."

Part I, Chapter I

(U.B. 294/43.—C.A.F.O. P.575/44.) mid-air, the cap and vanes (which are screwed on to the external thread of the pistol) unscrew. This exposes a perforated brass disc (see Fig. 17). Under the disc is a thin brass diaphragm which is dished so that it holds a thin needle striker away from a capsule detonator. On impact (or immediately before) the diaphragm is pushed in and when it gets beyond the central position it springs inwards and pierces the detonator. A spring is fitted under the detonator head in order to keep it in close contact with the pistol.

15. No. 45 Nose Pistol

This pistol differs from the No. 44 Nose Pistol in *details of construction*. It has no shank. The pistol cuts off at the bottom of the threads as in the case of the No. 34 Nose Pistol (see Fig. 15).

t the end of the paragraph *add* "Also it has six vanes instead of five. The vanes re made in pairs and riveted to the cap as in fuze No. 873, Fig. 26, Chapter 1. There no fuzing wire, as the bombs are carried in containers."

(U.B. 294/43.—C.A.F.O. P.575/44.)

Bombs in which used.—G.P., Mark V, 250 lb. and 500 lb.

Note.—(1) Nose plug has a cross cut and is *not* a ring bolt as in Mark IVs.

(2) As for the No. 37 tail pistol, the vanes in the tail are painted red.

(3) There is an *anti-withdrawal device* which detonates the bomb if the pistol is unscrewed.

(4) When the tail is removed the part of the pistol which is exposed is painted red. It is about 1 in. in diameter and stands out from the bomb about the same distance. A spindle protrudes from the pistol and an arming fork is screwed on to this spindle when the pistol is unarmed. The fork is screwed off when the bomb falls. On impact, the pistol functions. (*N.B.*—Unlike the No. 37 pistol which does not depend on impact.)

(5) The normal safety clip, used for preventing the arming vanes from turning until the bomb is dropped (read the clip details of No. 28 tail pistol. A photograph of the clip is shown in Fig. 10).

After paragraph 16 *add* "17. *No. 52, Mark I, nose pistol* (for use in American ombs, *see* page 5). Similar to the No. 45 nose pistol (*see* Fig. 17, Chapter 1), but le locking ring has four lugs for the safety wire."

(U.B. 294/43.—C.A.F.O. P.575/44.)

evices and Action.—(a) The safety cap and vanes are held in position by a safety pin. This is withdrawn by the fuze setting control link when the bomb leaves the aircraft. In mid-air, the cap and vanes (which are screwed on to the external thread of the pistol) unscrew. This exposes a perforated brass disc (*see* Fig. 17). Under the disc is a thin brass diaphragm which is dished so that it holds a thin needle striker away from a capsule detonator. On impact (or immediately before) the diaphragm is pushed in and when it gets beyond the central position it springs inwards and pierces the detonator. A spring is fitted under the detonator head in order to keep it in close contact with the pistol.

15. No. 45 Nose Pistol

This pistol differs from the No. 44 Nose Pistol in *details of construction*. It has no shank. The pistol cuts off at the bottom of the threads as in the case of the No. 34 Nose Pistol (*see* Fig. 15).

16. No. 17 Long Delay Tail Pistol

Approximate Delay.—½ hour to 72 hours.

Used by F.A.A. only.

Bombs in which used.—G.P., Mark V, 250 lb. and 500 lb.

Note.—(1) Nose plug has a cross cut and is *not* a ring bolt as in Mark IVs.

(2) As for the No. 37 tail pistol, the vanes in the tail are painted red.

(3) There is an *anti-withdrawal device* which detonates the bomb if the pistol is unscrewed.

(4) When the tail is removed the part of the pistol which is exposed is painted red. It is about 1 in. in diameter and stands out from the bomb about the same distance. A spindle protrudes from the pistol and an arming fork is screwed on to this spindle when the pistol is unarmed. The fork is screwed off when the bomb falls. On impact, the pistol functions. (*N.B.*—Unlike the No. 37 pistol which does not depend on impact.)

(5) The normal safety clip, used for preventing the arming vanes from turning until the bomb is dropped (read the clip details of No. 28 tail pistol. A photograph of the clip is shown in Fig. 10).

Part I, Chapter I

SECTION 13.—MISCELLANEOUS

(a) Aircraft Bomb, Infantry Training, 6 lb., Mark I.

1. The bomb is a cardboard cylinder, 20 in. long and 3·75 in. in diameter. It is fitted with a No. 34 nose pistol (*see* Section 12).

2. The filling is 2½ lb. of C.E./T.N.T.

3. Carried in small bomb containers or light series carriers.

(b)

C.B.3126 - Amendment No.1

SECTION 13b - 250 lb. 'B' BOMB (see Fig. No.25)

1. Overall length: 6 feet
2. Length without tail and nose attachment 3' 6".
3. Maximum diameter: 14.3"
4. Used for attacks on ships in motion. The bombs sink when they strike the water and as they have buoyancy chambers, they then rise and fire on impact with the underside of the ship.

5. Fuzed in the tail by a No.850 Fuze which is armed hydrostatically.

6. If it **fails** to hit a ship, the bomb sinks after a short period.

7. The nose is concave and has an attachment which is convex. The attachment improves the ballistics until impact with the water. The space between nose and attachment is filled with grease.

8. On striking the water, the nose attachment is dished in and also the tail breaks away.

9. The buoyancy chamber is held onto the charge case by twelve nuts. There are twelve recesses in the side of the bomb to receive these nuts.

10. When the tail breaks away it uncovers a wheel shaped disc on the base of the bomb. This is the contact disc, i.e., firing disc. There are three chains attached to the disc, the other ends being fastened to the support ring on the bomb base. If these chains are **tight** the fuze is armed because the contact disc rises during the arming process.

C.A.F.O. P.6/45

Add new page 18a.

SECTION 13C.—60-lb. TRAINING BOMB, H.E.

The body (2) and tail unit (1) are in one piece and are manufactured of rolled and pressed paper.

2. The rolled paper charge container (3) containing pentalite, rests on a felt washer seated on a diaphragm in the body.

3. The head of the charge container is closed by a rolled paper head (5), pinned (4), treated with shellac and taped in position.

4. The head is recessed to house the pistol adapter.

5. The pistol adapter houses 3 C.E. pellets, a detonator and a No. 42 nose pistol to which a 6-in. extension rod is fitted by means of a spring washer after the arming vane cap has been removed.

(*T. 06720/44.—C.A.F.O. P.6/45.*)

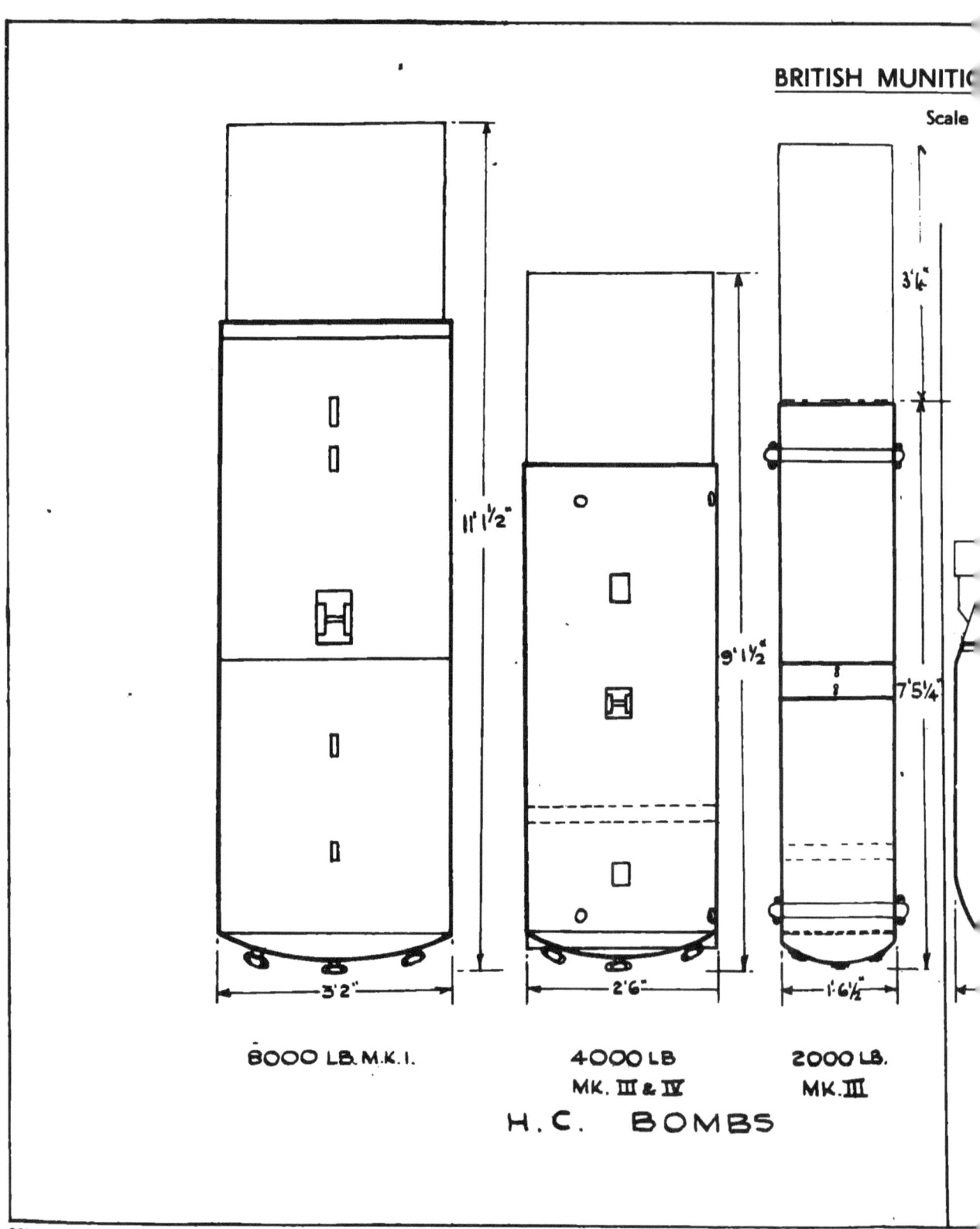

NS—H.E. BOMBS

Pt. 1. Chap. 1.
Diagram 1.

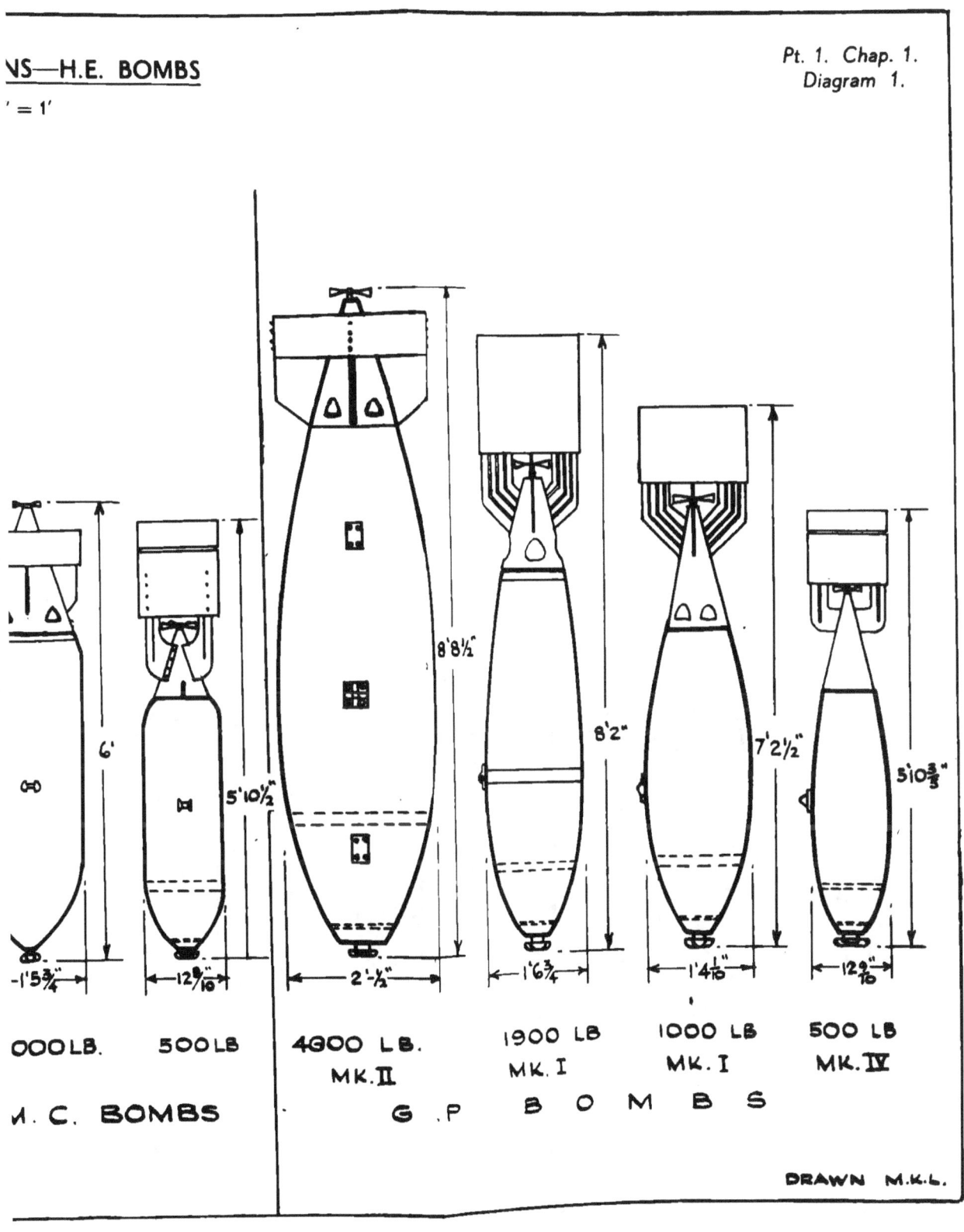

DRAWN M.K.L.

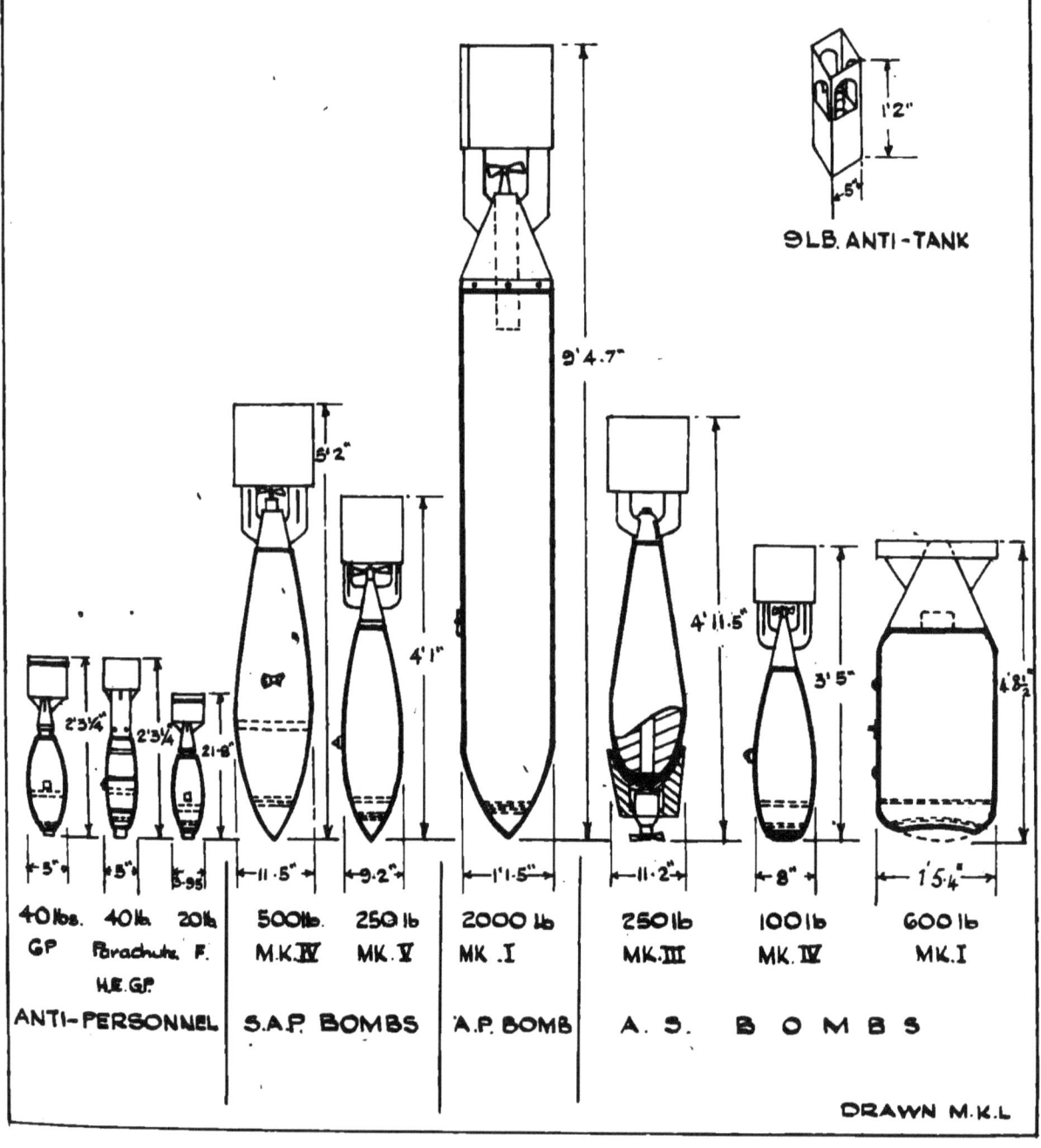

A.S. 35 LB. BOMB

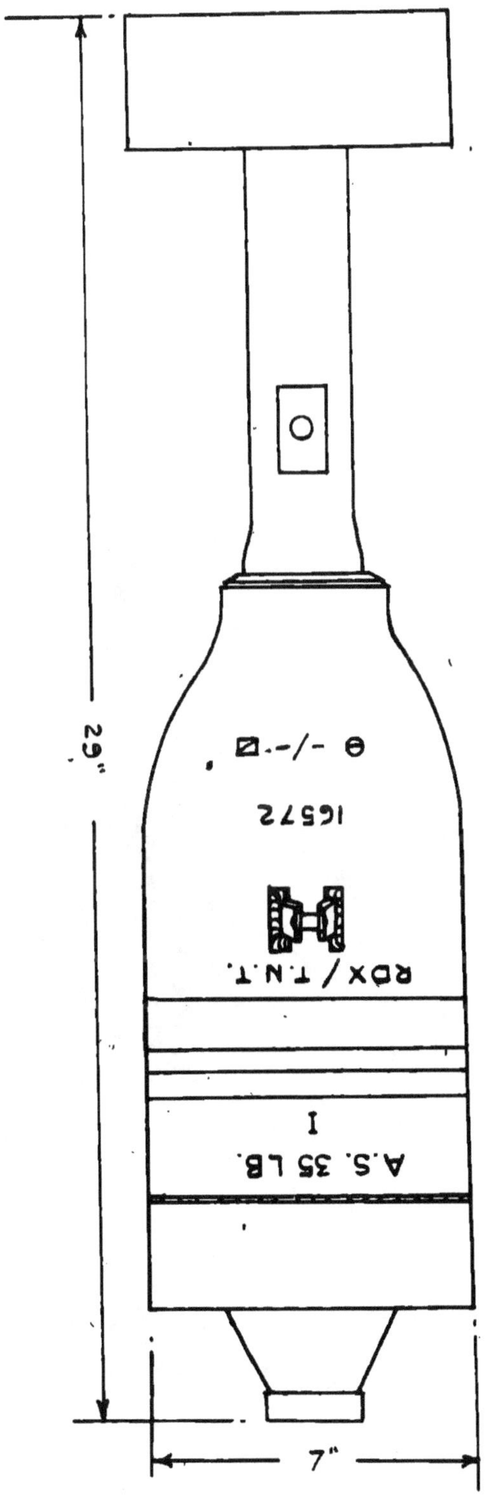

Pt. 1. Chap. 1.
Diagram 3. Section 7

29"

7"

A.S. 35 LB.
I

RDX/T.N.T.

16572

Pt. 1. Chap. 1.
Section 4.

Fig. 1

G.P. 250 LBS. Mk. IV

Pt. 1. Chap. 1.
Section 9.

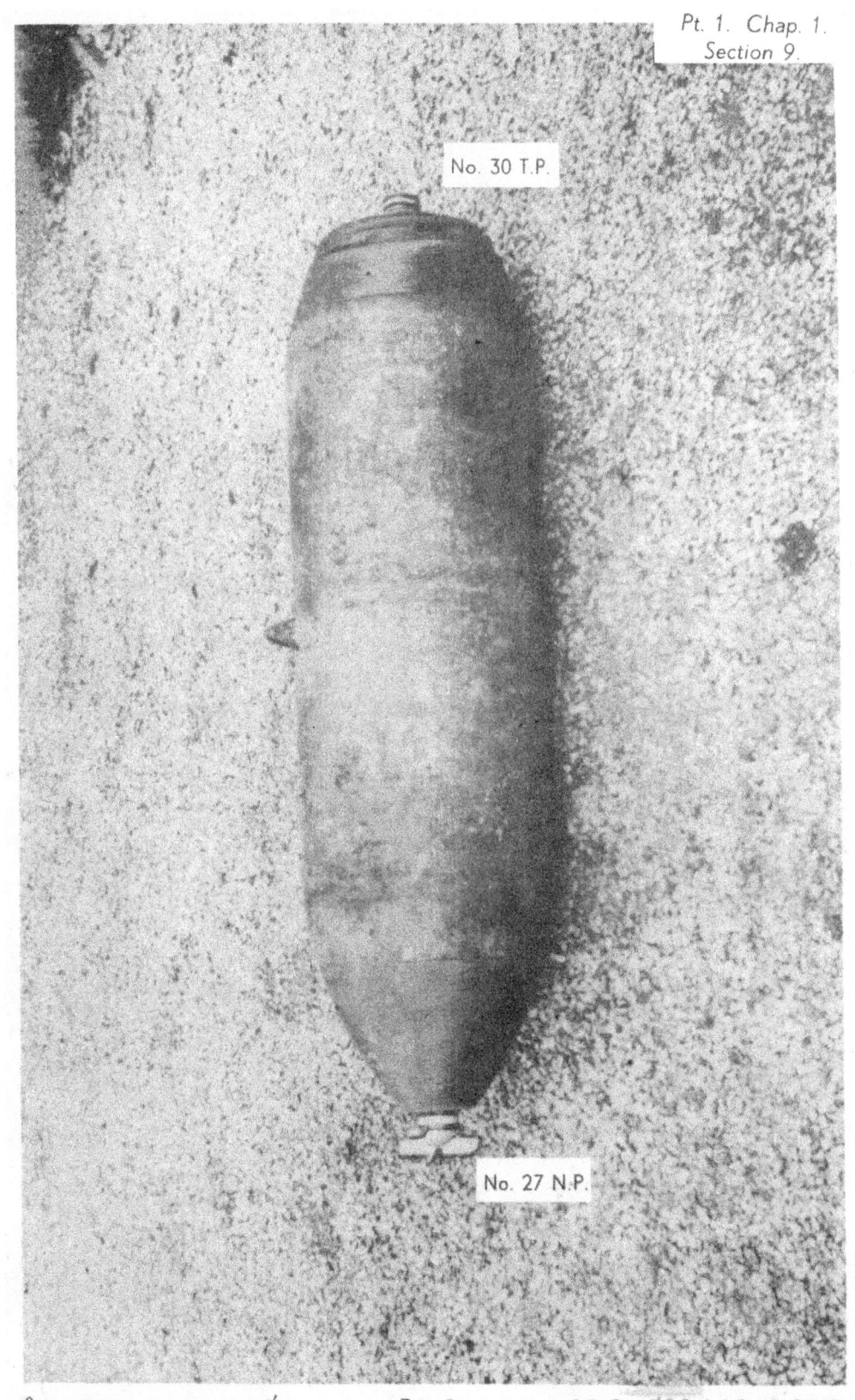

Fig. 2   M.C. 500 LBS. BOMB

Pt. 1. Chap. 1.
Section 11.

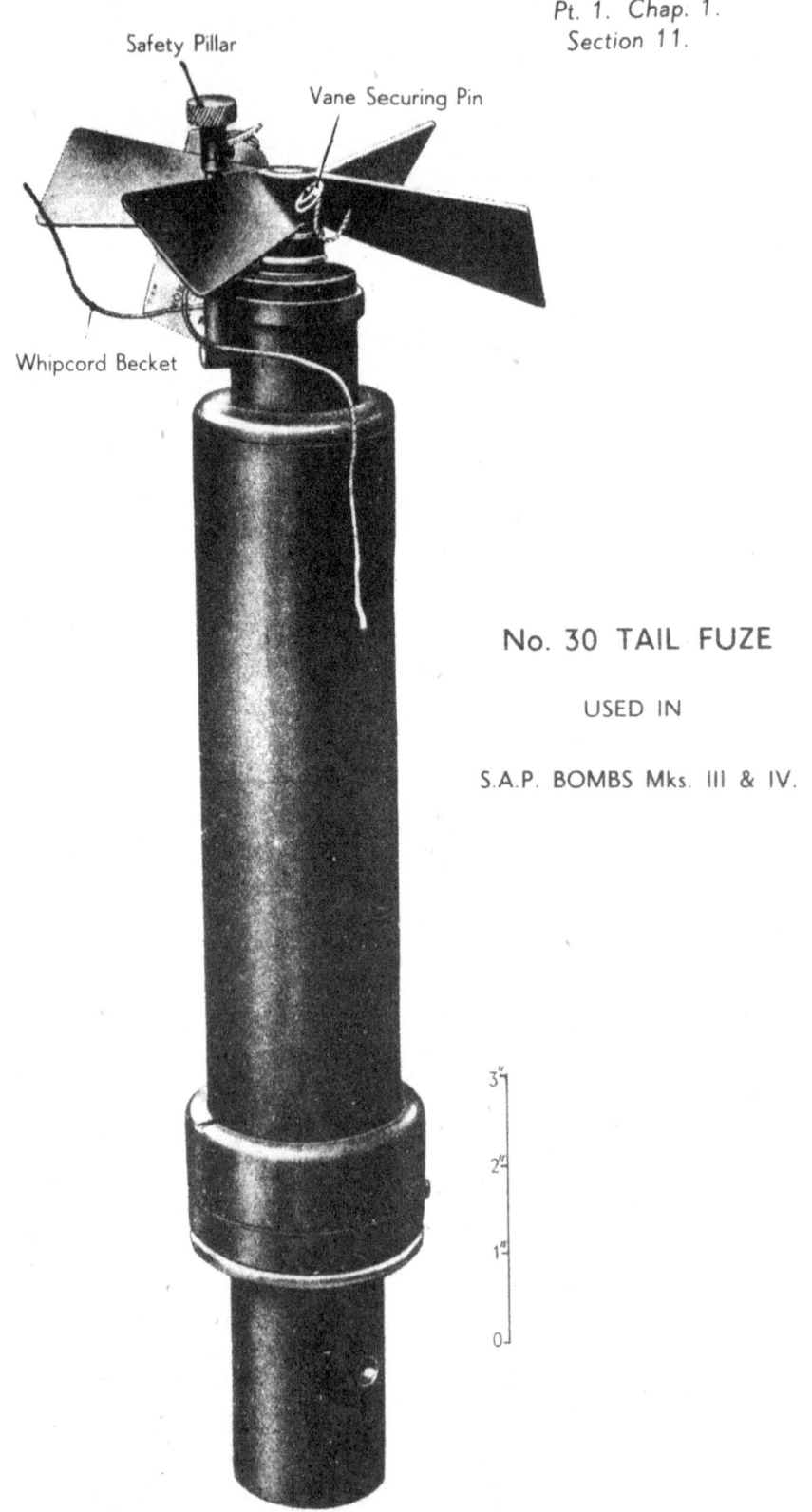

No. 30 TAIL FUZE

USED IN

S.A.P. BOMBS Mks. III & IV.

Fig. 3

Pt. 1. Chap. 1.
Section 11.

No. 32.
NOSE FUZE
USED IN A.S. BOMBS Mk. III.

No. 847.
TAIL FUZE
USED IN 9 LBS. ANTI-TANK BOMBS

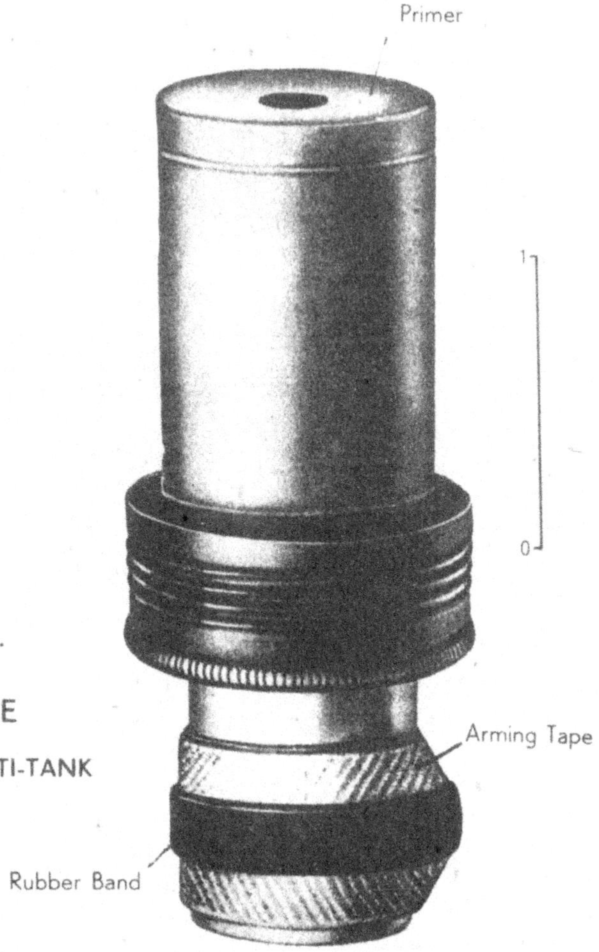

Fig. 4.

Fig. 5.

Pt. 1. Chap. 1.
Section 11.

No. 845 ANTI-DISTURBANCE

NOSE FUZE

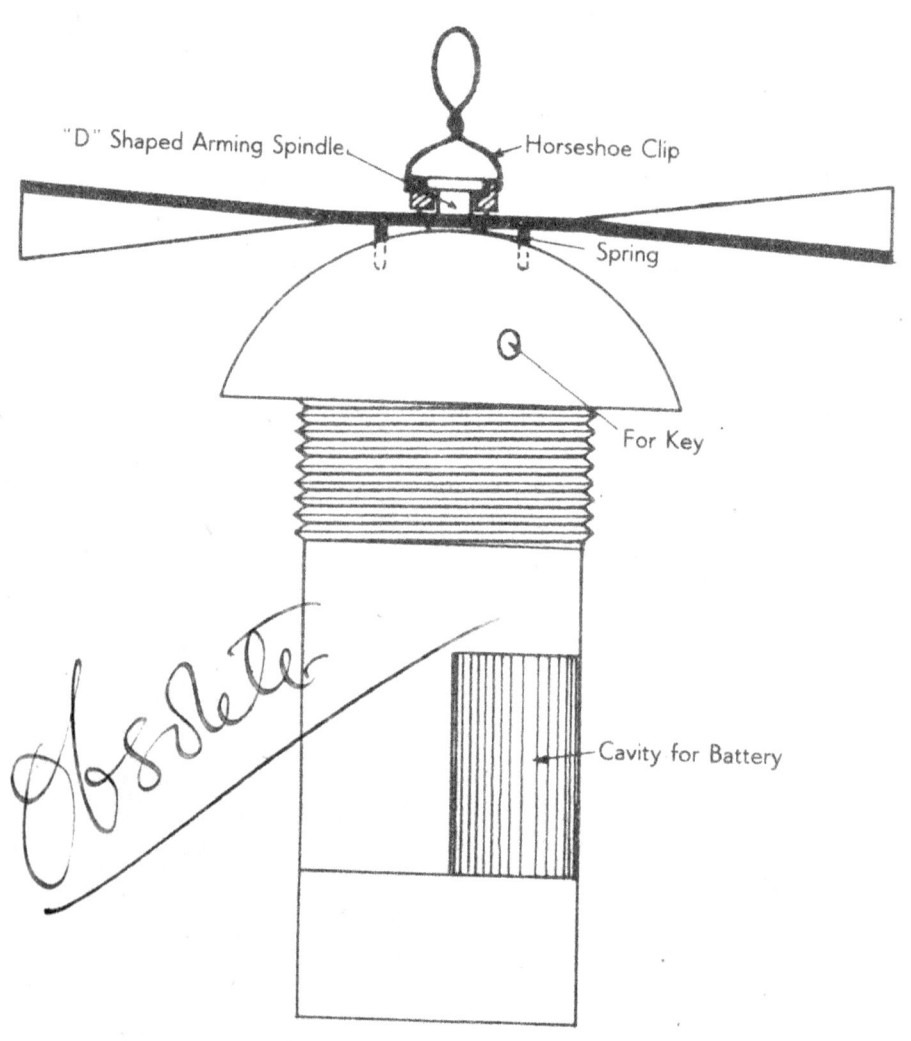

Fig. 6.

Pt. 1. Chap. 1.
Section 11.

No. 862 HYDROSTATIC TAIL FUZE

(USED IN THE 600 LBS. A.S. BOMB)

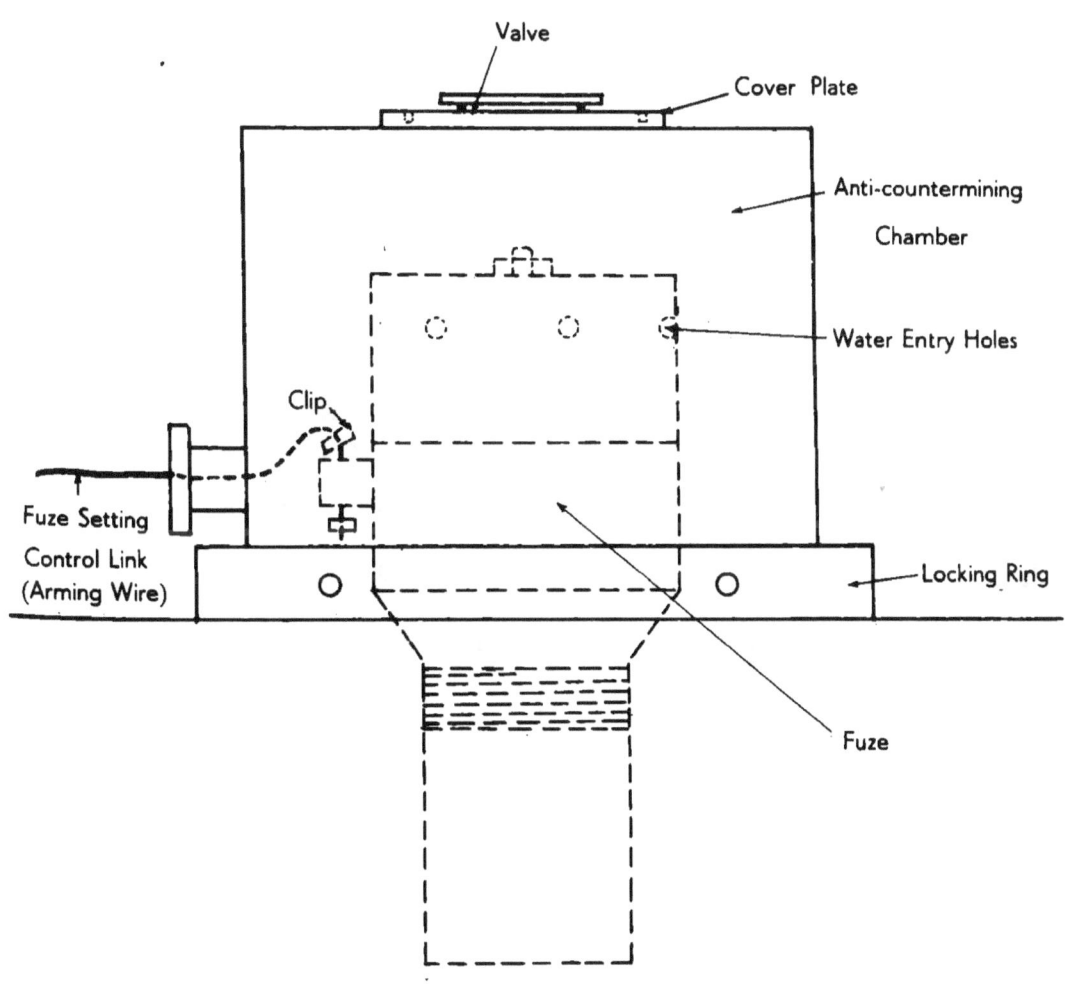

Fig. 7. Approx. Full Scale

Pt. 1. Chap. 1.
Section 12.

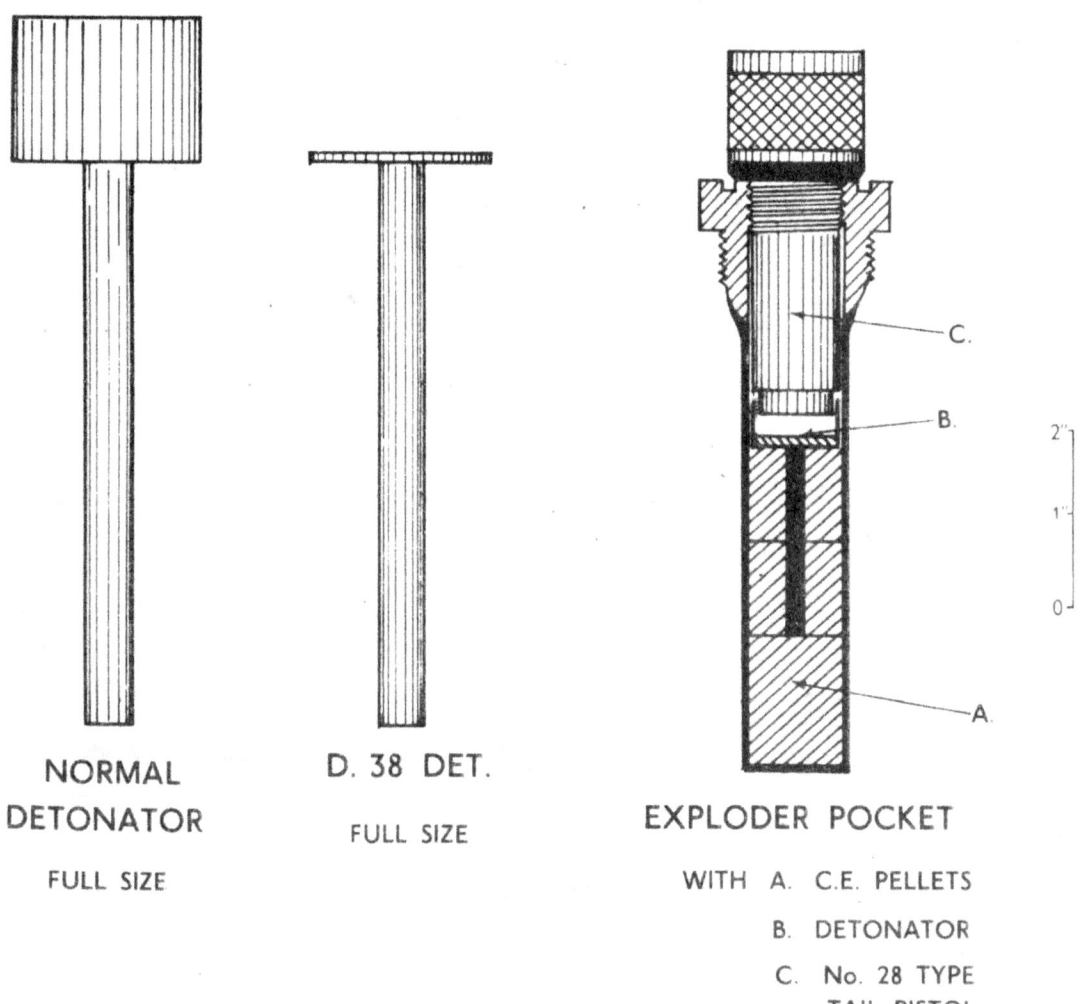

Fig. 8

Part 1. Chap 1.
Section 12.

USED IN G.P. BOMBS Mks. I - III

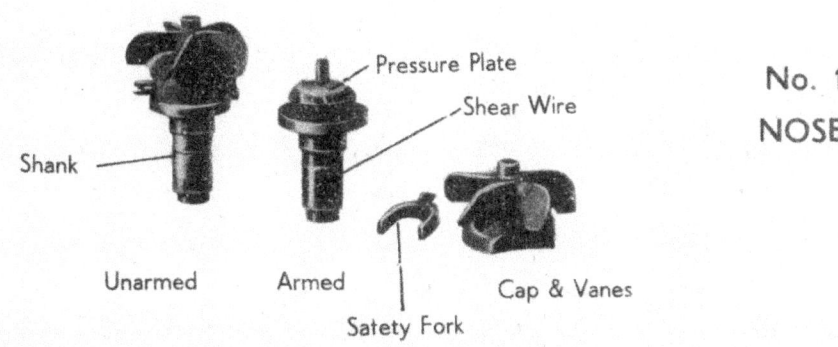

No. 22

TAIL PISTOL

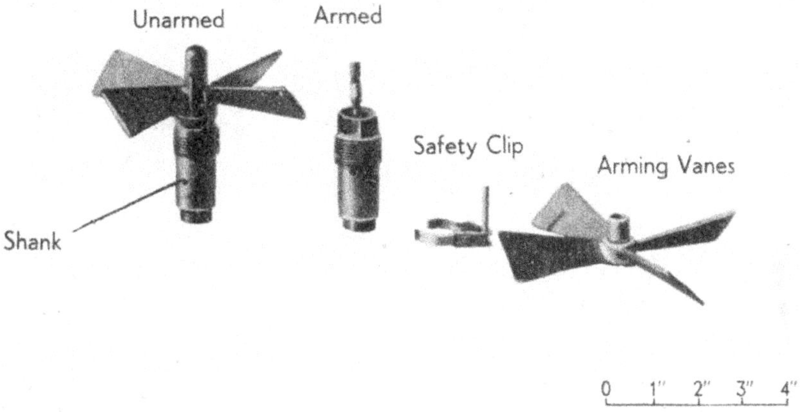

Fig. 10.

No. 19

NOSE PISTOL

Fig. 9

Pt. 1. Chap. 1.
Section 12.

No. 27 NOSE PISTOL

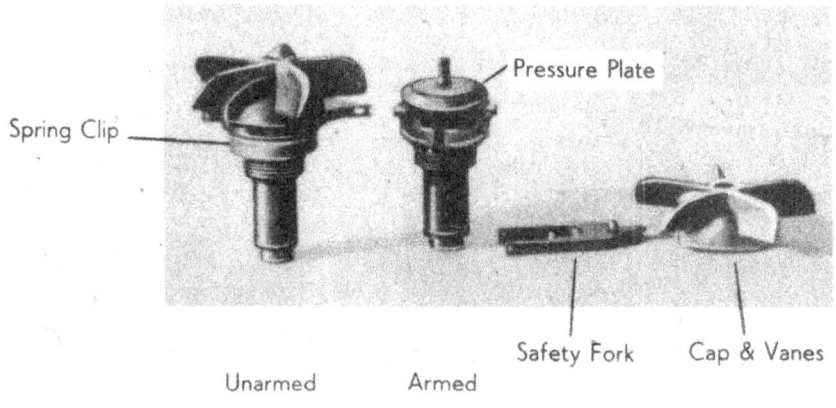

Fig. 11

No. 30 TAIL PISTOL

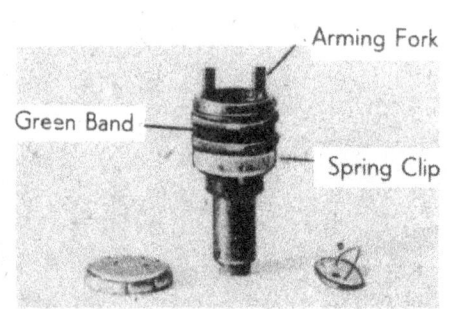

Fig. 12

Pt. 1. Chap. 1.
Section 12.

No. 37 TAIL PISTOL

LONG DELAY   N.B.—ALWAYS HAS RED ARMING VANES

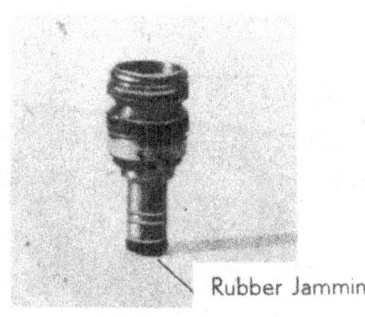

Rubber Jamming Washer for Anti Withdrawal Device

Fig. 13

No. 28 TAIL PISTOL

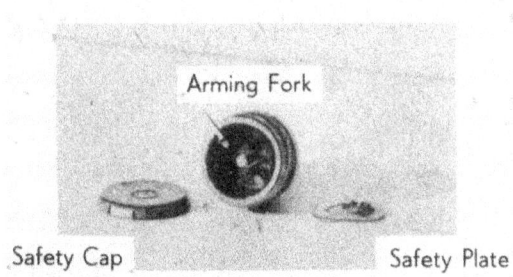

Fig. 14

Pt. 1. Chap. 1
Section 12.

No. 34 NOSE PISTOL

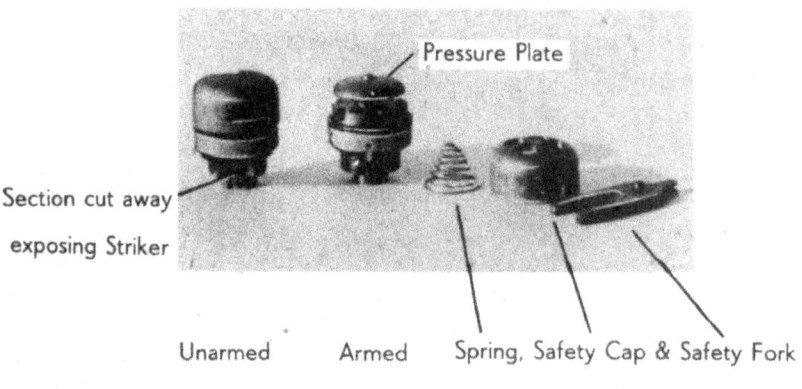

Fig. 15

No. 38 NOSE PISTOL

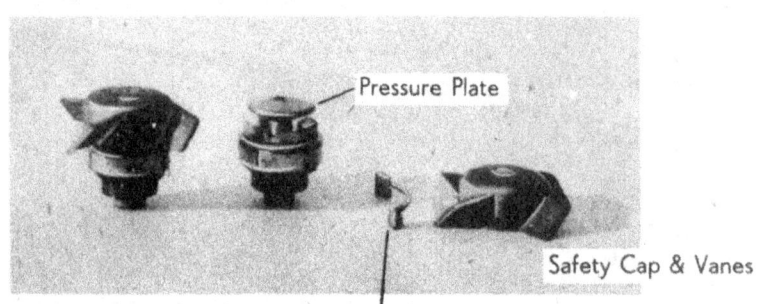

Fig. 16

Pt. 1. Chap. 1.
Section 12.

No. 44 NOSE PISTOL

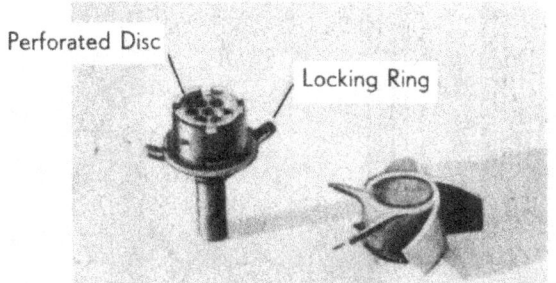

ARMED

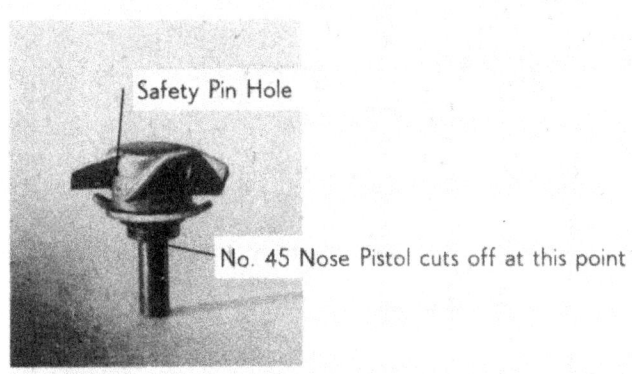

UNARMED

Fig. 17

Pt. 1. Chap. 1.
Section 12.

No. 33 NOSE PISTOL

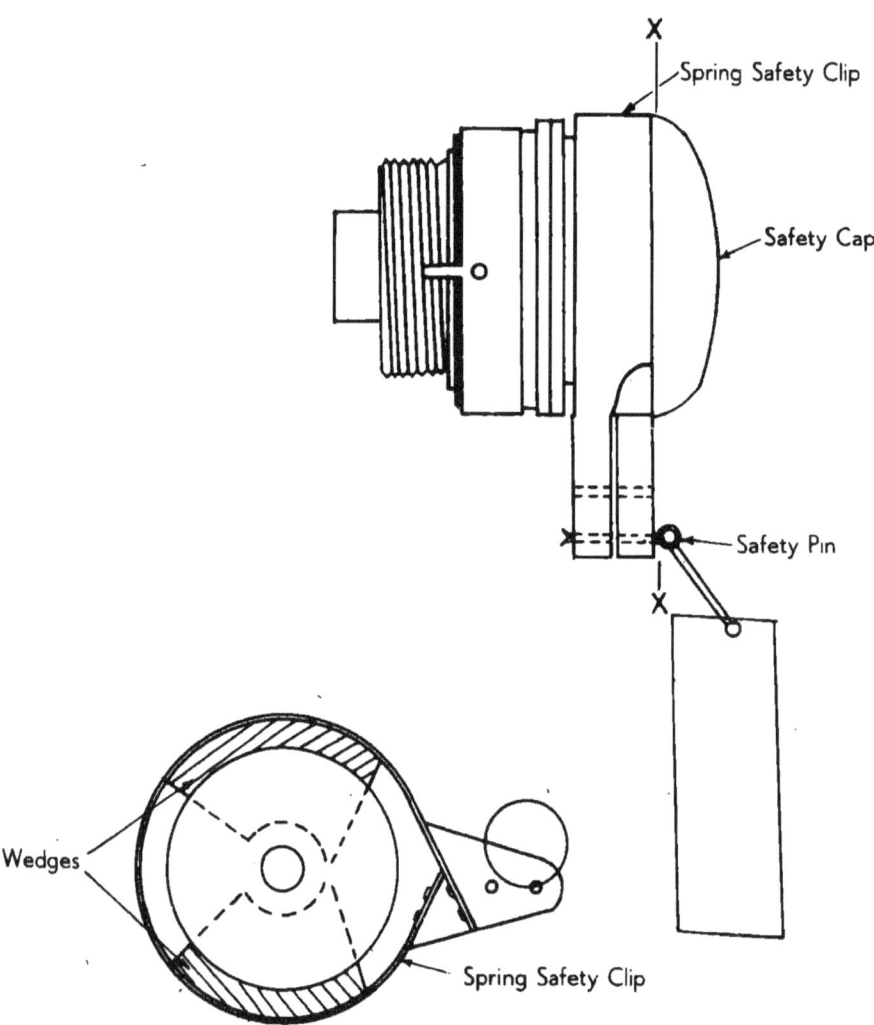

Fig. 18

FULL SIZE

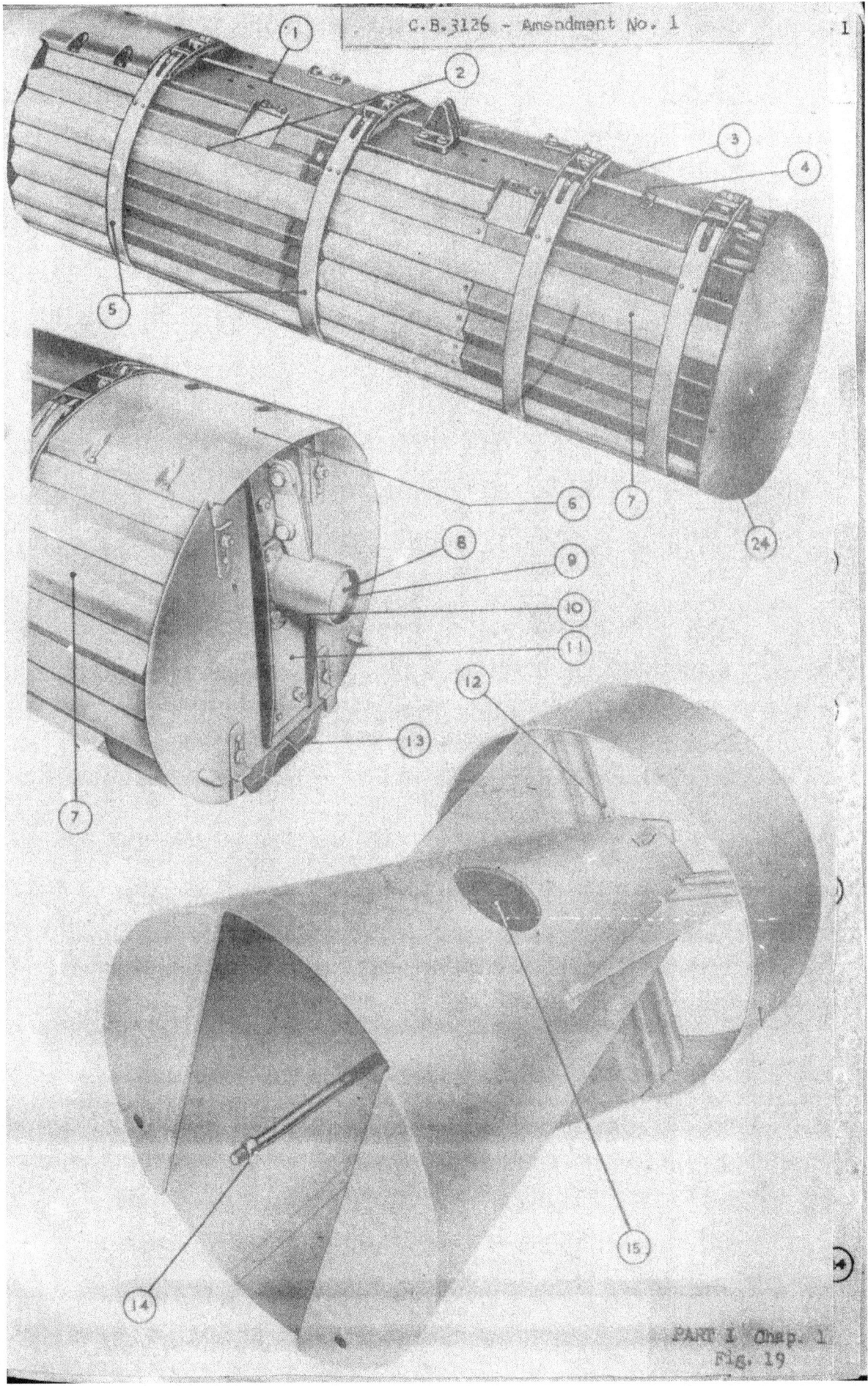

PART I Chap. 1
Fig. 19

C.B.3126 - Amendment No. 1   PART I Chap. I
                               Fig. 20

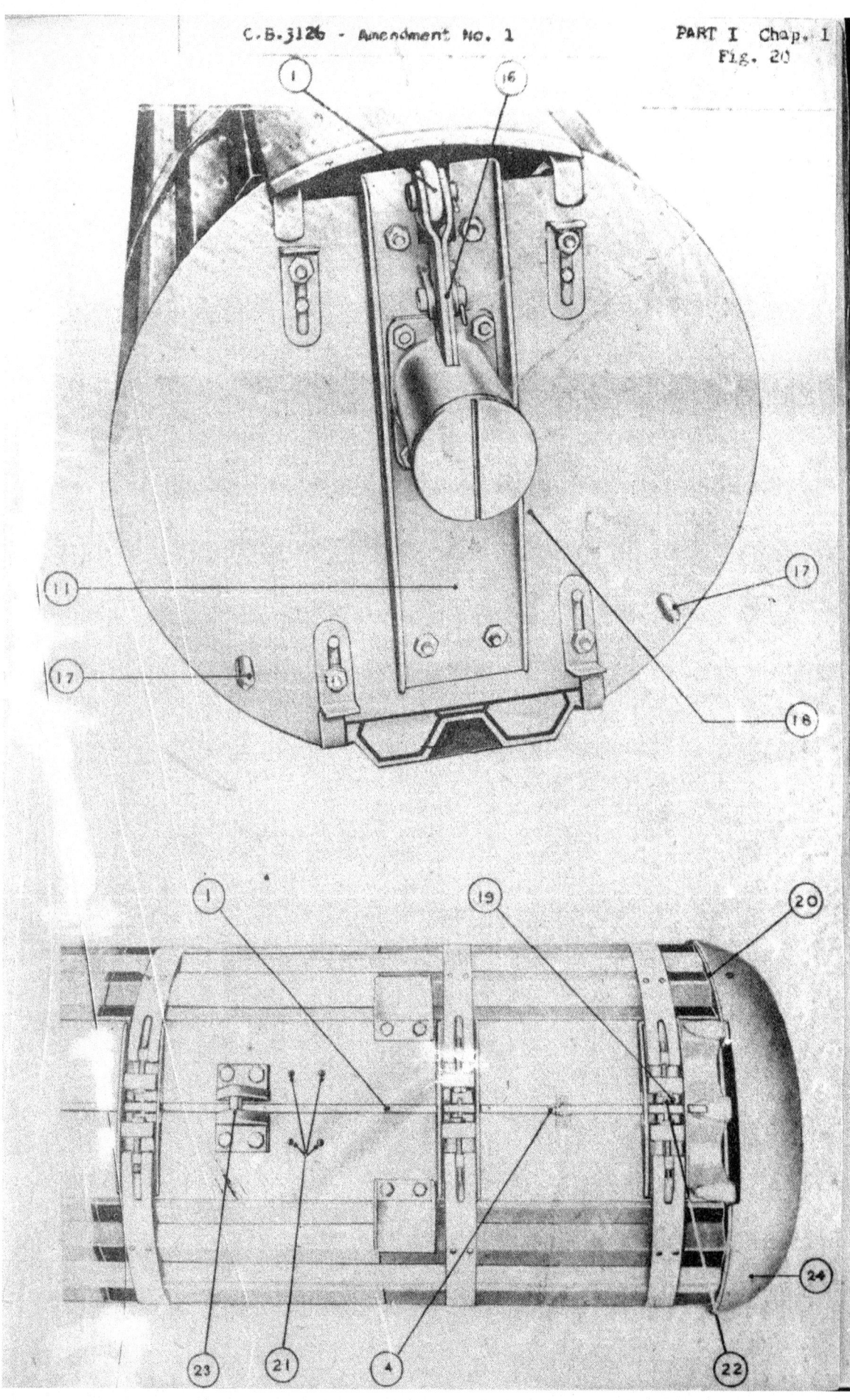

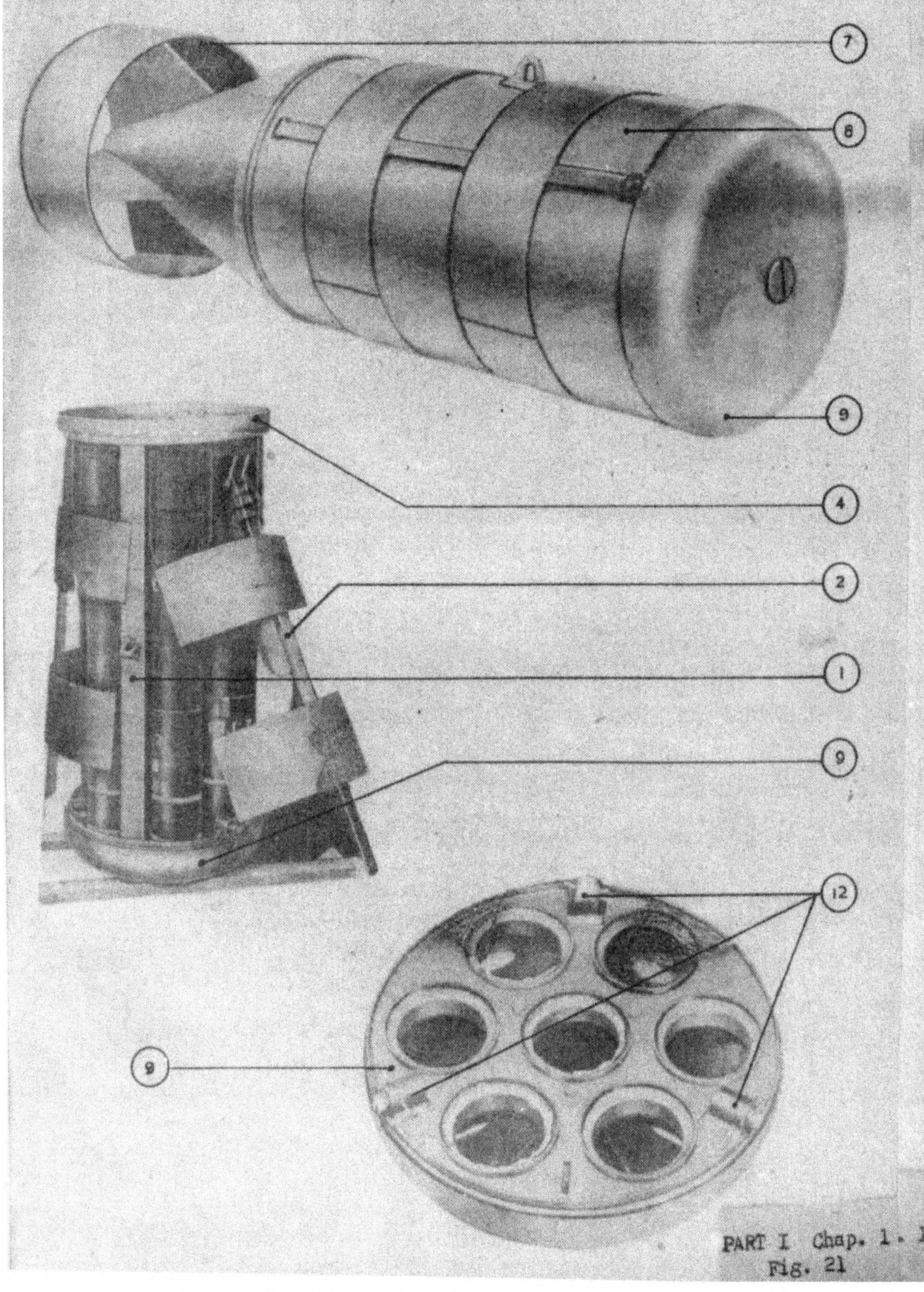

CONFIDENTIAL
C.B.3126 - Amendment No. 1

PART I Chap. 1.1
Fig. 21

C.B.5126 - Amendment No. 1

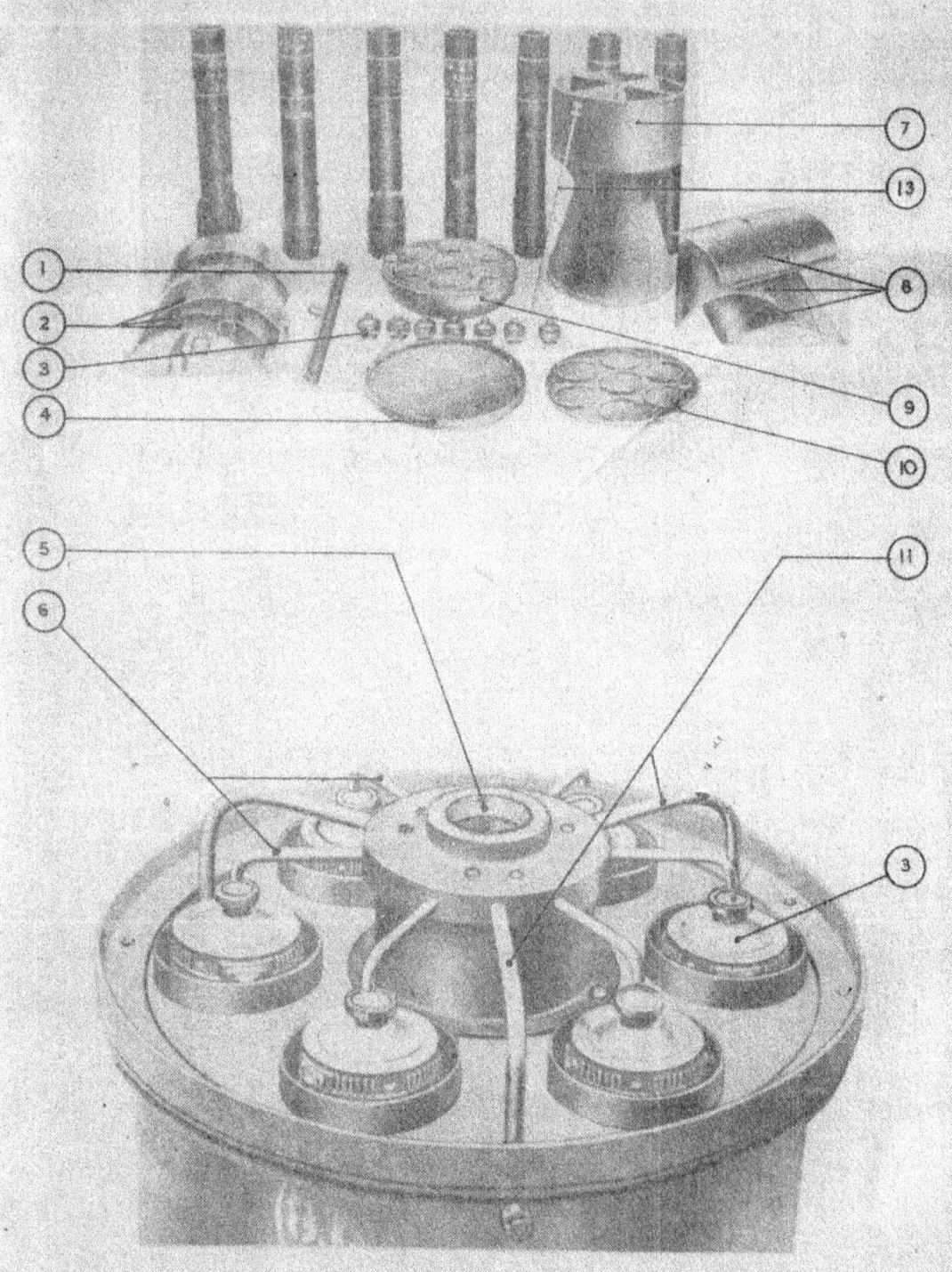

PART I Chap. 1
Fig. 22

C.B.3126 - Amendment No. 1

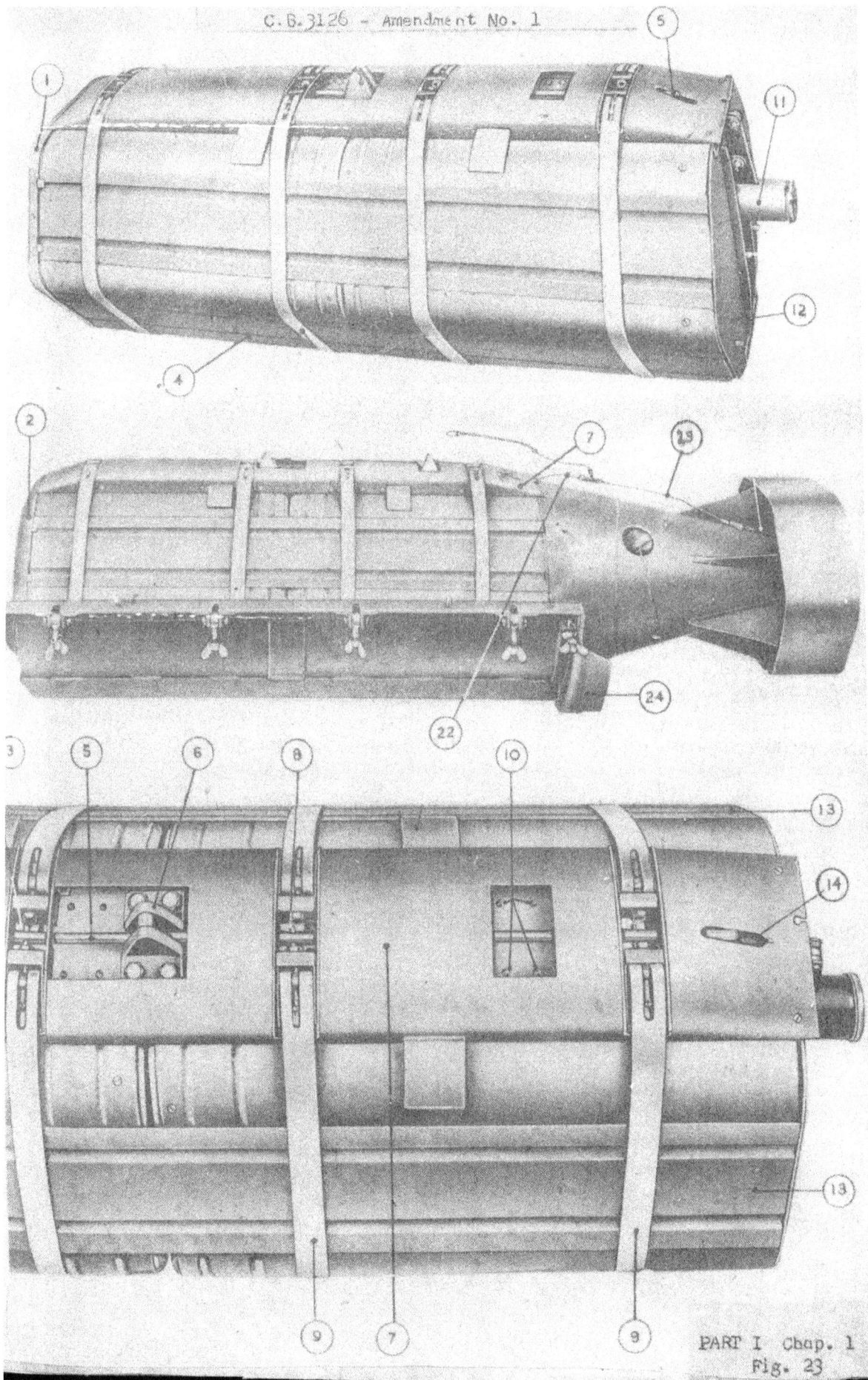

PART I Chap. 1
Fig. 23

CONFIDENTIAL.

C.B.3126 - Amendment No. 1

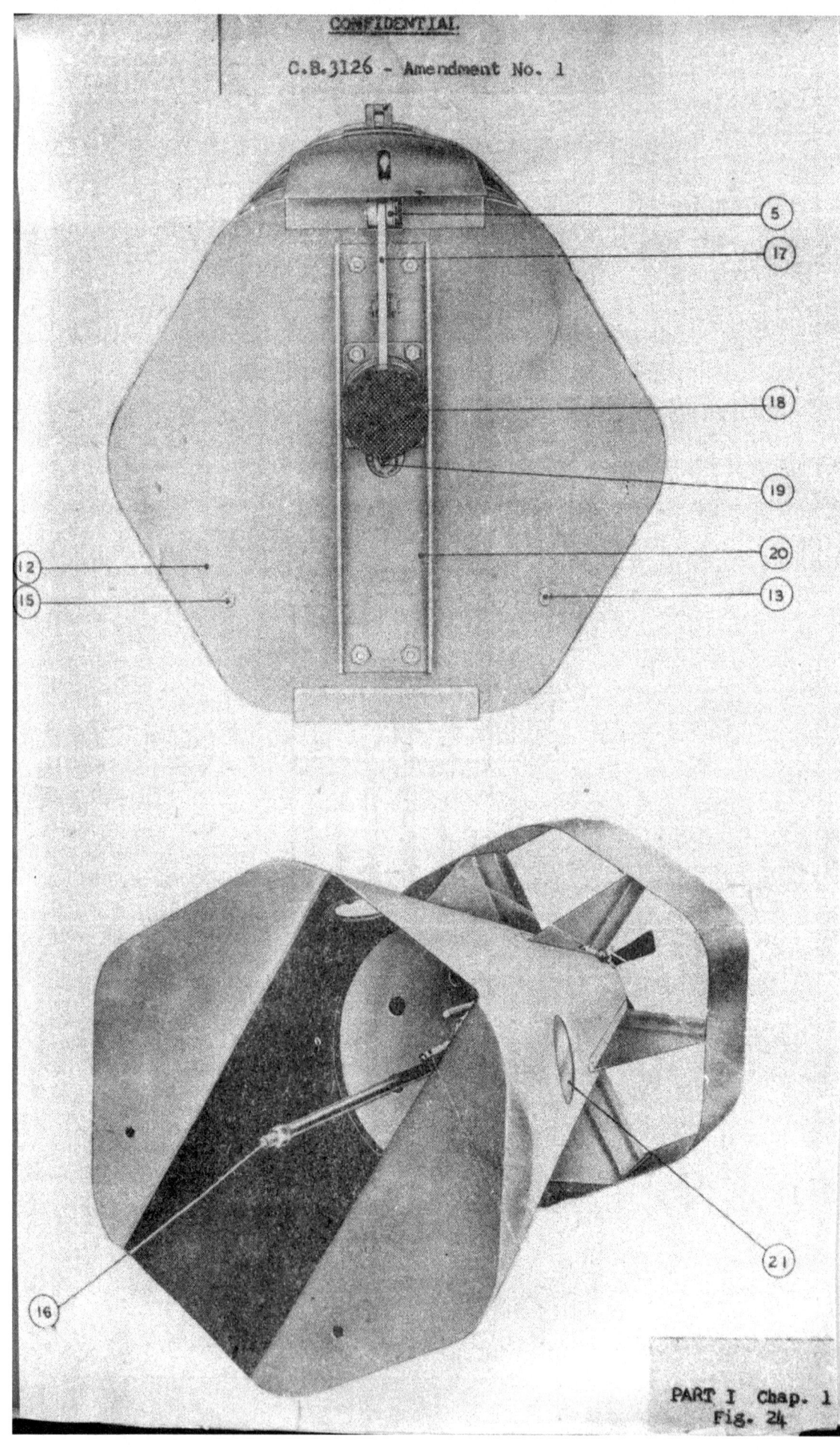

PART I Chap. 1
Fig. 24

CONFIDENTIAL
C.B. 3126 - Amendment No. 1

PART I
CHAP I.

250 LB 'B' BOMB. Mk III

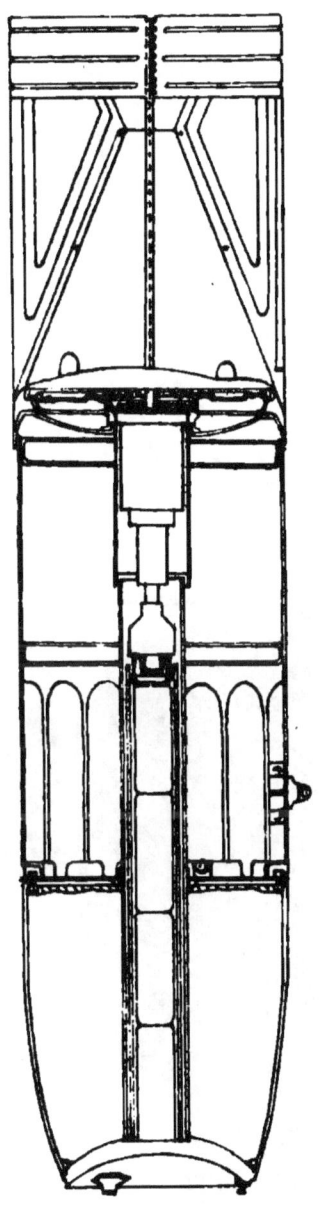

FIG. 25.

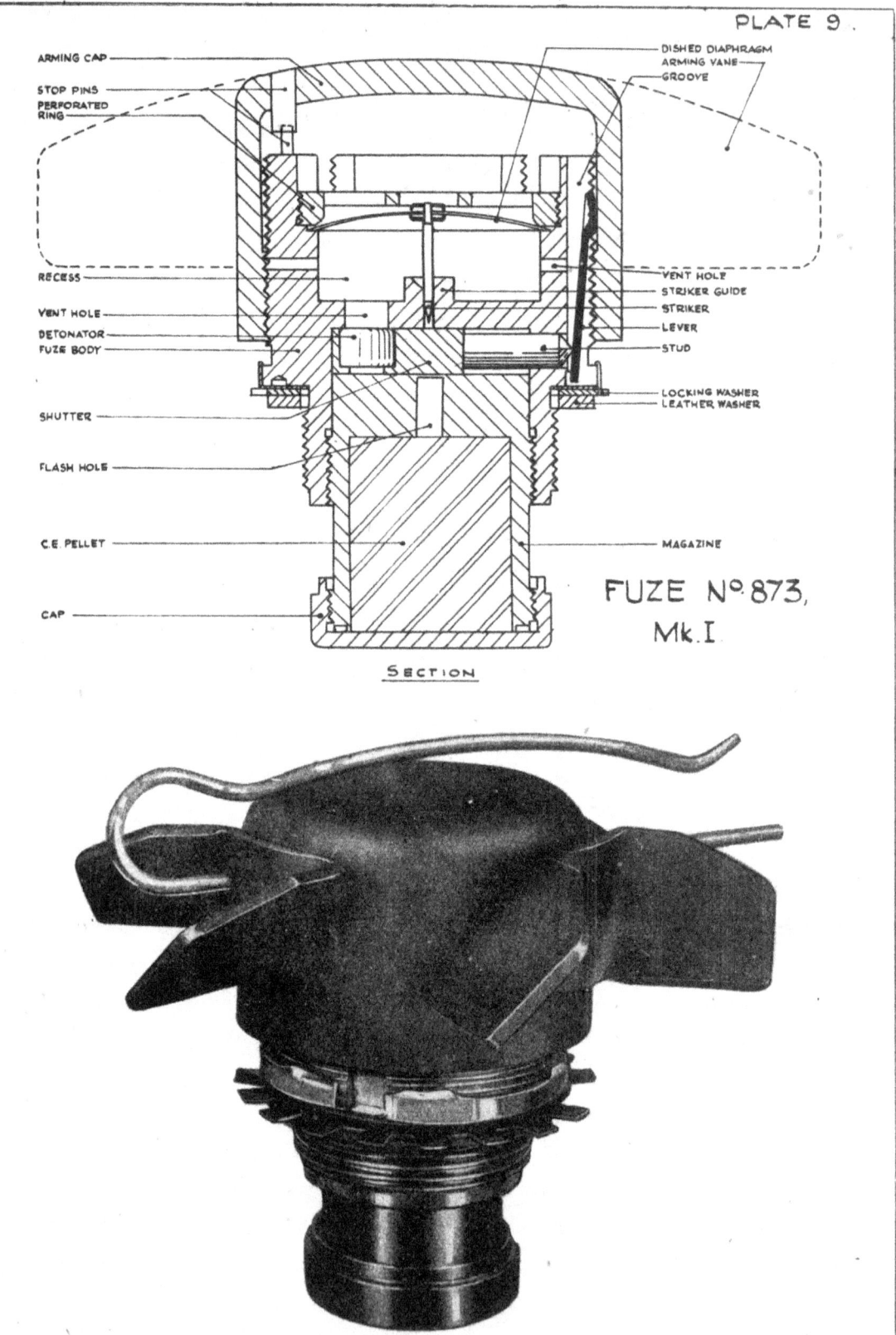

FUZE No. 873, Mk. I

C.A.F.O. "P" SERIES DIAGRAM 84/44 (1)

PLATE 10.

BRITISH 8lb. F BOMB

FIG 27.

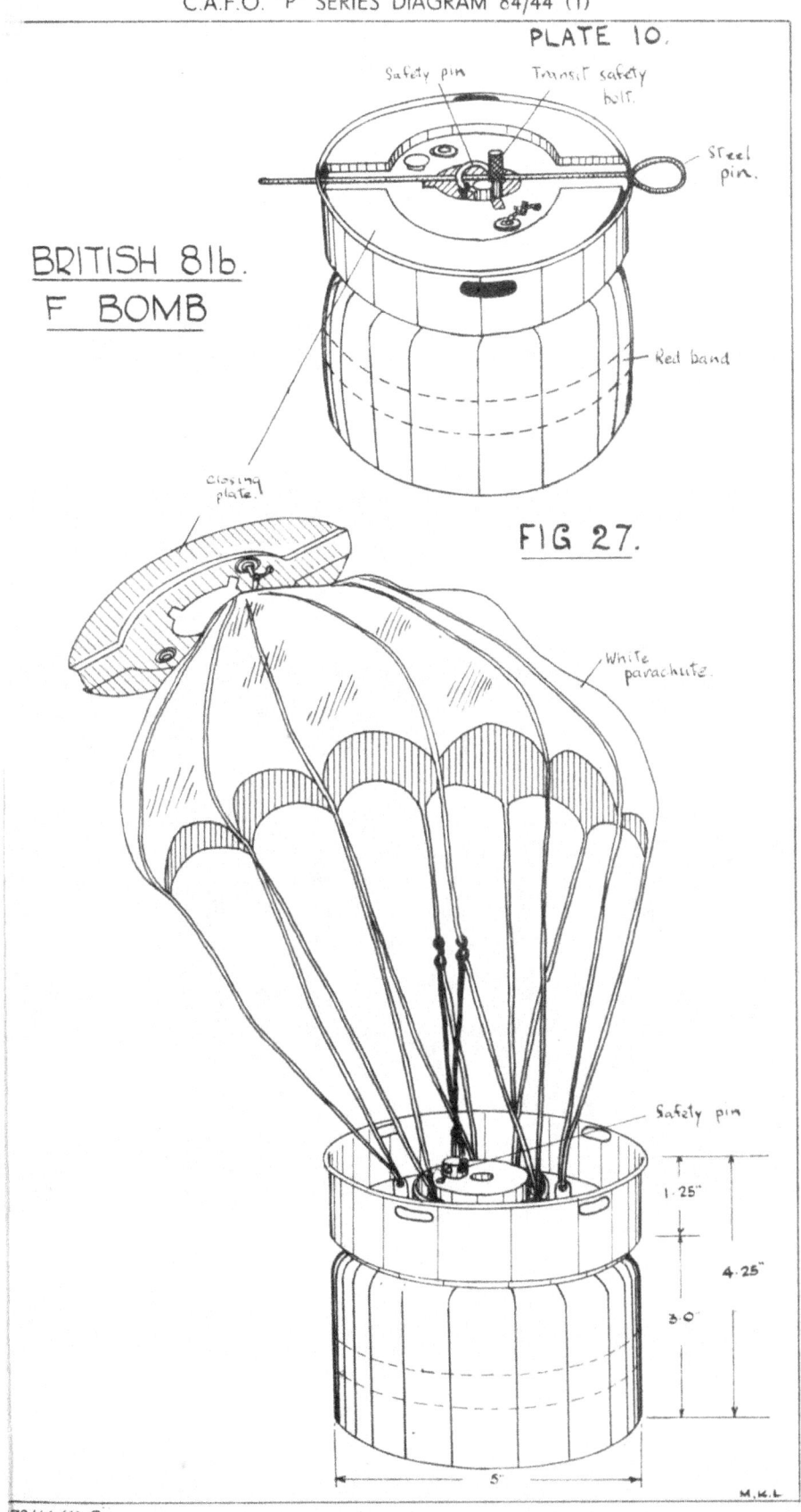

C.A.F.O. "P" SERIES DIAGRAM 84/44 (2)

PLATE II.

FIG. 28.

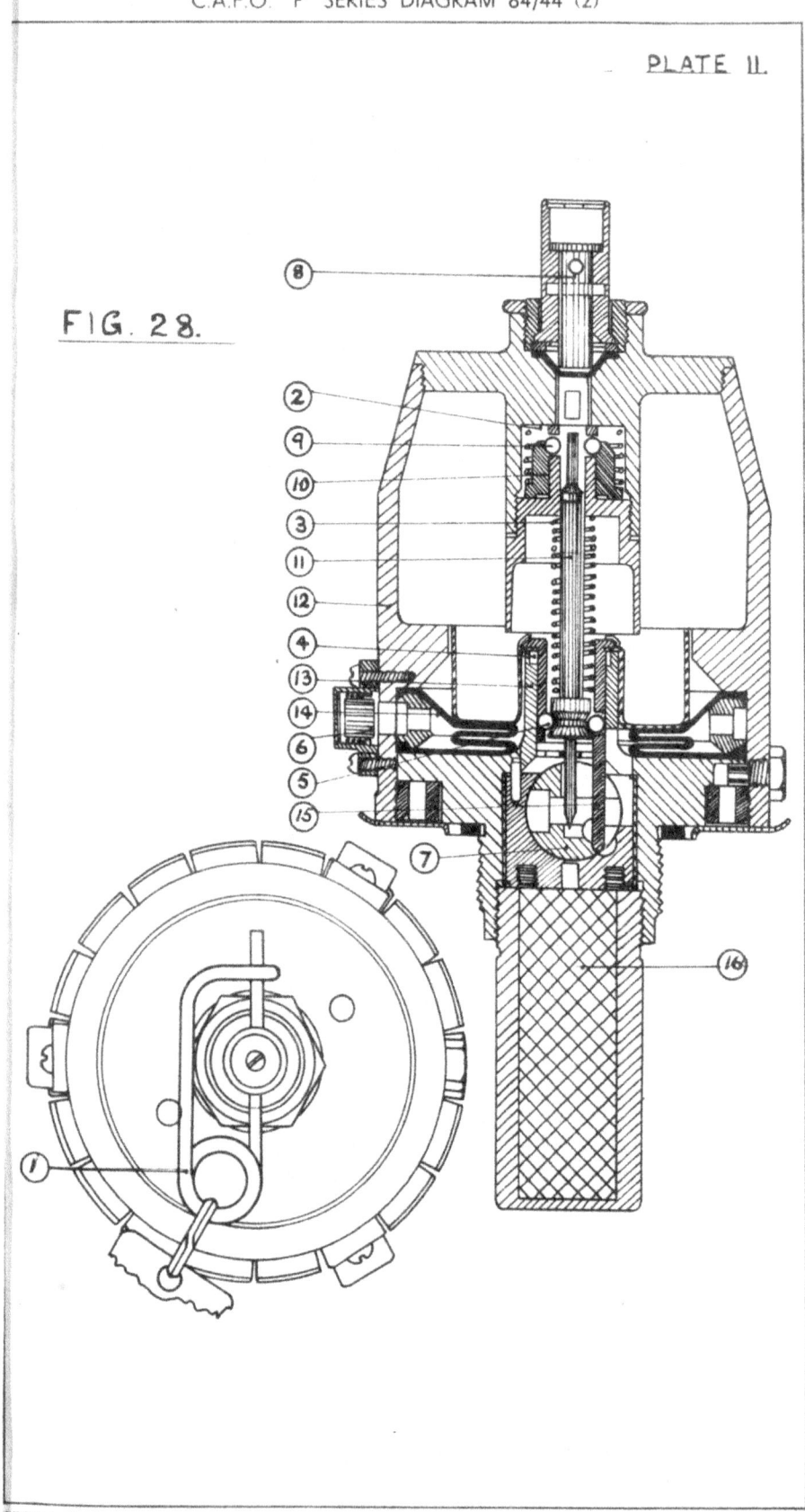

C.A.F.O. "P" SERIES DIAGRAM 84/44 (3)

PLATE 12

BRITISH NO. 54 MK.I. TAIL PISTOL

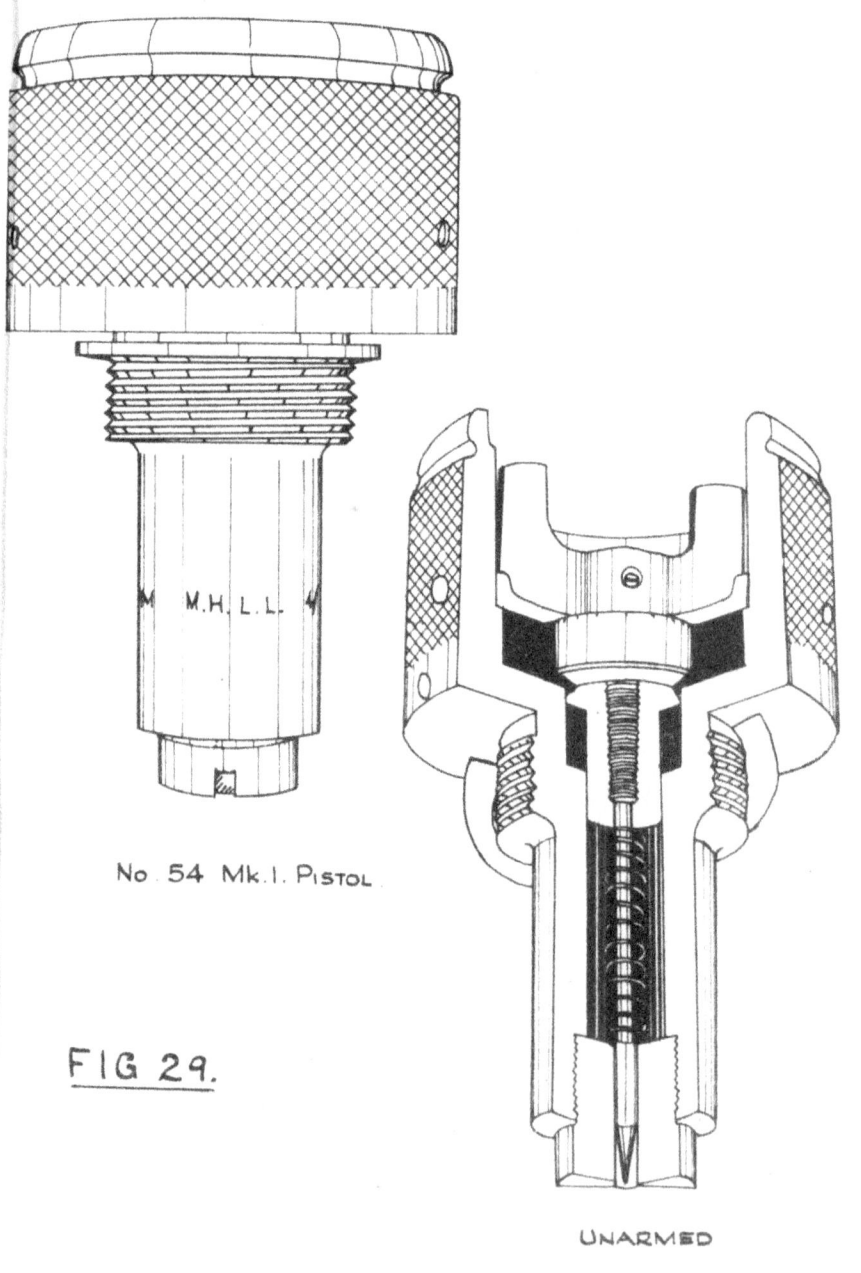

No. 54 Mk.I. Pistol

FIG 29.

UNARMED

C.A.F.O. "P" SERIES DIAGRAM 84/44 (4)

PLATE. 13.

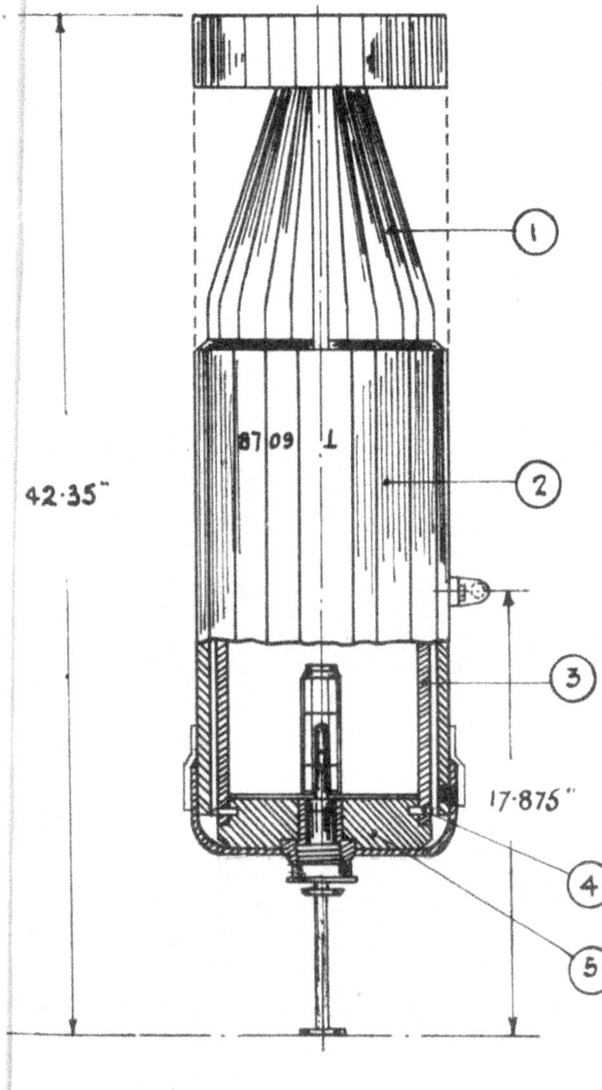

FIG. 30.

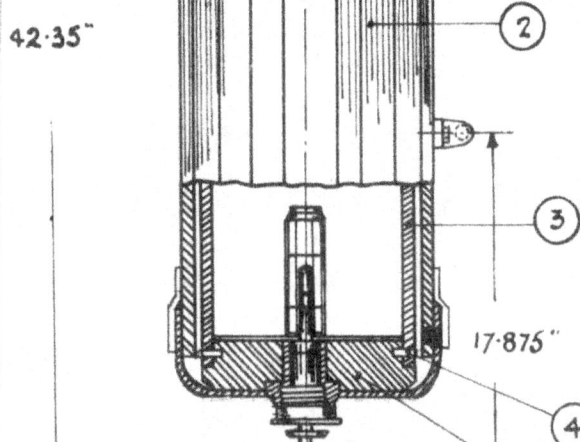

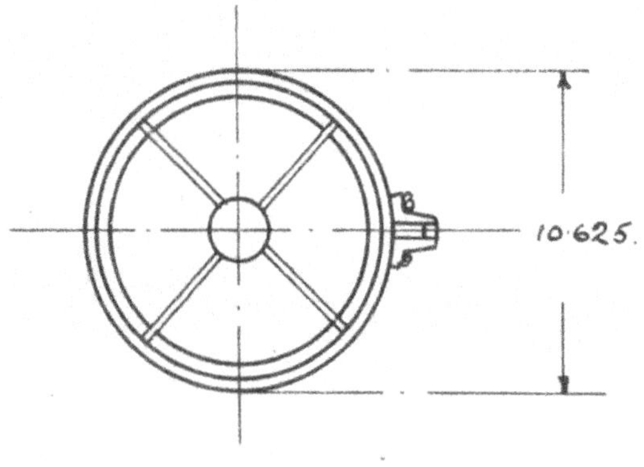

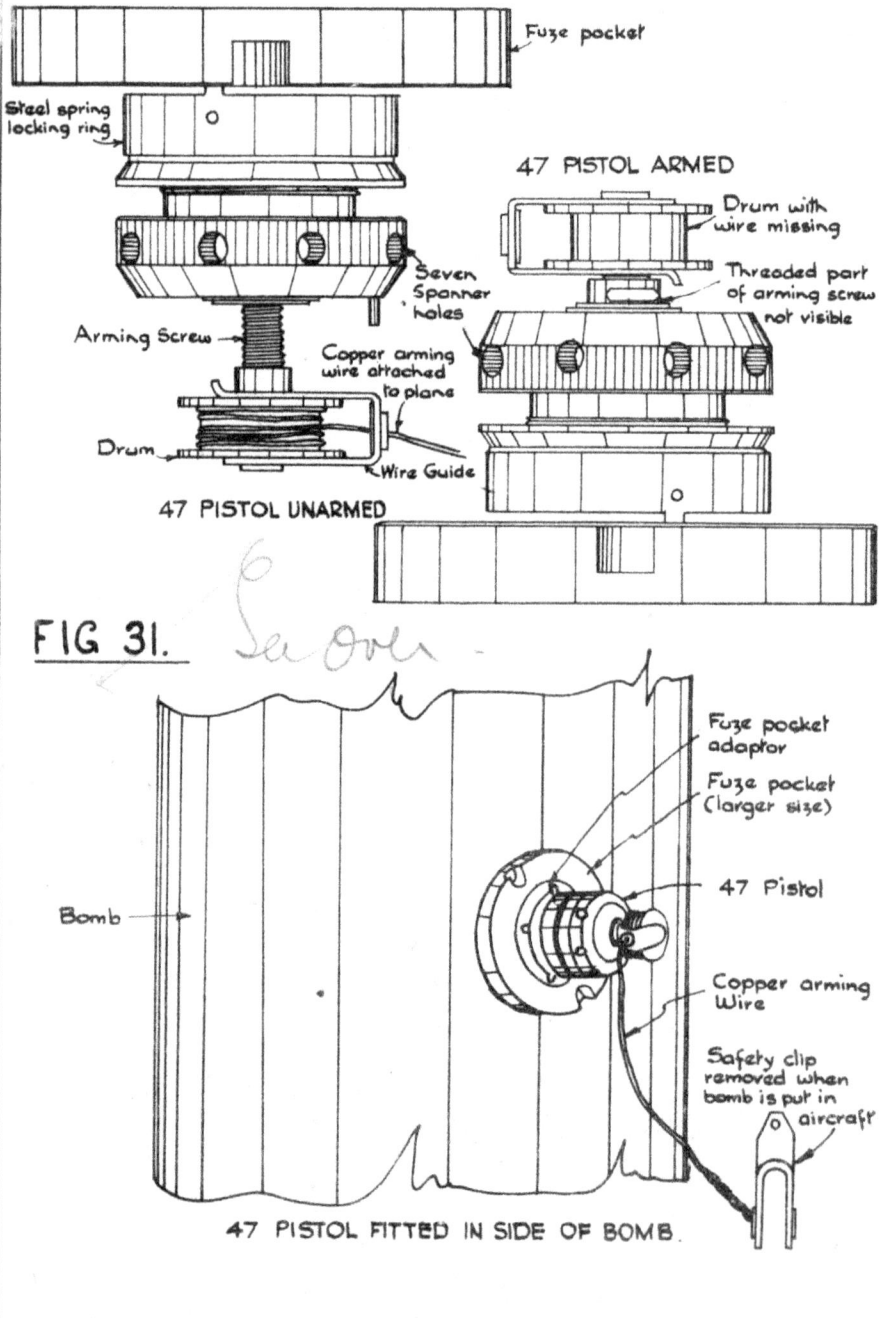
PLATE 14.

C.A.F.O. "P" SERIES DIAGRAM 84/44 (6)

PLATE 15.

FLARE AIRCRAFT RECONNAISSANCE. 7" HOODED MARK I.

See prev page
FIG 31.

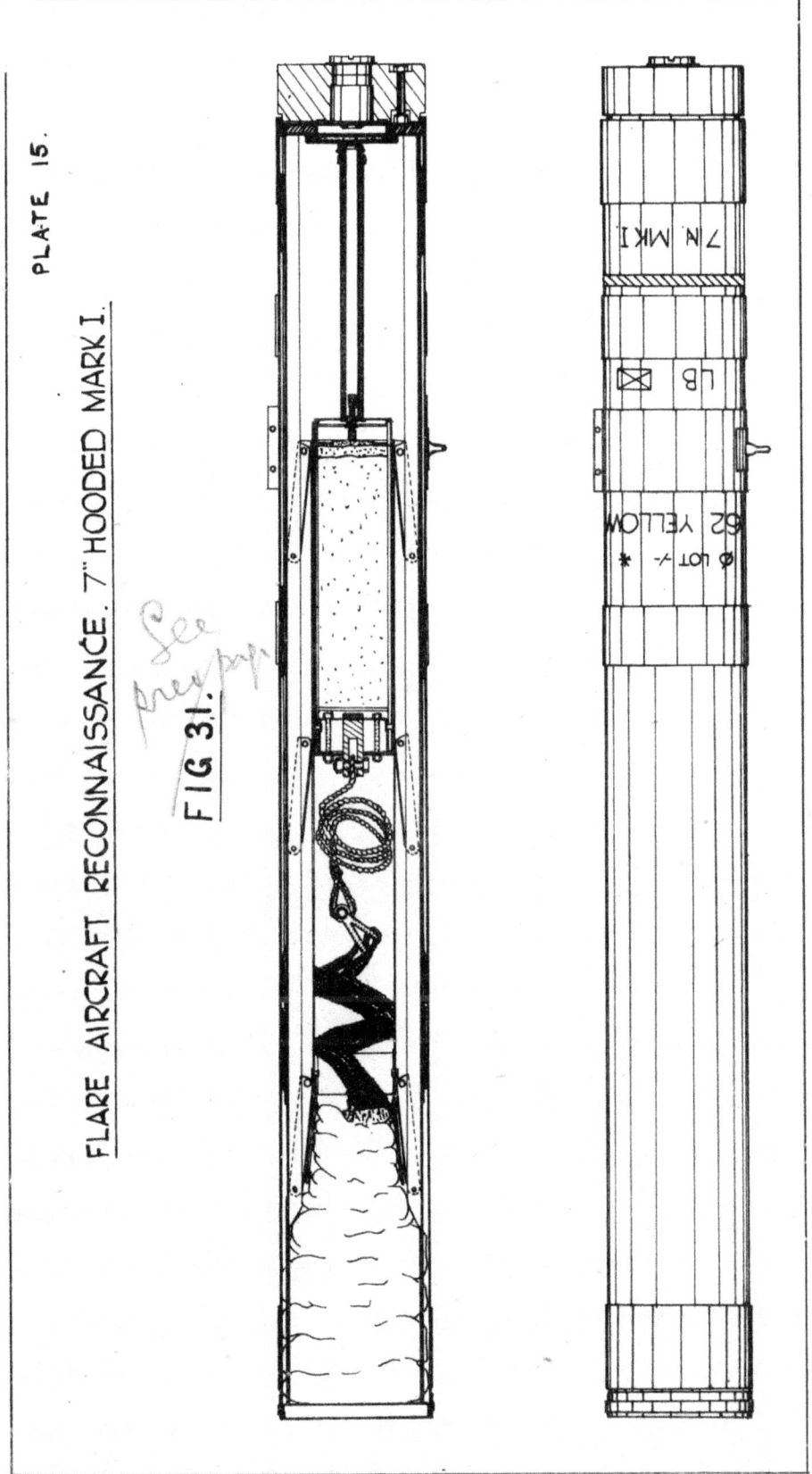

872/44 (6) C.

CHAPTER II

RECOGNITION

Incendiaries and Pyrotechnics

Section	Page
1A.—4-lb. Incendiaries	20
1B.—25-lb. Incendiary	20
1C.—30-lb. Incendiary	21
1D.—45-lb. Incendiary	21
1E.—250-lb., Mark I. Incendiary	21
1F.—	21a
1G—500-lb. Incendiary Bomb, Mark I	22
2D—500-lb. Smoke Bomb, Mark II	28
7D—T.I., 250 lb., No. 19, Mark II, Sea Marker	22
8E—Flame Aircraft Reconnaissance, 7 in., Headed, Marks I and II	29b

(*T. 06720/44.—C.A.F.O. P.6/45.*)

.... Bomb, 8½ lb., Break-up	23
3B.—Practice Bomb, 10 lb., Smoke and Flash	23
3C.—Practice Bomb, 11¼ lb., Smoke and Flash	23
4A.—Smoke Float No. 1, Mark IV	24
4B.—Smoke Float No. 2, Marks I and II	24
4C.—Smoke Float No. 3, Mark I	24
5A.—Smoke Generators No. 5, Mark II	25
5B.—Smoke Generators No. 6, Mark II	25
5C.—Smoke Generators No. 11, Marks I and II	25
5D.—Smoke Generators No. 15, Mark I	25
5E.—Smoke Generators No. 18, Mark I	25
6A.—Flame Floats, Mark II	26
6B.—Message Carrying, Mark I	26
6C.—Flame Float No. 3, Mark I	26
6D.—Flame Float No. 4, Mark I	26
6E.—Marker Marine, Mark I	26
6F.—Marker Marine, Mark II	27
6G.—Marker Marine, Mark III	27
7A.—Sea Marker, Mark I	28
7B.—Sea Marker, Mark III	28
7C.—Sea Marker, Mark V	28
8A.—Reconnaissance Flare, 4·5 in., Mark III	29
Reconnaissance Flare, 4·5 in., Mark IV	29
Reconnaissance Flare, 4·5 in., Mark V	29
Reconnaissance Flare, 4·5 in., Mark V, P.F.F.	29
8B.—Reconnaissance Flare, 5·5 in., Marks I and II	29
8C.—Target Flares, Mark I	29
8D.—Training 4-in. Flares	29
8E.—Reconnaissance 4 in., Mark I	29
"8.F - Flare A/C Skymarker 25 lb. Mark I White Drip"	29a
9A.—Photographic Flash Bomb, 4·5 in., Marks I and II	30
9B.—Heavy Photographic Flash, 4·5 in.	30
10.—12-in. Target Indicator Bomb	31
11.—Fuzes used in Flares, Photographic Flashes and Target Illumination Bombs	32
12.—Miscellaneous : (*a*) Calibrators, Altimeter, Flash, Mark I	33

CHAPTER II

RECOGNITION

Incendiaries and Pyrotechnics

Section		Page
1A.—4-lb. Incendiaries		20
1B.—25-lb. Incendiary		20
1C.—30-lb. Incendiary		21
1D.—45-lb. Incendiary		21
1E.—250-lb., Mark I, Incendiary		21
"1.F - 30 lb. 'J' Type Incendiary Bomb"		"21a"
2A.—4-lb. Smoke Bomb		22
2B.—100-lb. Smoke Bomb		22
2C.—120-lb. Smoke Bomb		22
3A.—Practice Bomb, 8¼ lb., Break-up		23
3B.—Practice Bomb, 10 lb., Smoke and Flash		23
3C.—Practice Bomb, 11¼ lb., Smoke and Flash		23
4A.—Smoke Float No. 1, Mark IV		24
4B.—Smoke Float No. 2, Marks I and II		24
4C.—Smoke Float No. 3, Mark I		24
5A.—Smoke Generators No. 5, Mark II		25
5B.—Smoke Generators No. 6, Mark II		25
5C.—Smoke Generators No. 11, Marks I and II		25
5D.—Smoke Generators No. 15, Mark I		25
5E.—Smoke Generators No. 18, Mark I		25
6A.—Flame Floats, Mark II		26
6B.—Message Carrying, Mark I		26
6C.—Flame Float No. 3, Mark I		26
6D.—Flame Float No. 4, Mark I		26
6E.—Marker Marine, Mark I		26
6F.—Marker Marine, Mark II		27
6G.—Marker Marine, Mark III		27
7A.—Sea Marker, Mark I		28
7B.—Sea Marker, Mark III		28
7C.—Sea Marker, Mark V		28
8A.—Reconnaissance Flare, 4·5 in., Mark III		29
Reconnaissance Flare, 4·5 in., Mark IV		29
Reconnaissance Flare, 4·5 in., Mark V		29
Reconnaissance Flare, 4·5 in., Mark V, P.F.F.		29
8B.—Reconnaissance Flare, 5·5 in., Marks I and II		29
8C.—Target Flares, Mark I		29
8D.—Training 4-in. Flares		29
8E.—Reconnaissance 4 in., Mark I		29
"8.F - Flare A/C Skymarker 25 lb. Mark I White Drip		29a"
9A.—Photographic Flash Bomb, 4·5 in., Marks I and II		30
9B.—Heavy Photographic Flash, 4·5 in.		30
10.—12-in. Target Indicator Bomb		31
11.—Fuzes used in Flares, Photographic Flashes and Target Illumination Bombs		32
12.—Miscellaneous : (a) Calibrators, Altimeter, Flash, Mark I		33

SECTION 1A.—4-LB. INCENDIARIES
(*See* Fig. 1.)

N.B.—(*a*) Section is hexagonal.

(*b*) The initiating system is in the tail. The tail is made of sheet steel and the body of a magnesium alloy.

(*c*) The nose is cast iron, about 2 in. long.

1. **Types** :—

Marks I to III	Striker and creep spring initiation.
Marks IV and V	No creep spring. Depends on forcing a small brass cross through an orifice on impact.
Marks I.E.–V.E.	Same as ordinary Marks I–V, but with an explosive element (gunpowder) in the nose.
Mark I.X	Like Marks IV and V, but with a C.E. pellet in the nose.

2. *Identification.*—(*a*) *Marks I–III.*—3¼ in. of nose are painted dull red. In the middle of this section are two black ½-in. bands with a ½-in. bright red band between them.

(*b*) *Marks IV and V.*—2 in. of the nose painted bright red.

(*c*) *Marks I.E.–V.E.*—Same as the Marks I–V, with an additional ½-in. bright red band ½ in. aft of the other nose colouring and with the base of the tail painted bright red.

(*d*) *Mark I.X.*—Same marking as the Mark IV.E and V.E, but with the base of the tail unpainted and a black cross stencilled on the side of the nose, together with a number 2 or 4. The number indicates the time before the C.E. pellet will detonate (in minutes) after impact. There is a plug screwed into the nose which gives further indication of an " X " type of bomb.

3. **Safety Devices.**—(*a*) Creep spring or brass cross.

(*b*) A spring loaded plunger on the side of the tail unit. This is held in by the other bombs until the bombs are released from the aircraft.

4. **Cases.**—These are metal boxes carried three per small bomb container. Each box usually carries 30 4-lb. incendiaries, but some carry only 20 bombs. The cases are retained in the aircraft.

Usually the " E " types are mixed with ordinary bombs, but the " X " types are kept in separate cases.

SECTION 1B.—25-LB. INCENDIARY
(*See* Fig. 2.)

1. *Colouring.*—Dull red with two ½-in. black bands round the nose with a ½-in. bright red band between them.

2. *Notes.*—(*a*) There are two main types : one has a parachute in the cylindrical tail, the other has no parachute.

(*b*) Both types are fired by a striker pellet in the tail. It is held until impact by a shear wire and a creep spring.

(*c*) A safety rod which is about 6 in. long is screwed in the striker pellet. The position of the rod is as indicated in the diagram. This rod is unscrewed before the bomb is dropped.

(*d*) The parachute type is like the above, but the safety rod is removed. A striker rod replaces it and is held at the top end by a retaining ball system. When the parachute opens, the pull compresses a spring and the balls system is drawn back. The retaining balls drop into a groove and the striker rod is released. On impact the additional weight of the striker rod makes up for the lower terminal velocity of the bomb with its parachute, and the striker pellet shears its wire and moves down.

(*e*) When the bomb fires the tail unit is blown off and then the bomb throws out seven fire pots, one after another. Finally the nose is left and, being itself filled thermite, acts as a separate incendiary.

(*f*) They can be carried in small bomb containers or in light series carriers.

SECTION 1C.—30-LB. INCENDIARY
(*See* Fig. 1.)

Colour : Dull red all over.

1. *Marks II and III.*—There are two bright red bands round the bomb. One near the nose indicates the bomb is filled and the other near the tail indicates that it is fuzed.

2. *Mark I* has only one bright red band to indicate that it is filled.

3. *Filling.*—Benzine and rubber with white phosphorus round the fuze cavity.

4. *Carried.*—Eight in a small bomb container.

5. *Mark I.*—(*See* the section drawing in Fig. 1) :—
   (*a*) Fuzed No. 38 N.D. (non-delay) Mark II nose fuze (*see* Fig. 3).
   (*b*) The fuze has a brass body and is screwed into the bomb, then a hemispherical nose faring fits over the fuze and on to the shoulder of the bomb. It is held in position by a circlip engaging in a groove round the nose of the fuze.
   (*c*) The bolt in the nose of the fuze is also the striker. When it is screwed right out, the fuze is safe. When the striker is screwed in, the fuze is armed. There is a locking nut to hold the striker in position.
   (*d*) The fuze fires by an inertia pellet overcoming a creep spring and bending four thin brass prongs before hitting the striker. The brass prongs are in the same plane as each other and are fixed regularly round the inertia pellet channel.

6. *Marks II and III* (*see* sectional drawing of Fig. 1).—(*a*) Fuzed No. 846 nose fuze, Mark I (*see* Fig. 4).
   (*b*) The bomb has no nose faring, but has itself a rounded nose. There is a nose plug for the bomb. The fuze is screwed to the nose plug. The safety pin is replaced by the safety plunger which is screwed into the nose plug. The whole is then screwed into the bomb.
   (*c*) The safety plunger, which keeps a retaining ball in position, is unscrewed before the bomb is dropped (or placed in the container). On impact the inertia pellet overcomes a creep spring and brass prongs before hitting the striker.

N.B.—The magazine of both the No. 38 fuze and the No. 846 fuze are filled with gunpowder.

The filling plug is in the base of the bomb and the tail is attached by being screwed onto the base plate.

" 7. Marks IIM and IIIM - These bombs differ from the Marks II and III very slightly. They have pads of metal welded on to the bomb near the point of balance. These pads act as positioning shown in the base of the bomb. There is a flexible tube lead weighted at the end, attached to the valve opening inside the bomb. The end always drops to the bottom of the container so that the gas pressure forces practically all the liquid out before the pressure is lost by gas escaping. As the liquid issues from the valve it is ignited by the flame from the vent holes of the pistol housing. The Page 21a.

At bottom *add* " Recent types are more sensitive. The brass cross has had two arms removed and the bombs may fire if dropped from a height of 9 in. on to ped from a concrete." Page 21a. *Add* new Section 1G.

SECTION 1G.—500-lb. INCENDIARY BOMB, MARK I

1. *Filling.*—16 gallons (approx.) of liquid phosphorus.

2. *Colouring.*—Grey with a 3-in. bright red band 7 in. from the nose and a 3-in. dull red band 9 in. from the tail of the bomb.

   Letters I N C D Y
   500 lb. I
   L.P.

are stencilled in black between the bright red band and the suspension lug.

3. *Dimensions.*—41 in. long (66 in. overall), 13·1 in. diameter, Tail is 28 in. by 31·1 in.

4. *Fuzing.*—No. 30 tail pistol (plus separate burster charge in addition to the normal detonator).

5. *Tail.*—Secured to tail locating ring by four spring clips.

6. *Remarks.*—Bomb is adapted for loading either on British or American aircraft.

(*T. 06720/44.—C.A.F.O. P.6/45.*)

Part I, Chapter II

SECTION 1C.—30-LB. INCENDIARY
(See Fig. 1.)

Colour : Dull red all over.

1. *Marks II and III.*—There are two bright red bands round the bomb. One near the nose indicates the bomb is filled and the other near the tail indicates that it is fuzed.

2. *Mark I* has only one bright red band to indicate that it is filled.

3. *Filling.*—Benzine and rubber with white phosphorus round the fuze cavity.

4. *Carried.*—Eight in a small bomb container.

5. *Mark I.*—(*See* the section drawing in Fig. 1) :—
   (a) Fuzed No. 38 N.D. (non-delay) Mark II nose fuze (*see* Fig. 3).
   (b) The fuze has a brass body and is screwed into the bomb, then a hemispherical nose faring fits over the fuze and on to the shoulder of the bomb. It is held in position by a circlip engaging in a groove round the nose of the fuze.
   (c) The bolt in the nose of the fuze is also the striker. When it is screwed right out, the fuze is safe. When the striker is screwed in, the fuze is armed. There is a locking nut to hold the striker in position.
   (d) The fuze fires by an inertia pellet overcoming a creep spring and bending four thin brass prongs before hitting the striker. The brass prongs are in the same plane as each other and are fixed regularly round the inertia pellet channel.

6. *Marks II and III* (see sectional drawing of Fig. 1).—(a) Fuzed No. 846 nose fuze, Mark I (*see* Fig. 4).
   (b) The bomb has no nose faring, but has itself a rounded nose. There is a nose plug for the bomb. The fuze is screwed to the nose plug. The safety pin is replaced by the safety plunger which is screwed into the nose plug. The whole is then screwed into the bomb.
   (c) The safety plunger, which keeps a retaining ball in position, is unscrewed before the bomb is dropped (or placed in the container). On impact the inertia pellet overcomes a creep spring and brass prongs before hitting the striker.

N.B.—The magazine of both the No. 38 fuze and the No. 846 fuze are filled with gunpowder.

The filling plug is in the base of the bomb and the tail is attached by being screwed onto the base plate.

SECTION 1D.—45-LB. INCENDIARY BOMB, MARK I
(*See* Fig. 1. Note that actual bomb is broader than shown.)

1. *Colour.*—Dull red with a bright red band to show that it is filled.

2. *Notes.*—(a) It is the same size and shape as a 5-gallon petrol can. It has strengthening strips down the sides and two distance pieces on the top. There are three carried per small bomb container.
   (b) There is no fuze ; it just breaks open on impact and the filling of benzine, rubber and phosphorus sesqui sulphide, ignites spontaneously.
   (c) The tail is a drogue formed by a canvas strip.

SECTION 1E.—250-LB. INCENDIARY BOMB, MARK I
(*See* Fig. 1. Note the nose is more definitely hemispherical than shown.)

1. *Filling.*—Benzine and rubber. The filling plug is in the middle of the base of the bomb.

2. *Colouring.*—Dull red with a 3-in. bright red band 7 in. from the nose.

3. *Tail.*—Special bayonet joint clip-on tail.

4. *Fuzing.*—(a) No. 36, Mark II, N.D. nose fuze (*see* Fig. 5) with a No. 2, Mark I, ejector charge. The fuze has a brass body.
   (b) The safety pin of the fuze is unscrewed and replaced by another plug, which is kept screwed into the fuze body close beside the safety pin. This pin must be replaced if the bomb is ever unloaded. It is kept in the aircraft.
   (c) When the bomb is dropped the safety clip is withdrawn and allows the vanes to rotate. This screws the vanes system inwards and the striker, which is part of the system, moves up inside the fuze into the armed position. On impact the inertia pellet carries forward, overcoming a creep spring and hits the striker.
   (d) The ejector charge is a charge of gunpowder in a metal container which gives an additional bursting

Page 21.
Section 1.E, paragraph 4. *Add* sub-paragraph " (e) When the striker is in the ' safe ' position a red-painted groove is visible on the plug under the flange on which the safety clip fits."
(Fig. 30)
(*U.B. 294/43.—C.A.F.O. P.575/44.*)

Part I, Chapter II

SECTION 2A.—4-LB. SMOKE BOMB
(*See* Fig. 1.)

Time of smoke emission : 4 minutes (approximately).

1. *Colour.*—Green with a red band round the nose.

2. *Carried* 14 in a tin. Three tins per small bomb container.

3. *Description.*—It is a cylindrical sheet metal can. In the top of the can is fitted a No. 859 fuze. This fuze is a *sensitive allways* fuze. There is a bakelite cap cover with a strip of linen attached. When the bomb is dropped from the aircraft, the cap is pulled off. A tape with a piece of lead at the end unwinds from the fuze body and withdraws the safety pin. The fuze is then armed. The fuze body is of bakelite and it stands out about 1 in. from the bomb body and is about 1 in. in diameter. There is a shallow groove running round the fuze body which is about ½-in. wide. The arming tape is wound in the groove.

SECTION 2B.—100-LB. SMOKE BOMB

The same size and shape as the 45-lb. incendiary bomb (*see* Fig. 1 and also Section 1D).

1. *Colour.*—Green with a red band round the lower part of the body.

2. *Notes.*—(*a*) This bomb differs from the 45-lb. incendiary bomb in having a fuze. The fuze is the No. 854. It is fitted in the top of the can beside the filling cap.

(*b*) It is like the No. 859 (*see* Section 2A). It differs in that the safety cap is held on by a safety fork and is spring loaded and the safety pin is spring-loaded so that when the safety cap jumps off the safety pin is pushed out.

(*c*) The fuze screws into a burster charge tube and the burster charge tube screws into the bomb.

(*d*) The main filling is white phosphorus.

(*e*) The bombs are carried three to a small bomb container.

SECTION 2C.—120-LB. SMOKE BOMB, MARKS I AND II
(*See* Fig. 28.)

Overall Length.—31 ins.

Maximum Diameter.—10 ins.

Duration of Effective Smoke Emission.—20 mins.

Carried.—Two per small bomb container or in a bomb carrier.

Fuzing.—No. 864 Mark I nose fuze.
No. 36 Nose Fuze is also used. (Fuze description, Section 1E, paragraph 4).

1. This fuze is like a No. 38 nose fuze. See Chapter 2, Section 3, and Chapter 2, Fig. 3.

2. It can be distinguished by the number which is stamped on the shoulder.

Colour.—Dark green with a ½-in. red band round the nose.

Action.—On impact the fuze fires and after about ½-second delay the magazine is fired. This ignites the inner smoke container and also fires an ejection charge which blows the container out of the tail end of the bomb case. This container is blown to a height of between 20 and 500 ft. depending on the depth of penetration of the bomb.

SECTION 3A.—PRACTICE BOMBS: 8½-LB. BREAK-UP

(*See* Fig. 1.)

1. *Colour and Markings.*—White with two green bands towards the tail. Marked: BREAK UP.

2. *Body.*—Bakelite.

3. *Tail.*—Cylindrical vane of sheet metal.

4. *Notes.*—(*a*) The nose portion is weighted with lead shot in paraffin wax. This part ends at the point of maximum diameter and will unscrew from the rear portion.

(*b*) The tip of the nose is metal and is part of the striker system. The striker passes right through the nose section. The detonator is housed in the middle portion of the bomb, which is filled with metal balls. The smoke producing mixture is in the after end of the bomb.

(*c*) The striker is held by a shear wire. A safety pin also holds the striker until the bomb is dropped. During transit there is an additional spring-loaded safety pin which is held in position by a copper safety wire which passes right round the nose of the bomb and through the loop of the other safety pin.

(*d*) When the wire is cut the spring-loaded pin jumps out of the bomb. The spring-loaded pin and the wire are shown in position on the 10-lb. and 11¼-lb. bomb in the figure.

SECTION 3B.—10-LB. PRACTICE, SMOKE AND FLASH BOMB

(*See* Fig. 1.)

1. *Smoke.—Colour and Marking.*—White all over with two green bands towards the tail.

2. *Flash.*—White all over with a red band round the nose and two black bands round the tail end.

3. *Notes.*—(*a*) The body is all metal. The nose portion is made of cast iron.

(*b*) Details of the firing mechanism are the same as for the 8½-lb. break-up bomb. It is obvious from the position of the joint of nose and rear part of the bomb that the striker is much longer in the case of the 10-lb. bomb.

SECTION 3C.—11¼-LB. PRACTICE, SMOKE AND FLASH BOMB

1. As for the 10-lb. practice bomb, but the nose is a steel case filled with lead instead of being cast iron.

SECTION 2D.—500-lb. SMOKE BOMB, MARK I

Length of Bomb Body.—3 ft. 5 in.

Diameter.—13·1 in.

Smoke.—Screen 250 to 300 yards in length, persisting 15 to 20 minutes.

Fuzing.—No. 30 Tail Pistol (with an ejection burster) in addition to the detonator.

Tail.—Four fins support a cylindrical vane. There are two arming vanes arming the pistol. The vanes are held by a safety clip retained by an arming wire.

SECTION 3A.—PRACTICE BOMBS: 8½-LB. BREAK-UP

(See Fig. 1.)

1. *Colour and Markings.*—White with two green bands towards the tail. Marked: BREAK UP.

2. *Body.*—Bakelite.

3. *Tail.*—Cylindrical vane of sheet metal.

4. *Notes.*—(a) The nose portion is weighted with lead shot in paraffin wax. This part ends at the point of maximum diameter and will unscrew from the rear portion.

(b) The tip of the nose is metal and is part of the striker system. The striker passes right through the nose section. The detonator is housed in the middle portion of the bomb, which is filled with metal balls. The smoke producing mixture is in the after end of the bomb.

(c) The striker is held by a shear wire. A safety pin also holds the striker until the bomb is dropped. During transit there is an additional spring-loaded safety pin which is held in position by a copper safety wire which passes right round the nose of the bomb and through the loop of the other safety pin.

(d) When the wire is cut the spring-loaded pin jumps out of the bomb. The spring-loaded pin and the wire are shown in position on the 10-lb. and 11½-lb. bomb in the figure.

SECTION 3B.—10-LB. PRACTICE, SMOKE AND FLASH BOMB

(See Fig. 1.)

1. *Smoke.—Colour and Marking.*—White all over with two green bands towards the tail.

2. *Flash.*—White all over with a red band round the nose and two black bands round the tail end.

3. *Notes.*—(a) The body is all metal. The nose portion is made of cast iron.

(b) Details of the firing mechanism are the same as for the 8½-lb. break-up bomb. It is obvious from the position of the joint of nose and rear part of the bomb that the striker is much longer in the case of the 10-lb. bomb.

SECTION 3C.—11½-LB. PRACTICE, SMOKE AND FLASH BOMB

1. As for the 10-lb. practice bomb, but the nose is a steel case filled with lead instead of being cast iron.

SECTION 2D.—500-lb. SMOKE BOMB, MARK I

Length of Bomb Body.—3 ft. 5 in.

Diameter.—13·1 in.

Smoke.—Screen 250 to 300 yards in length, persisting 15 to 20 minutes.

Fuzing.—No. 30 Tail Pistol (with an ejection burster) in addition to the detonator.

Tail.—Four fins support a cylindrical vane. There are two arming vanes arming the pistol. The vanes are held by a safety clip retained by an arming wire.

Colour.—Green with various black stencilling, marks including " P.H.O.5."

Action.—On impact the bomb is disrupted by the burster charge and white phosphorus is scattered giving white smoke.

(*T. 06720/44.—C.A.F.O. P.6/45.*)

Page 23. Section 3A. *Add* new sub-paragraph 4 (*e*) :—

(*e*) The Marks II and III have a 3-in. extension rod in the nose.

(*T. 06720/44.—C.A.F.O. P.6/45.*)

Page 28. *After* Section 7c. *Add* new Section 7D :—

SECTION 7D.—T.I. 250-LB., No. 19, MARK I, SEA MARKER

Colour.—The bomb consists of the normal 250-lb. T.I. bomb casing painted black with a ½-in. red band near the nose.

The words " Sea Marker Flame " are stencilled in white both on the body and nose of the bomb, together with the number " 19 " in three places round the nose.

Fuzing.—The bomb is fuzed, nose No. 848 or No. 860, and a No. 1, Mark II, or No. 35, Mark I, tail unit is fitted. (The burster container holds a 3-oz. gunpowder burster charge.)

General Details

1. The main filling of the bomb, consisting of sodium phosphide and phosphorus, is contained in a thin steel canister.

2. The canister is divided into two parts by a thin dished plate, the upper part acting as a buoyancy chamber, and the lower containing the filling.

3. Water inlet holes and a charging hole are drilled through the lower part of the canister. Each inlet hole is covered with wire netting soldered to the inside of the canister, and the charging hole is sealed with a plug.

4. The canister is seated on an ejector plate and is retained in position by a thin metal diaphragm soldered to the bomb body below the tail plate and by six equispaced wooden battens extending between the ejector plate and the diaphragm.

(i) On release from the aircraft the bomb falls in a normal manner until the fuze functions.

(ii) The explosion of the burster charge forces off the tail plate and ejects the canister.

(iii) On impact the water percolates through the inlet holes and on surfacing the generated phosphine gas burns spontaneously, giving a luminous flame about 3 ft. long, and at the same time emitting a cloud of white smoke for about 5-8 minutes.

(*T. 06720/44.—C.A.F.O. P.6/45.*)

SECTION 4A.—SMOKE FLOAT No. 1, MARK IV
(See Fig. 6.)

1. *Colour.*—Green up to the tail. Tail yellow. A red band round the nose.

2. *Fuzing.*—No. 23 tail pistol which is like the No. 22 T.P. (Chapter 1, Section 12). Made of either metal or plastic.

3. *Notes.*—It emits white smoke for 6 minutes. Instructions are stamped on the side.

SECTION 4B.—SMOKE FLOAT No. 2, MARKS I AND II
(See Fig. 7.)

Mark I

1. *Colour.*—Green with a red band round the nose and a yellow band round the tail.

2. *Fuzing.*—No. 844 tail fuze. There is a safety pillar which is unscrewed when the float is loaded in the aircraft and a safety clip which is withdrawn when the float is released. The striker overcomes a creep spring on impact.

3. *Notes.*—Very dense white smoke is emitted for 8–10 minutes. It gives an effective screen 200 ft. high and 200 ft. thick for a distance of 1,000 yards.

Mark II

4. Like Mark I, but for 1 ft. of the body at the nose the diameter is greater than the remainder by about 1½ in. There are no bolts in the nose, which is convex with a projecting rim acting as a nose faring.

5. **Fuzing.—No. 48 Tail Pistol**

6. **Tail Pistol No. 48, Mark I** *(See Fig. 29)*

Safety Devices.—Safety pin and safety clip.

Length.—2¾ in. overall.

The safety pin is removed from the pistol when the float is loaded in the aircraft and the clip comes away as the float leaves the aircraft. On impact the striker overcomes the resistance of a creep spring and fires the detonator. The flash is carried by primed cambric to the smoke composition in the nose of the float.

SECTION 4C.—SMOKE FLOAT No. 3, MARK I
(No Diagram.)

1. Shaped like an ordinary tin box, size 10·1-in. by 6·7-in. by 5-in., with push-on lids on the small ends. There are handles to the lids and both lids are sealed with tape.

2. Instructions are on a label on the side.

3. It is used for signalling from rubber dinghies and gives red smoke for forty seconds.

4. *Colour.*—Half is yellow and the other half is green.

5. *To Fire.*—The lids are removed and the exposed press cap is removed by pressing on the middle to release it. The whipcord becket is pulled until it comes away together with the metal clutch to which it is attached. This releases the striker and after a few seconds' delay the smoke is emitted from the other end after bursting the seal over the emission holes.

N.B.—The initiation is of the pull percussion type.

SECTION 5A.—SMOKE GENERATOR No. 5, MARK II

(No Diagram.)

Colour.—Green.

Time of Smoke Emission.—6–8 minutes.

Description.—A cylindrical metal box with a lid sealed with tape.

Length.—6·2-in. Diameter, 3·6-in.

Instructions are on the lid.

Inside the lid is a wedge of wood covered with glasspaper which is used to strike the match composition exposed.

N.B.—The filling is liable to catch fire spontaneously if it gets wet, especially if wetted with sea water.

SECTION 5B.—SMOKE GENERATOR No. 6, MARK II

(*See* Fig. 8.)

Colour.—Green.

Time of Smoke Emission.—2¼ minutes (orange).

Notes.—(a) The generator is dropped from aircraft.

(b) The pistol screws into the generator in the portion of the plug shown in the figure. The safety pin is withdrawn when it is dropped and on impact the striker shears a wire and fires the generator initiator.

SECTION 5C.—SMOKE GENERATOR No. 11, MARKS I AND II

(*See* Fig. 9.)

Colour.—Green.

Time of Smoke Emission.—Mark I, 30 seconds (red) ; Mark II, 55 seconds (orange).

The lid, which is sealed with tape is removed when the generator is put in the aircraft. The generator is fired electrically while still in the aircraft and is jettisoned after the emission of smoke ceases because the case, which is lined with cardboard, smoulders.

SECTION 5D.—SMOKE GENERATOR No. 15, MARK I

Colour.—Green.

Time of Smoke Emission.—8 minutes (white).

1. *Description.*—It is a sheet metal cylindrical box with a lid sealed with tape. The bottom of the tin has pressed threads on to which the cover screws. There is a handle to the lid.

2. *Size.*—6·2-in. long ; 3·6-in. diameter.

3. *Notes.*—It is fired electrically, the terminals being under the lid.

SECTION 5E.—SMOKE GENERATOR No. 18, MARK I

The same as No. 5, Mark II.

SECTION 6A.—FLAME FLOAT, MARK II

(*See* Fig. 10 without the message-carrying plug.)

Colour.—The light part in the figure is yellow; the rest is red.

N.B.—The yellow case is the buoyancy chamber.

Time of Flame Emission.—5 mins. bright, but a dull flame for about 2 hours.

Length : 23·4 in. Diameter : 5·85 in.

Notes.—(a) Before dropping, the punch attached to the tail is hammered into the base of the float in order to break the seal. The pin is then pulled from the nose and the metal cover removed; this exposes a copper dome.

(b) On striking the water the copper dome collapses, causing a striker to pierce a diaphragm and also the inner body (the yellow part) is pushed right out of the outer container, breaking three wires (marked " Shear Wire " in the figure). The water enters and the float burns spontaneously, the flame emerging from the top of the central tube.

SECTION 6B.—FLAME FLOAT, MESSAGE CARRYING, MARK I

(*See* Fig. 10.)

Details are as for 6A, with the addition of the plug and message-carrying device shown in the figure.

SECTION 6C.—FLAME FLOAT No. 3, MARK I

(*See* Fig. 13.)

Time of Bright Flame.—5 minutes.

Length : 18·5 in. Maximum diameter : 2·9 in.

Colour.—Yellow.

Buoyancy chamber is at the tail end.

Instructions for use are near the tail fins.

Notes.—The dome on the rear of the float has to be removed before dropping. The rupture disc is then broken, either by pulling the ring on the small pillar exposed, or by pushing the pillar sideways. The cords which are held to the side of the store, are attached to the nose tear-off strip and this must be pulled off before the float is dropped. The water entering causes the float to give a flame through the tail of the central tube.

SECTION 6D.—FLAME FLOAT No. 4, MARK I

Is identical with the inner body of the Mark II flame float.

SECTION 6E.—MARKER MARINE, AIRCRAFT, MARK I

(*See* Fig. 14.)

Colour.—Upper half, yellow. Lower half, red.

N.B.—Yellow end is the buoyancy chamber.

Time of Bright Flame.—2 hours (further dull flame about 6 hours).

Length : 26·75 in. Diameter : 5·8 in.

Notes.—(a) Before dropping, the three press cap overseals are removed, the wire and plug attached to the tail press cap being withdrawn with the cap.

(b) The marker is then dropped and the water entering causes the float to give a flame through the tail central tube. The flame is visible 3 miles away during the day and 20 miles away at night.

SECTION 6F.—MARKER, MARINE, AIRCRAFT, 19 LB., MARK II
(*See* Fig. 15.)

1. The **tail central tube** is sealed with a dome held on by adhesive tape. The whole nose has a cover held on by tape as shown. There is a bakelite disc which covers the central tube under the nose cover, this breaks on impact with the water.

2. Otherwise general details are similar to the Mark I.

SECTION 6G.—MARKER, MARINE, AIRCRAFT, 21 LB., MARK III

1. Like the Mark I, but incorporates a clockwork delay mechanism in the nose.

Length : 34 in.   *Diameter* : 6 in.

Clockwork delay : 0 to 6 hours.

2. The transit cap must be removed from the tail and the clock set at the required delay before the marker is dropped. The water inlet valve is released at the end of the delay period.

3. There is a spoiler on the nose which is centrally recessed to receive the clock. There is a screw on cover over the recess. Two holes in the body, just below the spoiler, allow water to enter.

SECTION 7A.—SEA MARKER, MARK I
(*See* Fig. 11.)

Size.—4·5 in. by 3·5 in. by 3·5 in.

Colour.—Aluminium.

It is a paper-sided cube filled with aluminium powder. During transit it is carried in the box shown.

SECTION 7B.—SEA MARKER, MARK III
(*See* Fig. 16.)

Colour.—Aluminium.

Length : 23·1 in.   *Diameter* : 4·4 in.

The body is sheet metal and the nose is steel. It contains aluminium powder and a burster charge. The whole firing system is like the 10-lb. practice bomb (*see* Section 3B). There is an additional safety device. The main safety pin is spring loaded and held in position by a further pin which is at right angles to it and passes through it. There is a withdrawal wire attached to this second pin.

SECTION 7C.—SEA MARKER, MARK V
(*See* Fig. 12.)

Colour.—Aluminium.

Note.—For packing the cylindrical tail telescopes over the body as shown in the figure.

Length telescoped : 12·6 in.   *Length extended* : 20 in.   *Diameter* : 3 in.

Notes.—(*a*) There is a bag of aluminium powder contained in the lower body. It is held by thread to a bar across the inside of the nose. The nose is sealed with paper and the tail with millboard discs. There are cutters in the tail just beneath the millboard discs:

(*b*) On impact with the water the paper nose seal is broken and the bag is carried back, the thread holding it breaking. The millboard washers are ejected and the bag is ripped open by the cutters

SECTION 8A.—RECONNAISSANCE FLARE, 4·5 IN., MARKS III, IV, V AND V P.F.F.

(*See* Fig. 18.)

Colour.—Black with a red band near the nose.

Overall length.—33 in.   *Diameter of parachute.*—11 ft.

Nose Fuzing (see Section 11).—No. 42, Mark II, fuze or No. 848, Mark V, fuze or No. 860, Marks I or II. (The 860 can only be used if specially authorized.)

1. *Time of Illumination.*—3 to 4 minutes.

2. *Notes.*—(a) The figure shows a Mark V flare. This has a 2-minute delay in the candle.

(b) Mark V P.F.F. has a 4-minute delay.

(c) Mark IV flare has no delay.

(d) Mark III flare has no delay and the tail is shaped like the tail shown in Fig. 21.

(e) The flare drops complete from the aircraft and, after a time, the fuze functions. This fires a powder charge which ejects the candle and parachute out of the tail. The closing dome is pushed off. The candle is housed in the nose of the flare, and the parachute in the tail.

(f) The details of the type of flare are marked clearly on the case.

SECTION 8B.—RECONNAISSANCE FLARE, 5·5 IN., MARKS I AND II

Colour.—Black with a red band near the nose.

Length.—48 in.

Fuzing (Section 11).—No. 42, Mark II, or No. 848, Mark V, or No. 860, Marks I or II (if specially authorized).

Time of Illumination.—3¼–4¼ minutes.

Notes.—As for the 4·5-in. flares (*see* Section 8A).

SECTION 8C.—TARGET FLARES, MARK I

(*See* Fig. 17.)

Details are the same as the 4·5-in. reconnaissance flare, Mark IV, except for the stencilled markings. Also, when falling, the target flares give either a red or green steady colour with seven stars of the other colour thrown out at intervals.

SECTION 8D.—4 IN. TRAINING FLARES

(*See* Fig. 20.)

Colour.—Black with a red band near the nose.
Length.—30 in.
Diameter of Tail.—5·5 in.
Diameter of Body.—4 in.
Duration of Illumination.—3¼ minutes.
Diameter of Parachute.—11 ft.

Notes.—(a) There is no fuze.

(b) The lanyard shown tucked in the canvas packet in the tail is called the static cord. When the flare leaves the aircraft the cord is held and draws out the parachute before breaking at a weak point. When the parachute opens, the jerk fires a pull-percussion igniter in the base of the candle. The flash is passed down a central tube and starts the flare burning at the nose. There is a small powder charge which blows off the nose plate at the same time.

SECTION 8E.—RECONNAISSANCE FLARE, A.S.4 IN., MARK I

1. This flare has the same structure as the 4-in. training flare but it burns with great intensity for 50 seconds only.

2. The delay before lighting is 5 seconds. The type of flare is stencilled on the body.

Section 8.F

(Part I Chapter II)

Flare A/C Skymarker 25 lb. Mk.I: Whitedrip

This flare is a modification of the 4.5" reconnaissance flare. Differences :-

1. The flare candle of the reconnaissance flare is replaced by a sheet iron cylinder containing a hollow magnesium casting filled with incendiary composition.

2. When the flare finishes burning there is a small explosion.

3. Type of flare is stencilled on the body.

SECTION 9A.—PHOTOGRAPHIC FLASH, 4·5 IN., MARKS I AND II

(*See* Fig. 21. Mark I is on the left. Mark II is on the right.)

N.B.—It is important to distinguish between flares and flashes.

1. Points to observe are :—
    (i) " FLASH " is stencilled on the nose of the photographic flashes.
    (ii) The tail of the flash is RED. The rest of the body is black except for a red band round the nose.
    (iii) Eight rivets round the body at the junction of the red and black parts of the flash.
    (iv) On removal of the tail dome of a flash, there is no parachute or shackle visible.

Remember the presence of the shackle indicates that there has *been* a parachute there and, therefore, the store will *not* be a flash.

2. *Nose Fuzing* (*see* Section 11).—No. 849, Mark I, fuze. No. 28, Marks IIB or III, fuze. No. 848, Mark V, fuze. No. 860, Marks I and II, fuze (if specially authorized).

3. *Notes.*—(*a*) The body is filled with flash powder which gives a brilliant flash when the fuze fires. All the fuzes should function in mid-air.

SECTION 9B.—HEAVY FLASH, PHOTOGRAPHIC, 4·5 IN.

(40 LB. Weight.)

1. Externally it is the same as the ordinary 4·5-in. flash (Section 9A), except for the stencilled words " HEAVY FLASH " round the body.

2. *Fuzing.*—The American M.111 nose fuze (*see* Fig. 27, and also the D.U.B.D. Instructions on American Bombs).

3. The fuze is a mechanical time fuze which has a fuze adapter in order to fit it into the British flare.

4. When the " flash " is loaded the arming wire is fitted through the second hole in the arming pin ; it also passes through the arming vane lock (in the same way as the sealing wire passes through in the figure). The safety fork, label and sealing wire are then removed. When the " flash " leaves the aircraft, the spring loaded arming pin flies out, the clockwork starts. The delay may be 5 seconds to 93 seconds, and this is set by unscrewing the screw plug on the right in the figure and turning the fuze body until the setting line is opposite the required delay. The fuze will not fire until the safety vanes have rotated enough for the safety segments to fall free.

SECTION 8E.—FLARE, AIRCRAFT RECONNAISSANCE, 7-in., HOODED, MARK I and II

Mark I

Note.—These flares cannot be used in clusters but are released singly.

Description

The flare, aircraft reconnaissance, 7-in., hooded, Mark I, weighing approximately 85 lb., consists of a flare candle unit (9) contained in a thin metal case (3) measuring 5 ft. 3 in. long by 7 in. diameter, painted black with a red band near the nose.

The casing, which is fitted with a heavy nose (18), is closed at the tail end by a metal closing cap (1).

A suspension band (10) fitted with a suspension lug (19) is fastened round the body in addition to two reinforcing bands (8).

Housed in the rear of the casing is the parachute (2) attached by the shackle (6) to the candle unit (9).

A metal tube (15) containing a primed cambric tube connects the powder puff (16) in the nose of the flare with the candle cap (12).

A length of Bickford fuze (13) sealed each end with a celluloid cap (14) containing a small gunpowder charge, passes through the candle cap to the gunpowder charge (11) contained in the nose of the candle.

Attached to the side of the candle unit (9) is a frame (7) to which is fixed the sheet asbestos hood (5).

The frame which folds round the candle unit has a square cross-section when open and extends beyond the ends of the candle unit.

The tail end of the hood is partially closed by a deflector (4).

The flare is fuzed, nose No. 848 (*see* Section 11).

Action

On release from the aircraft the flare falls in a normal manner until the fuze functions.

The flash from the fuze magazine ignites the powder puff (16) and the resultant explosion forces the parachute and candle unit out of the metal case, at the same time igniting the primed cambric.

The primed cambric ignites the celluloid cap (14) of the Bickford fuze and after a short delay the Bickford fuze fires the gunpowder charge (11) in the nose of the candle.

The explosion of the gunpowder forces off the candle cap (12) at the same time igniting the flare composition.

The short delay in the Bickford fuze allows the parachute and hood to open before the flare functions.

Mark II

This flare has been designed for use with the cluster projectile aircraft, 18-in., No. 3, Mark I.

Description

The flare aircraft reconnaissance, 7-in., Mark II, is similar to the Mark I, differing from it only in that the heavy nose and suspension band are omitted thereby reducing the weight to 58 lb.

(*T. 06720/44.—C.A.F.O. P.6/45.*)

SECTION 10.—12-IN. TARGET ILLUMINATION BOMB

(Same shape and size as the 250-lb. incendiary bomb (Section 1E and Fig. 1).)

1. *Fuzing.*—No. 860 fuze (*see* Section 11).
No. 848, Mark I, fuze may be used until No. 860 fuzes are available.

2. *Colouring.*—Black with a band round the nose indicating the colour of the flares and a 1-in. red band 3 in. from the nose to denote that the bomb is filled.

Towards the rear a red cross is painted if explosive candles are present. The colour of the flares is also stencilled on the bomb.

3. *Notes.*—(a) The bomb is filled with 60 candles, each 1 ft. long, which are all blown out of the tail end of the bomb when the fuze fires in mid-air. The candles are ignited by the bursting charge of gunpowder firing primed cambric. The candles are cylindrical or sometimes they are modified 4-lb. incendiaries (the incendiaries are always white burning).

(b) The candles are marked on the ends to indicate the type, *e.g.*:—
RED N.D. means red-burning candle without a delay.
RED 2½ means a red-burning candle with 2½ minutes delay.
RED 2½ with a cross over printing the delay means a red-burning candle with a delay of 2½ minutes and then an explosion.

4. *Possible Ways of Filling with Candles.*—
   (i) 60 non-delay.
   (ii) 56 non-delay and 4 explosive.
   (iii) 20 non-delay and 40 delay.
   (iv) 16 non-delay, 4 explosive and 40 delay.
   (v) 30 non-delay and 30 delay.
   (vi) 36 non-delay, 4 explosive and 20 delay.

5. Tracers are attached to the tail unit. These are functioned by a pull mechanism.

Page 31.
Section 10. *For* "Target illumination bomb" *read* "target indicator bomb."
(*U.B. 294/43.—C.A.F.O. P.575/44.*)

Part I, Chapter II   32

SECTION 11.—FUZES USED IN FLARES, PHOTOGRAPHIC FLASHES AND T.I. BOMBS

1. **Nose Fuze No.**   **Where Used.**
   No. 28B, II and III   Photographic flash only.
   No. 42, II   ..   4·5-in. reconnaissance flare.
                               5·5-in. reconnaissance flare.
                               4·5-in. target flare.
   No. 848, V   ..   4·5-in. reconnaissance flare.
                               5·5-in. reconnaisance flare.
                               4·5-in. target flare.
                               4·5-in. photographic flash.
                               12-in. T.I. bomb.
   No. 849, I   .. .. 4·5-in. photographic flash.
   No. 860, I and II   ..   12-in. T.I. bomb.

No. 873 Nose fuze. Also in flares and photographic flashes with special authorization.

2. **Fuze No. 28B, II and III** (*see* Fig. 24).—*Action.*—(*a*) The safety clip has the tag attached in the figure. It has two pins, one of which goes through the vanes spindle and the other through the firing rod. The clip is removed when the store is in the carrier of the aircraft. On release from the aircraft the firing rod is withdrawn. This allows a striker to fire a detonator which starts a delay train burning. The vanes wind out (but do not fall away) and the movement of the vanes spindle exposes a flash channel so that when the time ring finishes burning the flash passes to the magazine.

(*b*) The delay is set by turning the ring into which the setting rod is screwed.

3. **Fuze No. 42, Mark II** (*see* Fig. 22).—(*a*) The body of the fuze will separate as indicated in the Fig. 23 of the No. 848 fuze. The base is identical with that of the No. 848 fuze. A spring shutter has to be clipped on one side and then a delay capsule (containing a coil of safety fuze) fitted in position. The safety pin is withdrawn when the store containing the fuze is in position in the carrier.

(*b*) When the store containing the fuze is dropped from the aircraft, the lug and lanyard are retained and this fires a pull percussion igniter. The igniter starts the delay capsule burning and after a given time the magazine in the base of the fuze fires.

4. **Fuze No. 848, Mark V** (*see* Fig. 23).—The safety pin is withdrawn when the store containing the fuze is finally in place on the carrier. On release the metal cap on the top of the fuze is held by an arming wire on the aircraft. This exposes arming vanes. When the vanes rotate they withdraw the arming vanes spindle until the balls of a cup and retaining ball system release a spring loaded striker. This fires the igniter cap and the action is then the same as for the No. 42, Mark II, fuze.

5. **Fuze No. 849, Mark I** (*see* Fig. 25).—The initiating system is the same as for Fuze No. 848. The flash ignites a time ring whose delay can be adjusted from the outside by turning the pointer on the face of the fuze.

6. **Fuze No. 860, Marks I and II** (Fig. 26, approximate only).—(*a*) This fuze is a barometric fuze which fires at a definite height from the ground. Adhesive tape covers the air entry holes until the bomb containing the fuze is in position in the carrier.

(*b*) Under the safety cap there are vanes as in the No. 848 fuze.

(*c*) The upper part of the fuze body is aluminium colour and the lower part is zinc colour. A safety pillar is screwed into the base of the fuze as indicated in the diagram. This is removed when the bomb is in the carrier. The safety pillar is replaced by a grub screw.

Page 12.

List of fuzes. *After* "No. 845 nose fuze," write "Obsolete."
No. 30 tail fuze. Paragraph 2, line 6. *Alter to read* "The fuze is fired by two strikers moving forward against the resistance of creep spring."
    (*U.B. 294/43.—C.A.F.O. P.575/44.*)

No. 845 anti-handling nose fuze. Write clearly across paragraphs 9 to 15 "Obsolete".
Fig. 6, Part I, chapter 1. Write clearly across the diagram "Obsolete".
Section 11. At the end of the list of fuzes *add* "No. 873 nose fuze."
No. 32 nose fuze. Paragraph 8, line 1. *Delete* "and a" and *insert* "on to a"

SECTION 12.—MISCELLANEOUS

(a) **Calibrator, Altimeter Flash, Mark I.**—*Colour.*—Red.

Notes.—The calibrator is a cylinder 9 in. long by $4\frac{5}{8}$ in. in diameter.

The nose is closed with a metal plate. The tail end is open. In the centre of the nose is a threaded hole to take the striker. There is another hole to one side, in which the striker is screwed until the calibrator is to be dropped. In the centre of the nose inside is an adaptor into which fits an ordinary 4-in. by $1\frac{1}{2}$-in. signal flash cartridge. There is a spring inside the adaptor which acts as a creep spring for the cartridge which acts as an inertia pellet.

(b)

Part I, Chapter II

SECTION 11.—FUZES USED IN FLARES, PHOTOGRAPHIC FLASHES AND T.I. BOMBS

1. **Nose Fuze No.**   **Where Used.**

Nose Fuze No.	Where Used
No. 28B, II and III	Photographic flash only.
No. 42, II	4·5-in. reconnaissance flare.
	5·5-in. reconnaissance flare.
	4·5-in. target flare.
No. 848, V	4·5-in. reconnaissance flare.
	5·5-in. reconnaisance flare.
	4·5-in. target flare.
	4·5-in. photographic flash.
	12-in. T.I. bomb.
No. 849, I	4·5-in. photographic flash.
No. 860, I and II	12-in. T.I. bomb.

No. 873 Nose fuze. — Also in flares and photographic flashes with special authorization.

2. **Fuze No. 28B, II and III** (*see* Fig. 24).—*Action.*—(*a*) The safety clip has the tag attached in the figure. It has two pins, one of which goes through the vanes spindle and the other through the firing rod. The clip is removed when the store is in the carrier of the aircraft. On release from the aircraft the firing rod is withdrawn. This allows a striker to fire a detonator which starts a delay train burning. The vanes wind out (but do not fall away) and the movement of the vanes spindle exposes a flash channel so that when the time ring finishes burning the flash passes to the magazine.

(*b*) The delay is set by turning the ring into which the setting rod is screwed.

3. **Fuze No. 42, Mark II** (*see* Fig. 22).—(*a*) The body of the fuze will separate as indicated in the Fig. 23 of the No. 848 fuze. The base is identical with that of the No. 848 fuze. A spring shutter has to be clipped on one side and then a delay capsule (containing a coil of safety fuze) fitted in position. The safety pin is withdrawn when the store containing the fuze is in position in the carrier.

(*b*) When the store containing the fuze is dropped from the aircraft, the lug and lanyard are retained and this fires a pull percussion igniter. The igniter starts the delay capsule burning and after a given time the magazine in the base of the fuze fires.

4. **Fuze No. 848, Mark V** (*see* Fig. 23).—The safety pin is withdrawn when the store containing the fuze is finally in place on the carrier. On release the metal cap on the top of the fuze is held by an arming wire on the aircraft. This exposes arming vanes. When the vanes rotate they withdraw the arming vanes spindle until the balls of a cup and retaining ball system release a spring loaded striker. This fires the igniter cap and the action is then the same as for the No. 42, Mark II, fuze.

5. **Fuze No. 849, Mark I** (*see* Fig. 25).—The initiating system is the same as for Fuze No. 848. The flash ignites a time ring whose delay can be adjusted from the outside by turning the pointer on the face of the fuze.

6. **Fuze No. 860, Marks I and II** (Fig. 26, approximate only).—(*a*) This fuze is a barometric fuze which fires at a definite height from the ground. Adhesive tape covers the air entry holes until the bomb containing the fuze is in position in the carrier.

(*b*) Under the safety cap there are vanes as in the No. 848 fuze.

(*c*) The upper part of the fuze body is aluminium colour and the lower part is zinc colour. A safety pillar is screwed into the base of the fuze as indicated in the diagram. This is removed when the bomb is in the carrier. The safety pillar is replaced by a grub screw.

(*d*) The Mark I fuze has the zinc-coloured section of the fuze of a greater diameter than the rest of the body.

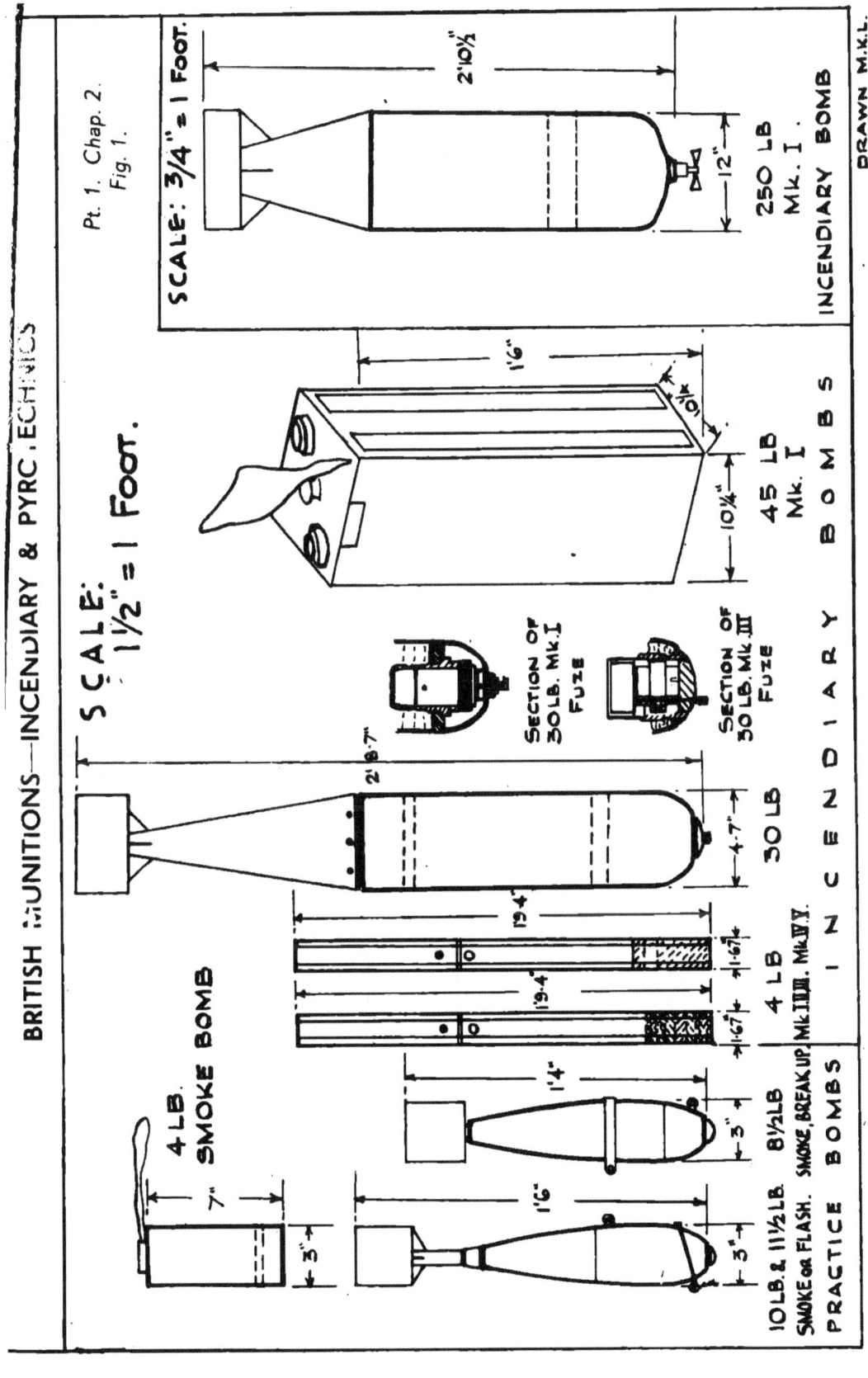

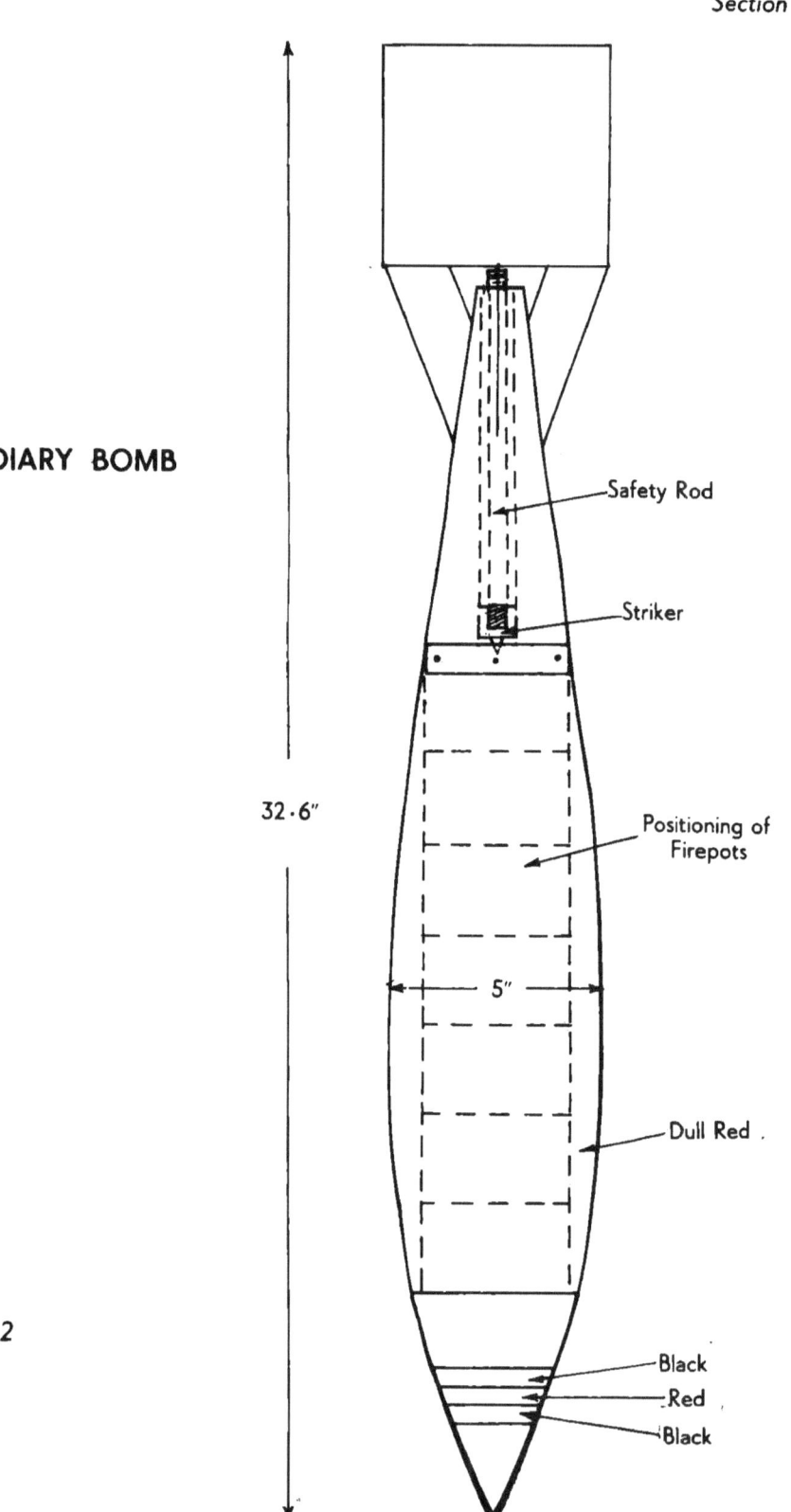

Pt. 1. Chap. 2.
Section 1B.

25 LB. INCENDIARY BOMB

Fig. 2

Pt. 1. Chap. 2.
Section 1C.

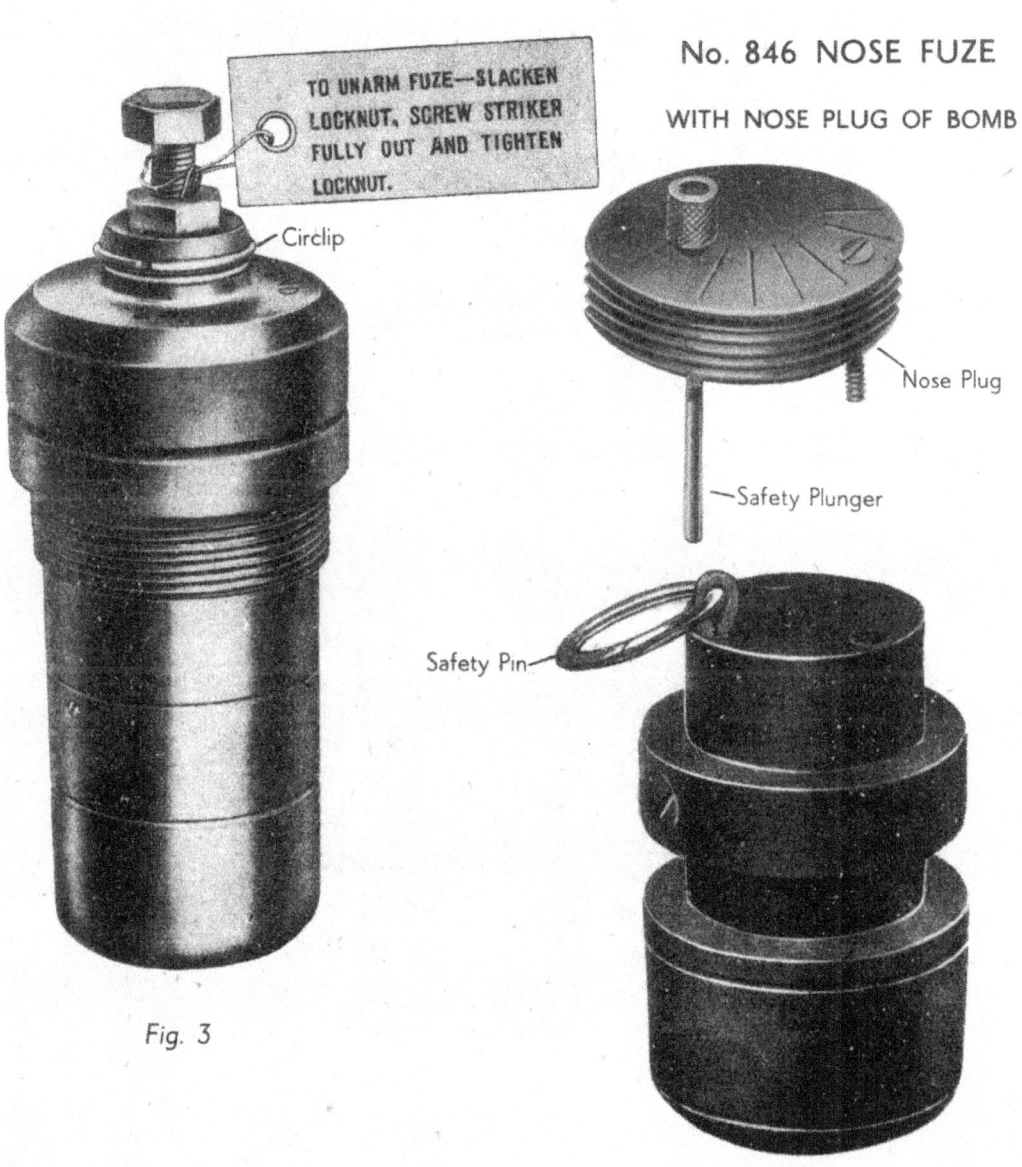

No. 38 N.D. NOSE FUZE

TO UNARM FUZE—SLACKEN LOCKNUT, SCREW STRIKER FULLY OUT AND TIGHTEN LOCKNUT.

Circlip

Fig. 3

No. 846 NOSE FUZE

WITH NOSE PLUG OF BOMB

Nose Plug

Safety Plunger

Safety Pin

Fig. 4

Pt. 1. Chap. 2.
Section 1E.

No. 36 Mk. II NON-DELAY NOSE FUZE

Fig. 5.

Pt. 1. Chap. 2.

SMOKE FLOAT No. 1 Mk. IV

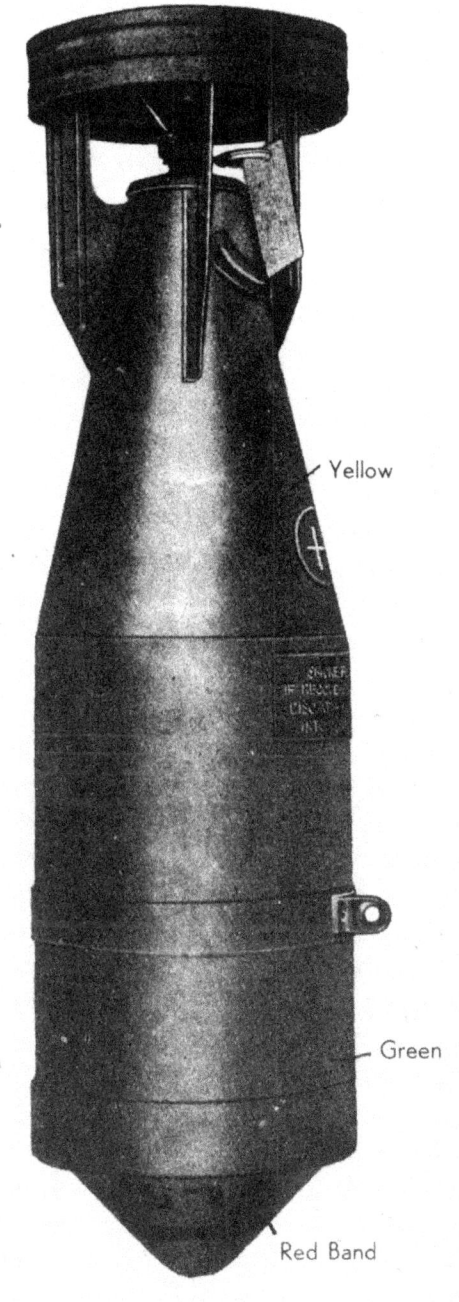

Fig. 6

SMOKE FLOAT No. 2 Mk. I

Fig. 7

SMOKE GENERATOR No. 6 Mk. II

Pt. 1. Chap 2.
Section 5B.

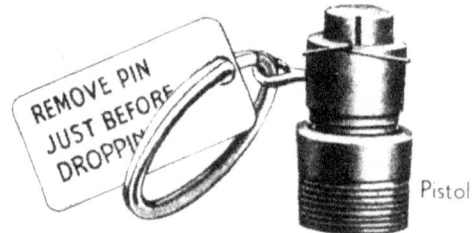

Fig. 8

Pt. 1. Chap. 2.
Section 5C.

SMOKE GENERATOR No. 11 Mk. II

Fig. 9

Pt. 1. Chap. 2.

FLAME FLOAT, MESSAGE CARRYING, Mk. I.

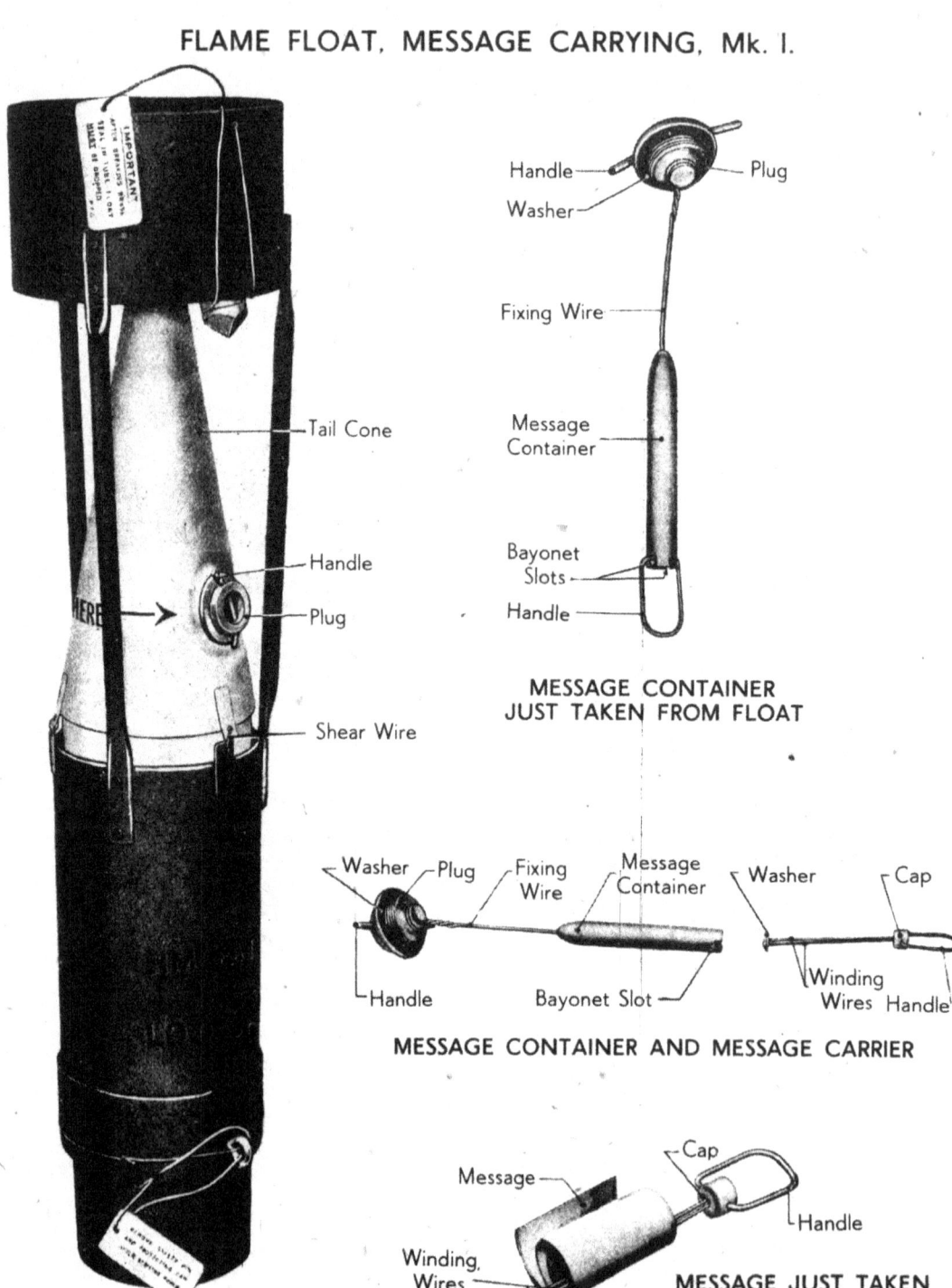

Fig. 10

SEA MARKER Mk. I

Pt. 1. Chap. 2.
Section 7.

Fig. 11

SEA MARKER Mk. V

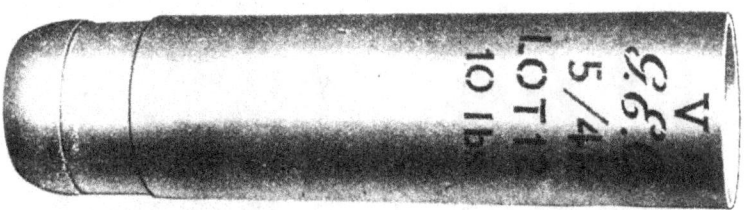

Fig. 12

FLAME FLOAT No. 3 Mk. 1

SECTION 6

Fig. 13

Pt. 1. Chap. 2.
Section 6.

MARKER MARINE Mk. I

Fig. 14

MARKER MARINE Mk. II

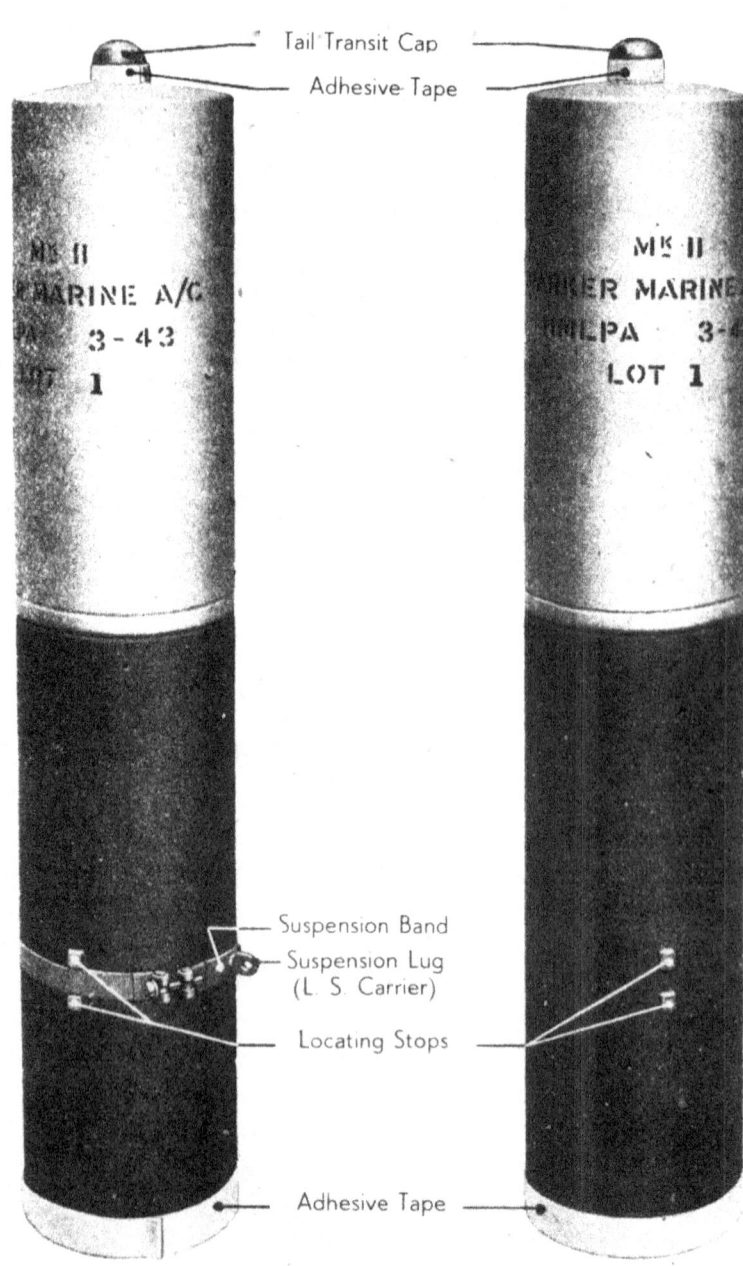

Fig. 15

Pt. 1. Chap. 2.
Section 7.

SEA MARKER Mk. III

Fig. 16

Pt. 1. Chap. 2.

4·5" TARGET FLARE

4·5" RECONNAISSANCE FLARE

5·5" RECONNAISSANCE FLARE

Fig. 17

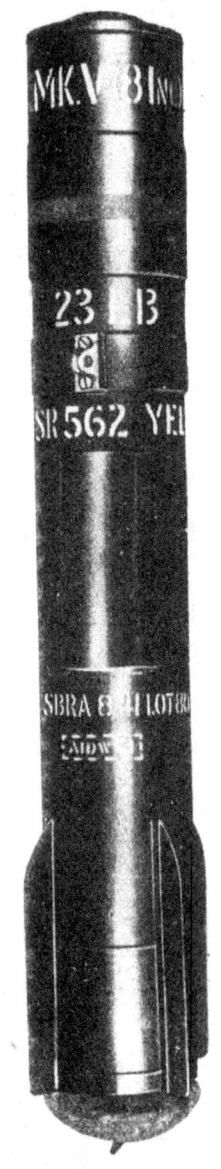

Fig. 18

Fig. 19

Pt. 1. Chap. 2.
Section 8D.

4" TRAINING FLARE

Fig. 20

4·5" PHOTOGRAPHIC FLASH

Fig. 21

Pt. 1. Chap. 2.
Section 11.

FUZE No. 42 Mk. II

Fig. 22

Pt. 1. Chap. 2.
Section 11.

FUZE No. 848 Mk. V

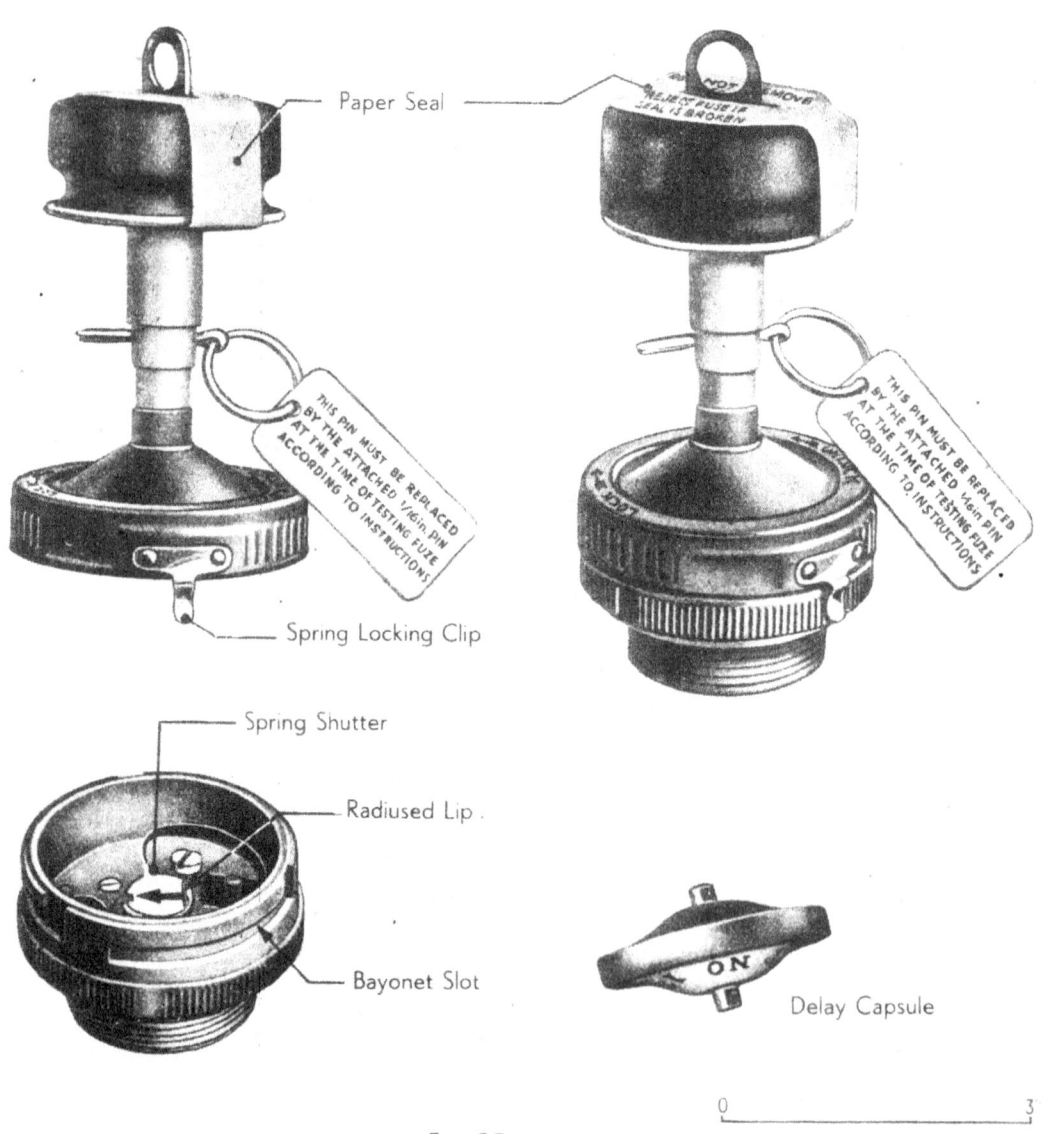

Fig. 23

Pt. 1. Chap. 2
Section 11.

FUZE No. 28 Mk. B III

- Firing Rod
- Setting Peg
- Locking Ring

Fig. 24

FUZE No. 849 Mk. I

Fig. 25

Pt. 1. Chap. 2.
Section 11.

FUZE No. 860 Mk. II

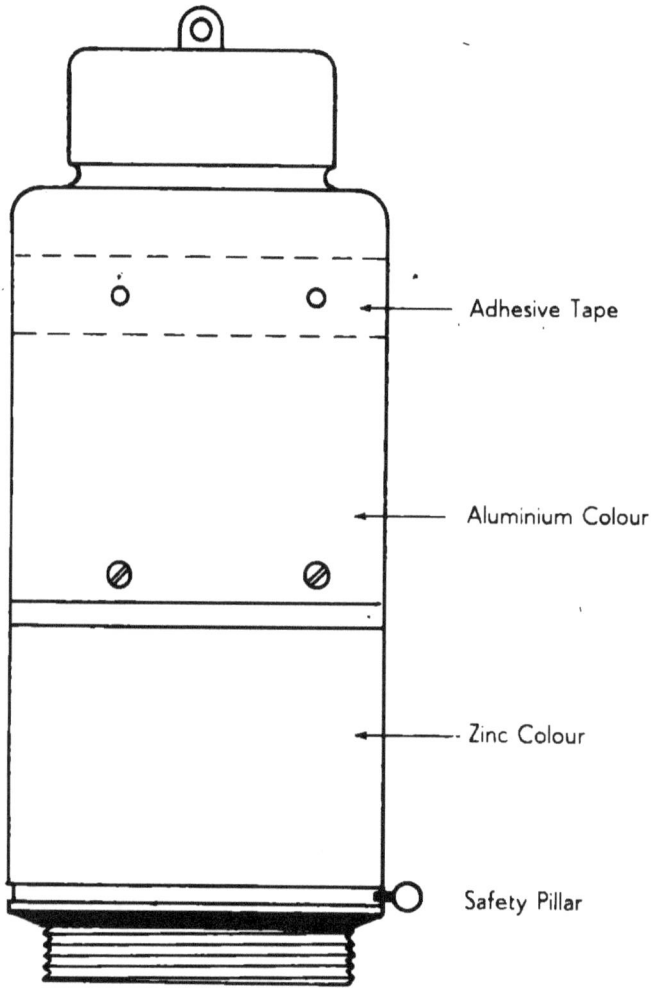

Fig. 26

A   AMERICAN FUZE M III

Pt. 1. Chap. 2.
Section 9.

Fig. 27

Pt. 1. Chap. 2.

Fig. 28

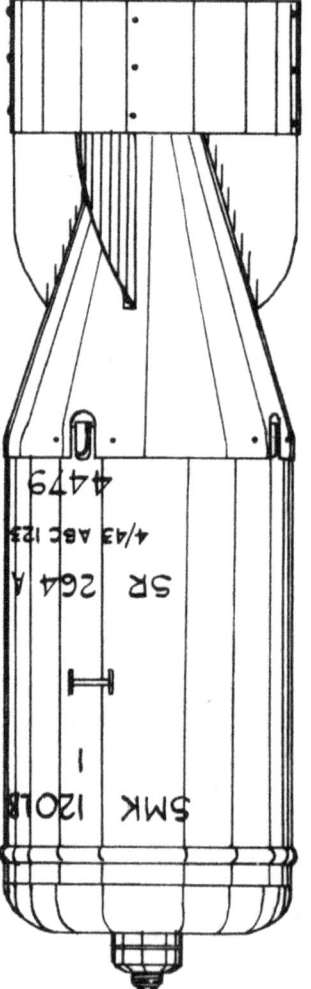

120 LB. SMOKE BOMB

Fig. 29

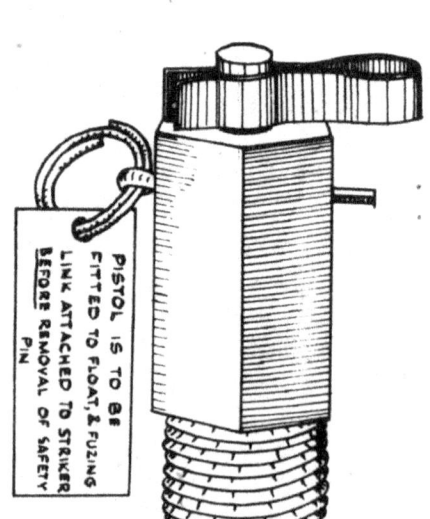

TAIL PISTOL No. 48

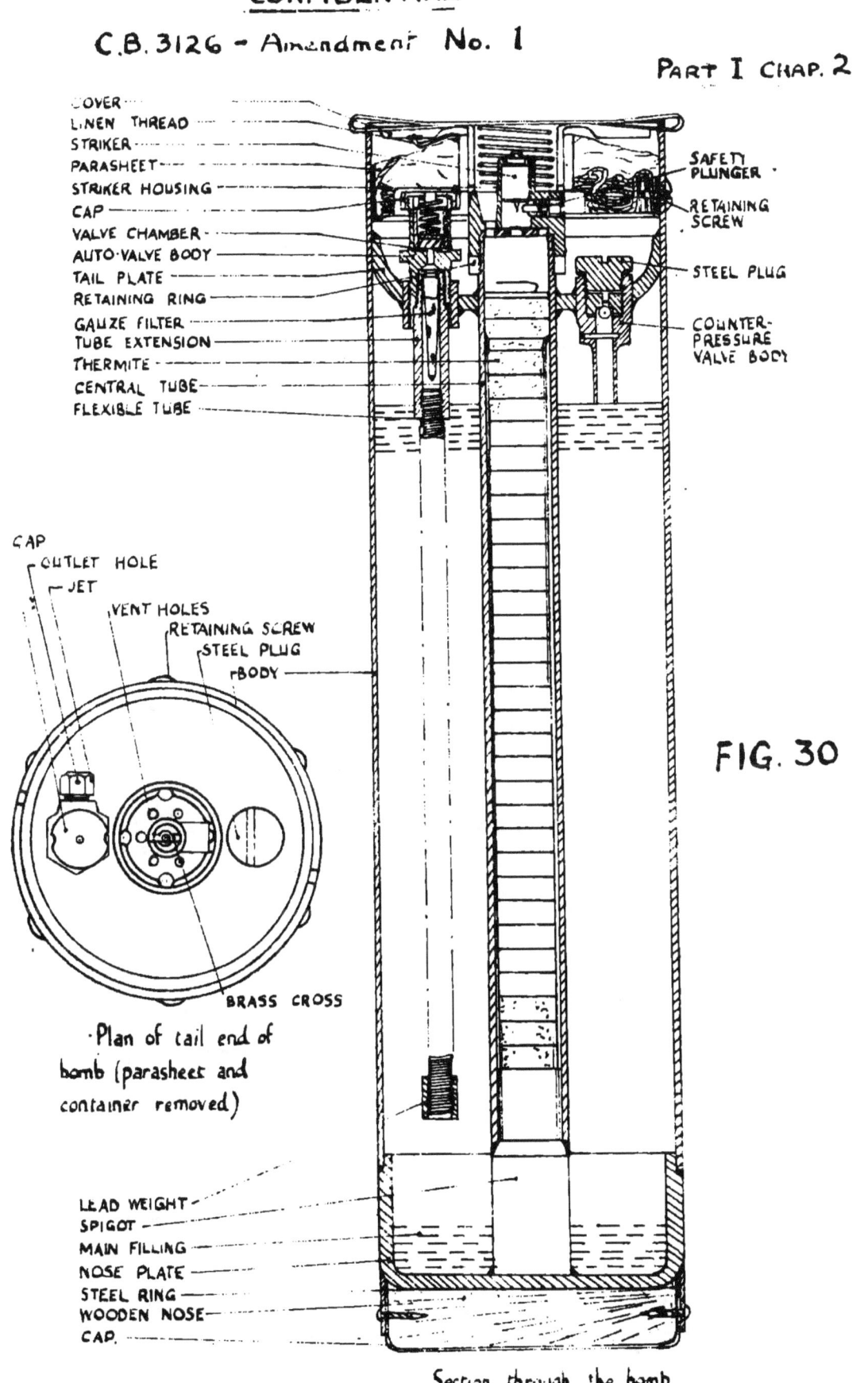

FIG. 30

Pt. 1. Chap. 3.

BRITISH MUNITIONS—DEPTH CHARGES

Scale 1/12" = 1"

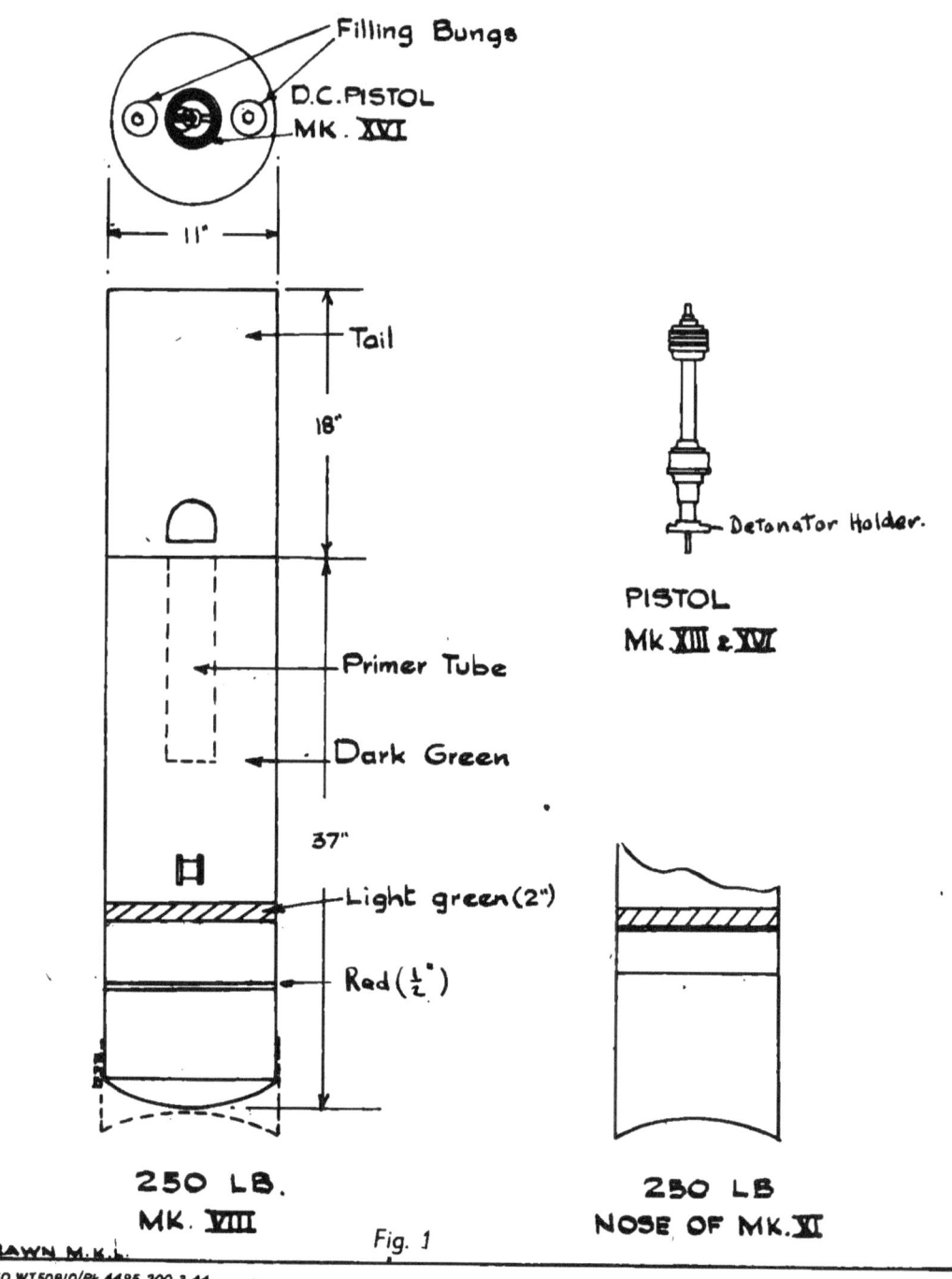

Fig. 1

CHAPTER III

DEPTH CHARGES DROPPED FROM AIRCRAFT, MARKS VIII AND XI

(*See* Fig. 1.)

1. *Colour.*—Dark green with a ½-in. red band near the nose to indicate that it is filled, and a 2-in. light green band near to the suspension lug, with stencilled markings to indicate the type of filling.

2. The nose of the Mark VIII D.C. is convex and usually there is a nose faring fitted (*see* dotted lines) to convert it to a concave nose. The Mark XI is already concave. Otherwise the D.C.s are identical.

3. The tails are hollow cylinders with three hand holes to give access to the tail retaining lugs.

4. The pistol fits into the primer pocket in the base of the depth charge. There are two filling bungs, one on either sde of the primer pocket.

5. The pocket contains a spring at the bottom, a metal-cased primer recessed to receive the detonator holder of the pistol, and the pistol itself. The pistol is held in position by a bayonet joint washer and locking ring. Under the washer there is a rubber sealing washer. The locking ring takes an Admiralty Pattern No. S.T. 6161 or 6588 (*see* Part II, Appendix). If these keys are not available a Mark II bomb disposal key for German bombs can be used.

6. There are three pistols in use. They are the Mark XIII, which is obsolescent, and Marks XVI and XIV (*see* Fig. 2 for the heads of Marks XIII and XVI pistols).

7. The Mark XIII pistol fires at depths of 50 ft., 100 ft. or 150 ft., depending on the hole into which the pillar is screwed which holds the setting arm. This setting arm is spring loaded and is held in the safe position by the clip holding it to a fixed pillar. This pistol is not necessarily safe if jettisoned with the clip in position because of possible distortion of a metal plate on impact.

8. The Mark XVI and Mark XIV pistols are similar and fire at one fixed depth of 20–24 ft. These pistols are definitely safe whatever depth of water they are in provided the safety clip is in position. The ordinary clips tend to jump off when the D.C. hits the water so that a new explosive type of safety clip is being fitted which will be certain to remain in position when the D.C. is jettisoned. These new clips are more elaborate than the ones shown in Fig. 2, but the pistol heads can still be recognized from that diagram.

9. The Mark XX pistol can only be used in the Mark XI D.C. This pistol is like the Mark XIV but the valve unit is screwed down on its seating by air vanes in the tail.

An arming wire is removed from the vanes when the D.C. is dropped.

(*T. 06720/44.—C.A.F.O. P.6/45.*)

BRITISH MUNITIONS—DEPTH CHARGES

Pt. 1. Chap. 3.
Fig. 2.

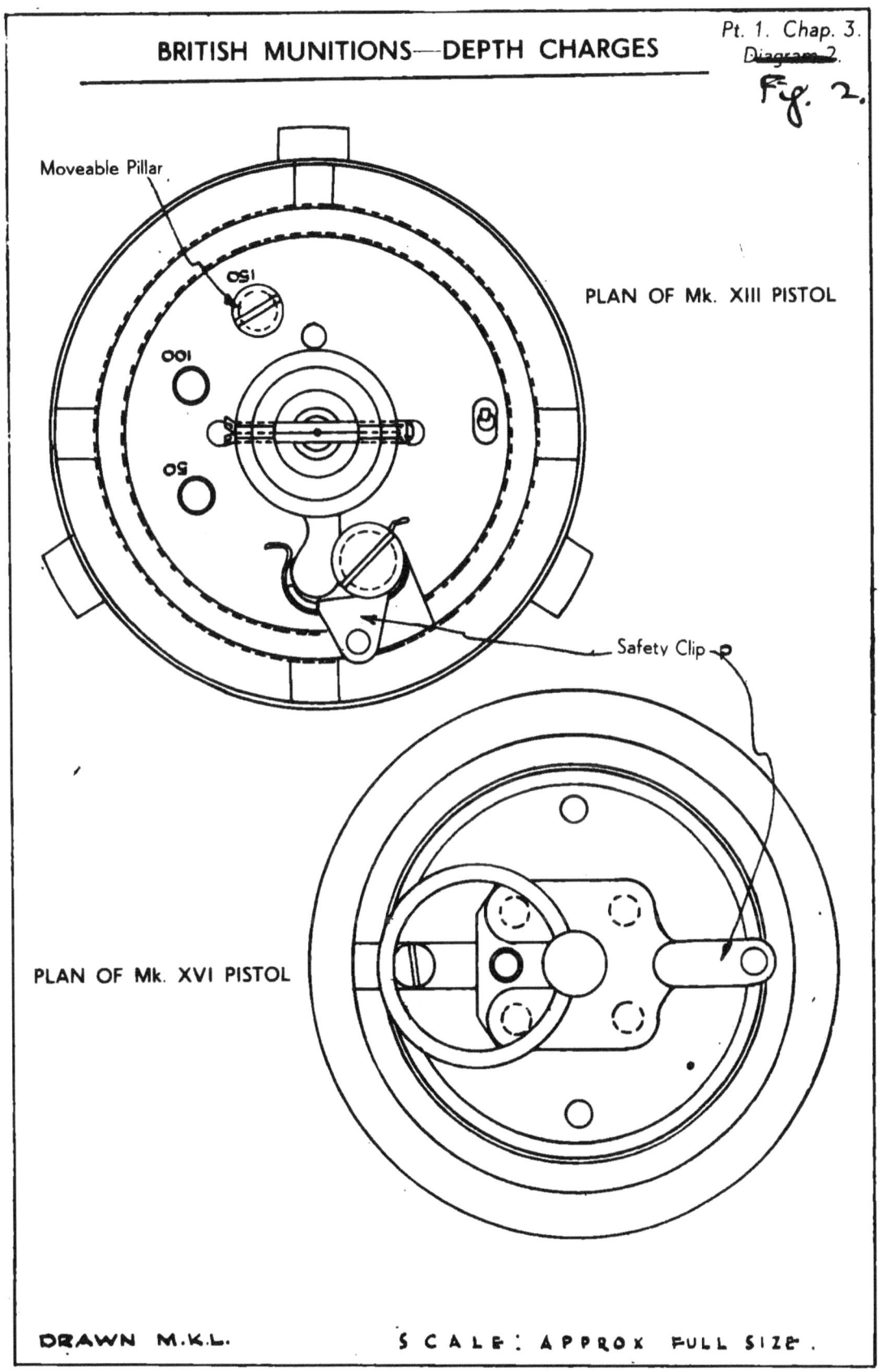

PLAN OF Mk. XIII PISTOL

Moveable Pillar

Safety Clip

PLAN OF Mk. XVI PISTOL

DRAWN M.K.L.   SCALE: APPROX FULL SIZE.

CHAPTER IV

AIRCRAFT-LAID MINES

Until notes are issued, reference should be made to C.B. 4105 or, if available, the newer C.B. 3115 (1).

CHAPTER V

ROCKET DEVICES

Section	Page
1.—Rocket Shell	
A.—H.E.	37
(i) " U " 5-in. Rocket Shell	
(ii) 60-lb. S.A.P. Rocket Shell	
(iii) 2-in. Rocket, Marks I, II and III	
B.—Incendiary	37
C.—Smoke	37

Part I, Chapter V

SECTION 1A (i).—"U" 5-IN. ROCKET SHELL WITH 722 FUZE

1. This projectile consists of a 29-lb. H.E. shell propelled by a 5-in. rocket, and is fuzed to arm in flight and fire on impact. (*See* Diagram 1.)

2. *Action of Fuze* (*see* Diagram 2).—In the unarmed position the arming vanes and striker mechanism are locked to the body of the fuze by the inertia collar, and the detonator shutter is held in the safe position by the striker. When the rocket is fired, the inertia collar, under the arming vanes, sets back and in so doing rotates slightly and unlocks the arming vanes from the fuze body. The vanes are then permitted to rotate and unscrew, taking with them the pin depressing the striker, thus allowing the striker to withdraw from the detonator shutter under the influence of the striker spring. The detonator shutter is then free to swing into the armed position.

3. The vanes will continue to rotate until the entire vane assembly and inertia collar is screwed off, leaving the striker pressure plate clear to be operated on impact.

SECTION 1A (ii).—60-LB. S.A.P. ROCKET SHELL

(*See* Diagram 3.)

1. This projectile consists of a S.A.P. H.E. shell, which is propelled by a standard 3-in. rocket and is fired from aircraft against soft shipping and certain types of land target, where a S.A.P. medium-weight shell is required.

2. The fuze, as shown in Diagram 4, is actuated by the heat generated by the rocket on leaving the aircraft. The black powder charge is contained in the chamber immediately behind the fuze, which is sufficiently sensitive to be fired by the heat given off by the rocket. The rapid burning of the black powder charge in the chamber immediately behind the fuze, sets up a high pressure which causes the diaphragm in the base of the fuze to be depressed, carrying with it a release arm which frees the detent balls from the striker and allows the detonator shutter to swing into the armed position. On impact, the striker sets forward, firing the first cap which, in turn, fires the very short delay which, in turn, fires the main detonator and detonates the shell.

3. A further type of this shell is in use, but instead of the projectile being filled H.E., it is of solid steel and is used merely as a large rocket-propelled bullet.

SECTION 1A (iii).—2-IN. ROCKET, MARKS I, II AND III

(*See* Diagram 5.)

1. This is a naval A.A. weapon, and blind rounds may have to be dealt with. It consists of a shell containing 9 oz. of T.N.T., screwed into a long tube fitted with four fins, and containing the rocket propellant.

The shell has an impact fuze in its nose armed by a wind vane and containing a self-destroying device.

2. *Functioning of the Fuze.*—The vanes are normally prevented from rotating by a safety pin with ring (*see* diagram) and also by two spring loaded detents—one outside the vane cap and one inside.

The safety pin is removed before firing. During flight, the detents set back owing to continued acceleration of the rocket and the vanes rotate in an anti-clockwise direction, looking from the nose. After five revolutions :—

(*a*) The fuze is armed and will fire on impact, since the main striker is held only by a shear wire. The vanes do not fall away, but remain, forming an extension of the striker.

(*b*) A secondary striker fires a time ring, which will cause the fuze to detonate 4 seconds after fuze arms.

3. Blind rounds are dangerous because, if armed, movement may fire the fuze and, if not armed, a slight extra turn of the vanes may initiate the self-destroying mechanism (*see* 2 (*b*)) and cause detonation in 4 seconds.

SECTION 1B.—"U" 5-IN. INCENDIARY SHELL

In appearance and dimensions this projectile is similar to the "U" 5-in. 29-lb. rocket shell and is fuzed Impact Fuze 721. This fuze is a simple direct action fuze which consists of a thin metal diaphragm, attached to the centre of which is a striker suspended over the cap in the "ready arm" position. The only safety precaution is a transit cap which is removed just before the projectile is fired.

SECTION 1C.—"U" 5-IN. SMOKE SHELL

This projectile is similar to the "U" 5-in. 29-lb. incendiary, except that it is filled smoke composition; colour markings are in accordance with the standard Navy colour code.

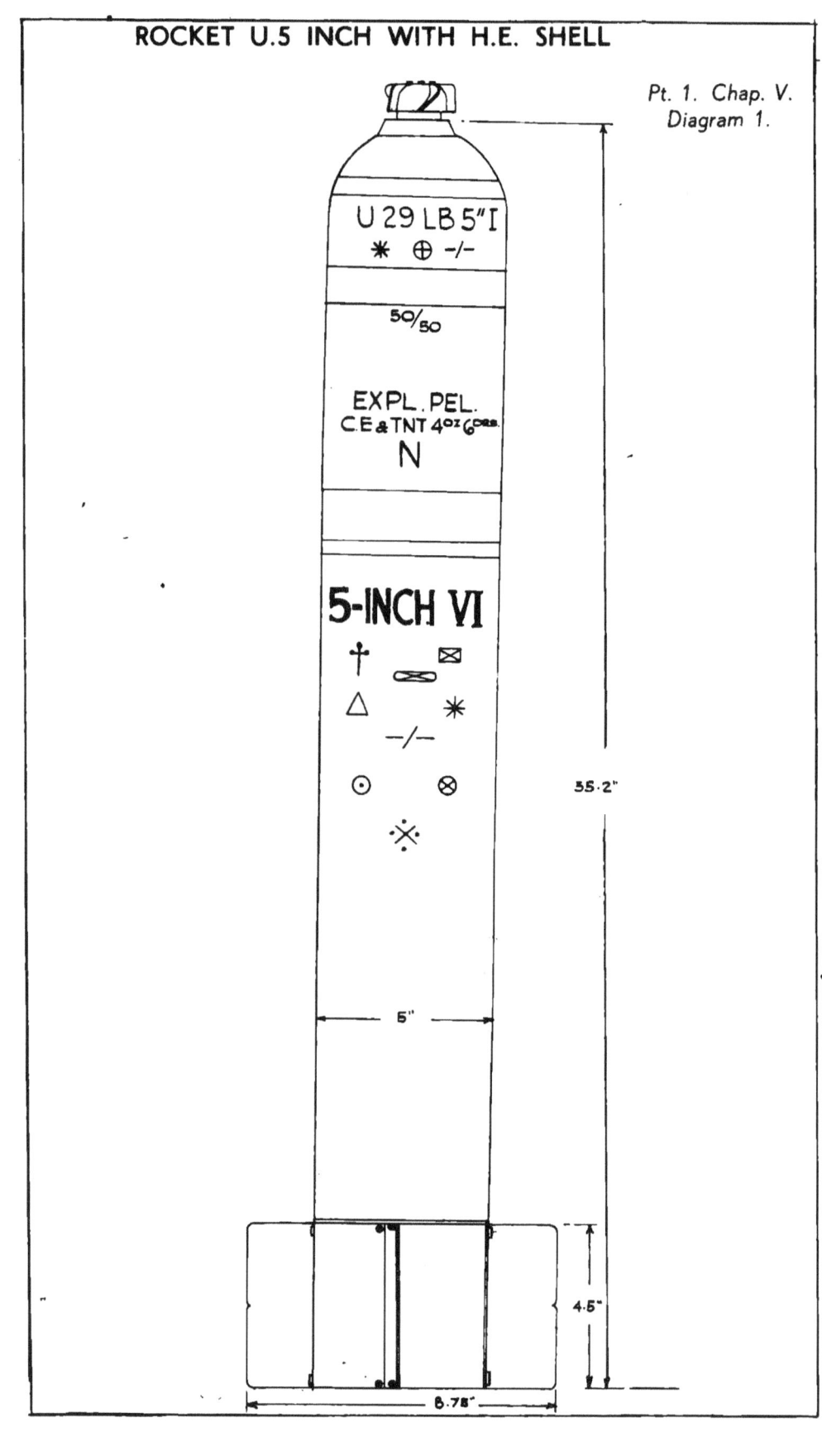

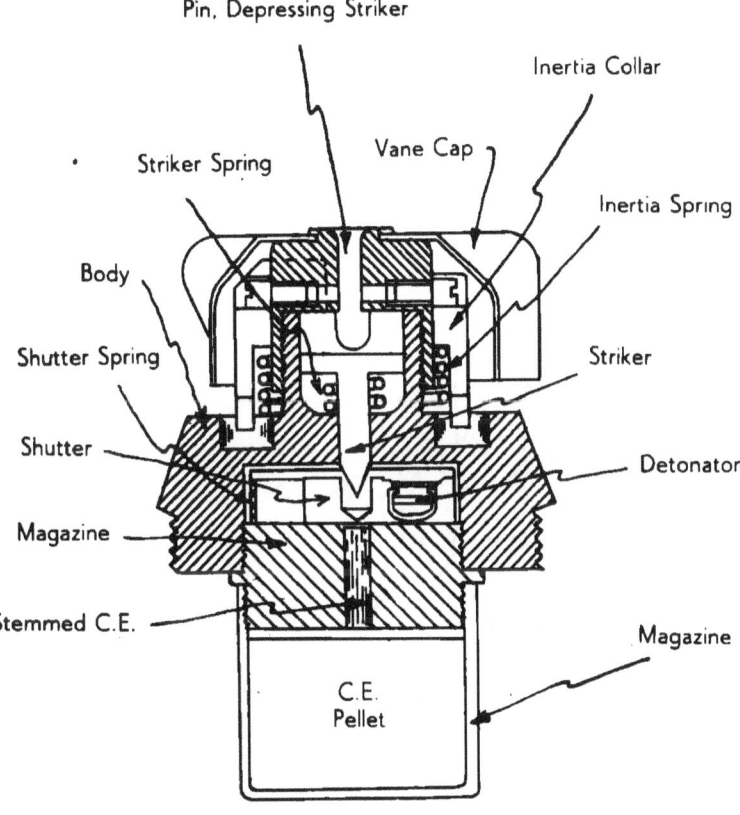

Pt. 1. Chap. V.
Diagram 2.

BRITISH FUZE No. 722 (DIRECT ACTION)
FOR USE WITH U.5 INCH ROCKET SHELL

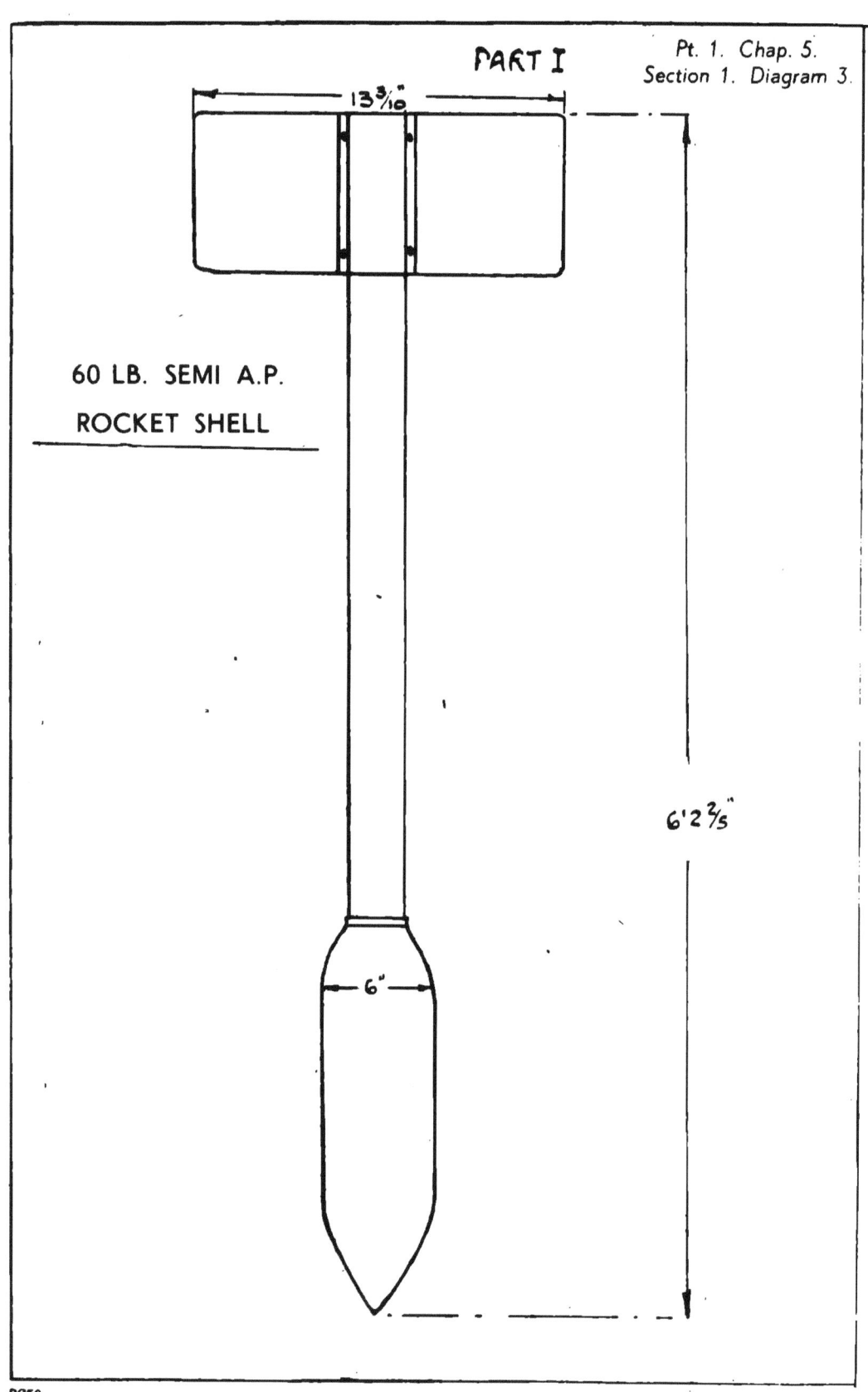

Pt. 1. Chap. V
Diagram 4.

CHAP. V

BRITISH INFORMATION

BRITISH FUZE No. 865 (DELAY) FOR USE 60 LB. S.A.P. ROCKET SHELL

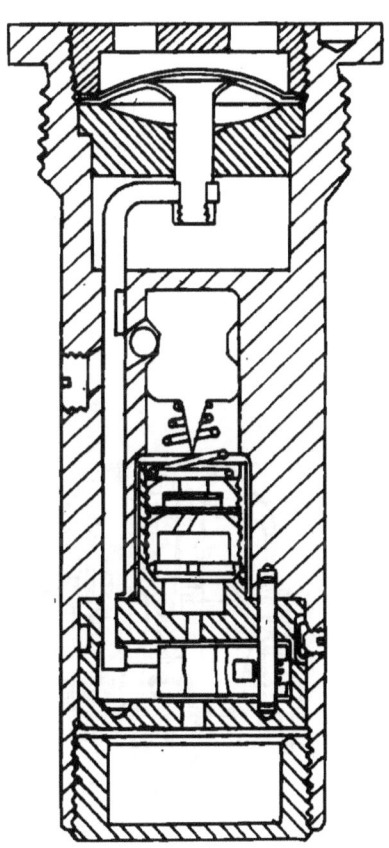

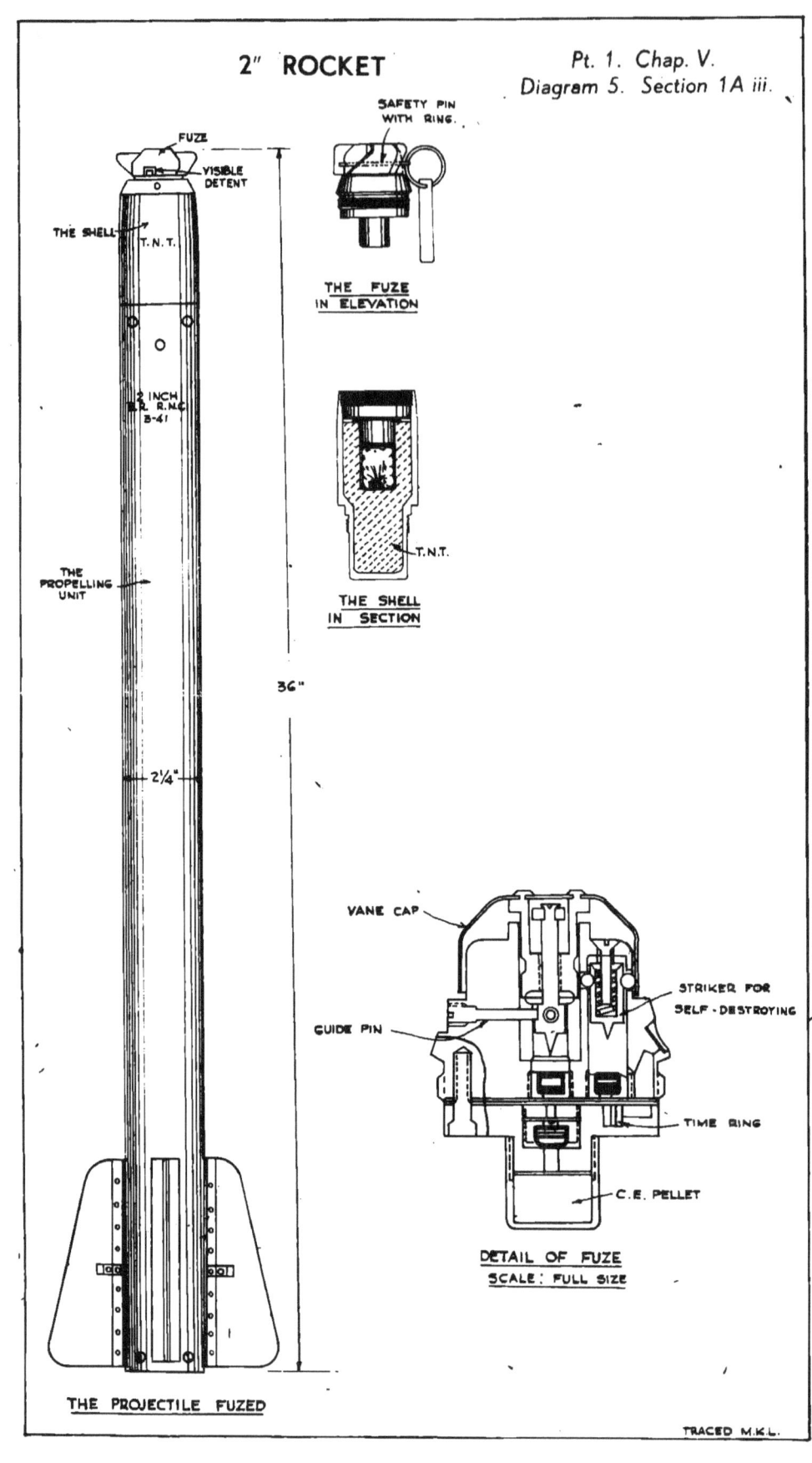

CHAPTER VI

MISCELLANEOUS DEVICES

Section	Page
1.—Mortars for use from Landing Craft	
(*a*).—Hedgerow	39
(*b*).—Unicorn	39

Part I, Chapter VI

SECTION 1 (a).—62-LB. HEDGEROW CHARGE, FUZED 152

(*See* Diagram 1.)

1. *Description.*—The projectile consists of a cylindrical charge head, tubular tail piece and stabilizing pins. The fuze 152 is housed at the end of a nose stick, 20 in. long, through which runs a length of Cordtex to transmit the detonation wave from the fuze to the main exploder in the charge head.

The detonating system is so designed to ensure that the projectile explodes at about 18 in. above the surface of the beach.

2. *Use.*—The " Hedgerow " is fired from landing craft in batches of 12 or 24 at a time by spigot mortars which are so placed as to give a different trajectory to each round, so causing the rounds to fall in a ripple.

3. The main purpose of the " Hedgerow " is to operate beach mines by making an umbrella of pressure just above level of the beach.

SECTION 1 (b).—35-LB. UNICORN

(*See* Diagram 2.)

1. *Description.*—The Unicorn round is shaped as shown in Diagram 2. The internal construction is on the Munro principle to form a shaped charge, similar to the Beehive.

2. The fuze is of the direct acting type and is armed on being fired from the spigot. The striker is covered by a thin copper cap which collapses on impact, so driving in the striker.

3. *Action of Fuze.*—On impact the striker fires a cap which, in turn, fires a small active charge contained in the fuze. The detonation wave passes up a central tube and detonates main charge from the tail end.

4. *Use.*—The Unicorn is intended for submarine attack and projected from ship by spigot motor device.

Pt. 1. Chap. 6.
Section 1. Diagram 1.

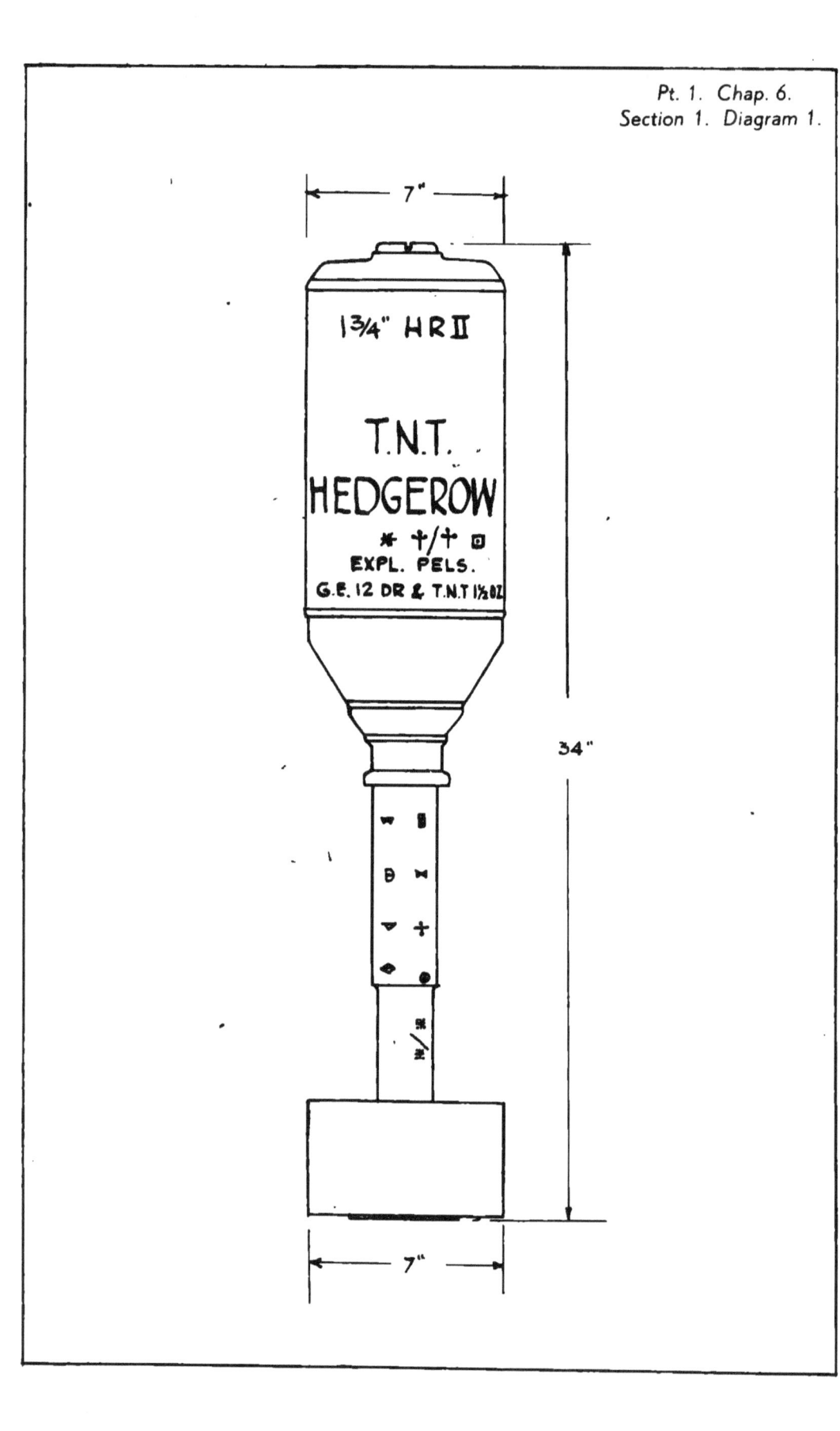

Pt. 1. Chap. 6.
Section 1. Diagram 2.

T.N.T.   T.N.T.
60/40

40 LB
UNICORN
M.OF.F. D.M.W.D 71/3/9

PART II

BRITISH MUNITIONS

RENDERING SAFE, AND DISPOSAL

Chapter	Page
I.—H.E. Bombs	41
II.—Incendiaries and Pyrotechnics	50
III.—Depth Charges dropped from Aircraft	66
IV.—Aircraft-laid Mines	67
V.—Rocket Devices	68
VI.—Miscellaneous Devices	70
Appendix.—Spanners, Keys, etc.	72

CHAPTER I

H.E. BOMBS

Section		Page
1.—General Procedure		42
2.—Bombs fitted with Tail Pistols and Fuzes (Section 4 gives detail)		43
3.—Bombs fitted with Nose Pistols and Fuzes (Section 4 gives detail)		44
4A.—No. 22 Tail Pistol		45
4B.—No. 28 Tail Pistol		45
4C.—No. 30 Tail Pistol		45
4D.—Nos. 30 and 37 Tail Fuzes		45
4E.—No. 487 Tail Fuzes		45
4F.—No. 862 Tail Fuze (Hydrostatic)		46
4G.—Nos. 19, 27 and 42 Nose Pistols		46
4H.—No. 34 Nose Pistol		46
4I.—No. 33 Nose Pistol		46
4J.—No. 38 Nose Pistol		46
4K.—Nos. 45 and 44 Nose Pistol		47
4L.—No. 32 Nose Fuze		47
4M.—No. 845 Anti-handling Nose Fuze and No. 37 Tail Pistol, Long Delay		47, 47a, 47b, 47c
4N.—No. 17 Long Delay Tail Pistol		47

After Section 4N. *Add* :—

4O.	No. 873 nose fuze	47d	48
4P.	No. 880, 881 and 882 (8-lb. F. bomb)	47d	49
4Q.	No. 895A, Mark I fuze	47d	
4R.	No. 47 long delay side pistol	47d	
4S.	No. 53 and 53a long delay tail fuze	47e	
4T.	No. 54, Mark I tail pistol	47e	
4U.	No. 885 tail fuze	47e	

(*T. 06720/44.—C.A.F.O. P.6/45.*)

SECTION 1.—GENERAL PROCEDURE
(*See* A.F.O.s.)

1. All incidents will be dealt with by R.A.F. personnel except :—
   (*a*) R.N.A.S. will be responsible for their own stations in all cases.
   (*b*) Naval bombs jettisoned on Admiralty property will be dealt with by B.S.O.s.
   (*c*) Bombs in crashed aircraft which interfere with important work on Admiralty property will, as far as possible, be rendered safe by B.S.O.s and a report passed to the Air Liason Officer attached to the Regional Controller.
   (*d*) R.A.F. B.D. Flights are authorised to call upon the B.S.O. whenever his services may be required to deal with jettisoned bombs.

2. Before proceeding to deal with these bombs, the following information should be obtained, if possible.
   (i) Details of the bombs and their pistols or fuzes.
   (ii) If jettisoned—whether they were jettisoned " safe " or " live " and also at what height they were released.
   In all cases the fuzes must be identified before a bomb is disturbed in any way.

3. Should any one of the fuzes be (i) long delay, (ii) anti-disturbance, (iii) unknown, or (iv) badly damaged, the bomb should be demolished in position if at all possible (*see* Part II, Chapter I, Sections 4M and N).

4. When dealing with a bomb, fuzed nose and tail, other things being equal, the tail fuze or pistol should be dealt with first.

5. After removal of a pistol, the detonator is to be extracted, using detonator extractor No. 2, Mark I. (*See* Appendix to Part II.)

6. If the bomb is in good condition the pistol or the appropriate transit plug is then to be screwed into the bomb, which is to be kept to await A.I.D. inspection with a view to bringing it back into service.

7. Detonators and fuzes are to be demolished with full precautions.

8. Where it is not possible to unscrew the pistol or fuze, the bomb should be demolished *in situ*.

9. In the following script, instructions are given in certain cases to tamp a charge. In all these cases the charge should be fired by cordtex. The detonator should be fitted only after all the tamping operations have been completed.

CHAPTER I

H.E. BOMBS

Section	Page
1.—General Procedure	42
2.—Bombs fitted with Tail Pistols and Fuzes (Section 4 gives detail)	43
3.—Bombs fitted with Nose Pistols and Fuzes (Section 4 gives detail)	44
4A.—No. 22 Tail Pistol	45
4B.—No. 28 Tail Pistol	45
4C.—No. 30 Tail Pistol	45
4D.—Nos. 30 and 37 Tail Fuzes	45
4E.—No. 487 Tail Fuzes	45
4F.—No. 862 Tail Fuze (Hydrostatic)	46
4G.—Nos. 19, 27 and 42 Nose Pistols	46
4H.—No. 34 Nose Pistol	46
4I.—No. 33 Nose Pistol	46
4J.—No. 38 Nose Pistol	46
4K.—Nos. 45 and 44 Nose Pistol	47
4L.—No. 32 Nose Fuze	47
4M.—No. 845 Anti-handling Nose Fuze and No. 37 Tail Pistol, Long Delay	47, 47a 47b 47c
4N.—No. 17 Long Delay Tail Pistol	47
5.—H.E. Bombs Overseas	48
6.—H.E. Bombs on Board Ship	49
7.—Miscellaneous	49a
(a) Aircraft Bomb, Infantry Training 6 lb. Mark I	
(b) 250 lb. 'B' Bomb	

SECTION 2.—BOMBS FITTED WITH TAIL PISTOLS AND FUZES

1. (*a*) Precautions during excavation :—

    (i) The bomb must not be moved in any way until the pistols have been exposed and dealt with.

    (ii) These pistols and fuzes even when jettisoned safe, may be so sheared off on impact, so that the striker is only held away from the detonator by a light creep spring.

    Great care is therefore to be exercised when excavating to uncover the bomb, since even a slight pressure or blow on such a floating striker would result in detonation of the bomb.

    The probe is therefore to be used only as a last resort and, in such circumstances, the man using the probe is to be the only person within the danger area.

    (iii) When the bomb is reached, the pistol is to be uncovered without moving the bomb in any way. (The tail unit, if present, is to be carefully removed if it obstructs the uncovering of the pistol.)

    (iv) Earth obscuring the state of a pistol or fuze is to be washed out, using a jet of water. A nose nozzle is to be fixed near to and pointing at the pistol or fuze (at an angle) and cold water forced through the hose, using pump *placed behind adequate cover*. This precaution is necessary since, if the striker has pierced the detonator which has failed to function, the washing away of the earth may release the striker which, under the influence of its spring, is withdrawn from the detonator. *It is possible that this movement of the striker will function the detonator and bring about detonation of the bomb.*

    (v) When the water has been turned off, approach is to be made to the bomb *by one man only* and the condition of the pistol or fuze ascertained.

(*b*) *Removal of Pistol or Fuze.*—(i) The pistol or fuze is to be unscrewed by remote control unless it is known to be in a safe condition (*see* items on individual pistols and fuzes). Badly damaged pistols are always to be unscrewed by remote control.

(ii) Bombs with badly damaged pistols, which cannot be unscrewed, would normally be demolished *in situ*. Should circumstances not permit of demolition *in situ*, trepanning and boiling out should be considered if the necessary gear is available.

Boiling out can only be resorted to if the fuzes or pistols are identified and are known to be of impact type. Bombs containing long delay pistols must not be boiled out.

(iii) If the pistol or fuze is known to be in a safe condition it may be unscrewed by hand.

(iv) If the pistol or fuze cannot be identified the bomb should be demolished *in situ*.

SECTION 3.—BOMBS FITTED WITH NOSE PISTOLS AND FUZES

1. (*a*) Precautions during excavations :—
    (i) The bomb must not be moved in any way until its pistols and/or fuzes have been exposed and dealt with.
    (ii) Provided no tail pistol is fitted, probing is permissible during the excavation. If a tail pistol is fitted, *see* 2(*a*).
    (iii) When the bomb is found the fuze is to be carefully exposed without moving the bomb in any way and the condition of the pistol ascertained. Any earth which may have become lodged round the pistol is to be washed away using a stream of water. This may be done using an ordinary stirrup pump.

    (*b*) Removal of nose pistols or fuzes :—
    (i) The pistol is to be removed by remote control unless it is known to be in a safe condition (*see* items on individual pistols). Badly damaged pistols are always to be unscrewed by remote control.
    (ii) Bombs with badly damaged pistols, which cannot be unscrewed, would normally be demolished *in situ*. Should circumstances not permit of demolition *in situ*, trepanning and boiling out should be considered if the necessary gear is available.

    Boiling out can only be resorted to if the fuzes or pistols are identified and are known to be of impact type. Bombs containing long delay pistols must not be boiled out.
    (iii) If the pistol or fuze is known to be in a safe condition it may be unscrewed by hand.
    (iv) If the pistol or fuze cannot be identified the bomb should be demolished *in situ*.

SECTION 4A.—TAIL PISTOL No. 22

1. (a) This pistol may be considered safe and unscrewed by hand :—
    (i) If the safety vanes and clip are in position.
    (ii) If the safety devices are missing and the red band on the striker spindle is visible. It should then be taped till rigid.

   (b) In all other conditions the pistol is to be unscrewed by remote control or the bomb demolished *in situ*.

SECTION 4B.—TAIL PISTOL No. 28

1. (a) This pistol may be considered safe and may be unscrewed by hand :—
    (i) When the safety fork is screwed fully down on the striker spindle.
    (ii) When the safety fork is partially unscrewed but not beyond the position where the top of the striker spindle is flush with the top thread of the safety fork (*see* Part I, Section 12).

   (b) In all other conditions it is to be unscrewed by remote control or the bomb demolished *in situ*.

SECTION 4C.—TAIL PISTOL No. 30

1. (a) The striker of the No. 30 tail pistol has a long, sharp point and, used with its appropriate detonator, is more sensitive than the No. 28 pistol with its anvil type detonator.

   It is therefore important that this pistol should be treated with special care. It can be distinguished from the No. 28 pistol by a $\frac{1}{4}$-in. groove painted green round the middle of the head.

   (b) This pistol may be considered safe and unscrewed by hand :—
    (i) When the safety fork is screwed fully down on the striker spindle.
    (ii) When the safety fork is partially unscrewed but not beyond the position where the top of the striker spindle is flush with the top thread of the safety fork (*see* Part I, Section 12).

   (c) In all other conditions it is to be unscrewed by remote control or the bomb demolished *in situ*.

SECTION 4D.—TAIL FUZES Nos. 30 AND 37

1. (a) If the safety clip is present the fuze may be considered safe. The procedure for removing the fuze is :—
    (1) Replace a safety pillar.
    (2) Remove the vanes and safety clip.
    (3) Remove the locking ring without removing the tail, if possible ; otherwise remove the tail first.
    (4) If the keys are not available remove the fuzed bomb to a safe place until such time as the keys become available, or remove the bomb to a demolition site and demolish it.
    (5) Put a wooden plug in the fuze pocket before transporting the bomb.
    (6) The safety pillar of the fuze should be wired in position before transporting.

   (b) When the safety clip is not present the fuze must be assumed to be armed and must be removed by remote control. The procedure laid down in (a) should be followed as nearly as possible.

   The No. 111 key will have to be adapted and used on the S.A.P., Mark IV, and the A.P. 2,000-lb. Mark I and II, as this is the only type of key which can be used for remote control. The Mark IV extractor will require a spring between the rotating head and the fixed base in order to keep the key in engagement with the locking ring. The locking rings of the S.A.P. Mark III and IV have left-hand thread and, when used, the extractor head must be placed on the after end of the shaft.

   The only other divergence from the procedure as for (a) is that the fuze must be demolished, taking all safety precautions. When moving the fuze it should be kept horizontal or with the arming spindle end inclined slightly downwards.

SECTION 4E.—No. 487 TAIL FUZE (ANTI-TANK, 9-LB.)

1. (a) If safety devices present, remove fuze by hand.
   (b) In any other condition the bomb is to be demolished in position.

SECTION 4F.—No. 862 TAIL FUZE (HYDROSTATIC)

1. (a) If the bomb has not been submerged to a greater depth than 15 ft. :—

   In all cases unscrew the locking ring with an R.A.F. implement ammunition No. 209 and unscrew the fuze by hand.

   (b) If the bomb has been submerged to a depth greater than 15 ft. *at any time* :—

   (i) If a safety wire is visible entering the anti-countermining chamber :—

   Remove the tail and unscrew the anti-countermining chamber cover with an R.A.F. implement ammunition No. 208. If the wire is correctly positioned, then the locking ring and fuze may be removed by hand.

   (ii) If the safety wire is not visible :—

   Demolish in position if possible. If this is not possible then tow the bomb to a suitable site from a safe distance and then demolish. It must be understood that movement of the bomb may cause detonation and therefore full precautions must be taken.

SECTION 4G.—NOSE PISTOLS Nos. 19, 27 AND 42

N.B.—The No. 42 pistol is more sensitive than the No. 27 and No. 19. It has a needle striker instead of an anvil striker.

1. (a) In these pistols the point of the striker is less than 1/16-in. from the detonator cap, and a small longitudinal movement of the striker is sufficient to cause it to strike the detonator.

   (b) These pistols may be considered safe and unscrewed by hand when the visible safety devices—arming dome and fork—are in position and the pressure plate shows no signs of having become depressed.

   (c) If the visible safety devices are missing, the fuze is still safe provided that the safety fork can be inserted in its normal position under the pressure plate. If a safety fork is not available, wedges can be used to hold the pressure plate in position.

   (d) In all other conditions the pistol is to be unscrewed by remote control or the bomb demolished *in situ*.

SECTION 4H.—NOSE PISTOL No. 34

1. (a) In this pistol the point of the striker is close to the detonator cap and a small longitudinal movement of the striker is sufficient to cause it to strike the detonator.

   (b) The pistol may be considered safe and unscrewed by hand when the visible safety devices, safety cap and safety fork are in position and the pressure plate shows no signs of having been depressed.

   (c) If the visible safety devices are missing, the fuze is still safe provided that the safety fork can be inserted in its normal position under the pressure plate. If a safety fork is not available wedges can be used to hold the pressure plate in position...

   (d) If the pressure plate is depressed the pistol should be removed by remote control or the bomb demolished *in situ*.

SECTION 4I.—NOSE PISTOL No. 33

1. (a) This pistol may be considered safe and unscrewed by hand if the safety spring clip is in position. This will usually mean that the parachute has not opened. Before unscrewing a safety pin should be inserted.

   (b) In all other conditions demolish the bomb *in situ* or, if it is essential to move the bomb, secure the pistol in the position found by adhesive tape and move carefully to the nearest position in which the bomb, complete with pistol, can be demolished.

SECTION 4J.—NOSE PISTOL No. 38

1. (a) This pistol may be considered safe and unscrewed by hand if the safety cap is in position and if the safety pin can be inserted.

   (b) In all other conditions the pistol is to be unscrewed by remote control or the bomb demolished *in situ*.

SECTION 4K.—NOSE PISTOLS Nos. 45 AND 44

1. (a) If the safety cap is present then the pistols may be removed by hand.
(b) In all other cases the pistols are to be removed by remote control or the bomb demolished *in situ*.

SECTION 4L.—NOSE FUZE No. 32

1. (a) This fuze may be considered safe and unscrewed by hand if the safety clip is present.
Procedure :—
   (1) Screw in a safety pillar.
   (2) Remove vanes and clip.
   (3) Remove ballistic cap of the bomb (first remove grub screw).
   (4) Remove the delay cover and set the delay to " Bridge " with a No. 126 key (R.A.F. implement ammunition) or an adjustable spanner. *N.B.*—Turn clockwise.
   (5) Loosen the locking ring with a No. 89 key (R.A.F. implement ammunition) or foot prints.
   (6) Remove the fuze. This will probably be stiff as luting is put on the threads when fuzing.

(b) In all other conditions demolish in position if possible. If this cannot possibly be accepted, the procedure laid down in (a) should be carried out, removing the ballistic cap and fuze by remote control. The fuze should then be demolished, taking all safety precautions. When moving the fuze it should be kept horizontal or with the nose inclined slightly upwards. The setting of the delay to " Bridge " does not make the fuze safe as it is possible for the fuze to fire by direct action of the second striker.

N.B.—It is not possible to tell by external examination whether or not the fuze is armed. When armed the fuze is in a highly dangerous condition and slight movement of the bomb may result in detonation.

SECTION 4M.—BOMBS, FUZED, ANTI-HANDLING AND LONG DELAY No. 845 NOSE FUZE AND No. 37 TAIL PISTOL

1. In general, bombs containing these fuzes are to be demolished in position. If, however, the safety devices are present and the bomb has received no severe jolt, *e.g.*, if an aircraft has made a forced landing, the bombs may be moved, but under NO circumstances must the No. 37 pistol be unscrewed or turned in the bomb. The bomb should be demolished at the nearest convenient site.

N.B.—The R.A.F. under the above circumstances recover the bomb, remove the No. 845 fuze, take off the tail, replace the safety devices of the No. 37 pistol, replace the warning tag from the safety clip to the pistol and re-use the bomb at a later date. Obviously if B.S.O.s have had to deal with the bombs the question of re-using the bombs will not arise.

In an extreme emergency a bomb fuzed No. 845 and No. 37 which has been dropped live can be dealt with as follows :—
   (a) Apply a modification of the " F " process to the No. 845 until the indications of the process reach the first green band on the bomb.
   (b) Apply a freezing process to the No. 37 pistol in order to slow down the delay process.
   (c) Extract the No. 845 fuze using a No. 104 key (R.A.F. implement ammunition).
   (d) Demolish the 845 fuze, taking full safety precautions.
   (e) Remove the bomb to a demolition site. If the bomb cannot be moved it is possible to apply the Mark IV extractor and remove the exploder pocket containing the No. 37 pistol. A grub screw which secures the pocket in the bomb must first be removed.
      N.B.—Remember that the pistol must NOT turn relative to the pocket.

"Continued on pages 47a - 47d"

SECTION 4N.—No. 17 LONG DELAY TAIL PISTOL

1. This pistol which is used in G.P., Mark V, bombs only, should be treated in the same way as a No. 37 tail pistol, except in the case of extreme emergency. In the latter case the No. 17 pistol can be frozen and the bomb moved immediately. There is no anti-handling device. The pistol must NOT be unscrewed as there is an anti-withdrawal device.

2. If the bomb is jammed and cannot be moved, the only possibility is to apply a freezing process and then remove the nose plug and try to withdraw the exploders and detonators from the nose of the bomb,

CONFIDENTIAL

47a

C.B.3126 - Amendment No. 1

(PART II Chap. 1)

(To be read after Section 4 M.)

The following is extracted from an Air Ministry Instruction. The details have been modified slightly so that B.S.C.'s equipment may be used.

1. <u>General</u> In view of the extremely erratic behaviour of No.37 pistols when fitted in bombs jettisoned from aircraft, or bombs which have been subjected to heat and/or shock in crashed aircraft, the following procedure should be adopted.

2(i) Bombs, other than priority which in all cases will be dealt with at once under the most appropriate method (see para.4), may only be approached or dealt with at the following specified times subsequent to impact :-

NOTE: Type of No.37 Pistol will only be known after receiving information from the aircraft or its home station

    No.37 pistol - within 1 hour or after 15 hours
    No.37A   "   - within 3 hours or after 26 hours.
    No.37B   "   - within 12 hours or after 80 hours.
    No.37D   "   - within 24 hours or after 150 hours.
    No.37E   "   - within 72 hours or after 300 hours.

(ii) The B.S.O. will decide which of the alternative methods of disposal (see para.2 below) are applicable and <u>immediately</u> initiate the necessary action.

3. <u>Disposal</u>

    (i) <u>Where demolition in situ is acceptable</u>

        (a) Except in the case of Priority bombs the time limitations, during which bombs may be approached, as given in para.1, sub.para.(i) are to be strictly observed.

        (b) Double the normal demolition charges are to be laid.

47b

    (c) These demolition charges are to be placed, the cable connected and run out to the firing point <u>at once</u> after which the bomb is not to be approached.

    (d) The bomb will then be demolished.

    (e) If the detonation of the demolition charge fails to demolish the bomb, it is not to be approached until a safety time equal to double the normal delay of the pistol has elapsed. Safety precautions are to be fully maintained during this period.

    (f) In the event of more than one bomb fuzed 37 pistol being present within a radius of 50 yds, they are to be demolished simultaneously providing the combined weight of the main fillings is not greater than 1,000 lb.

    (g) Double charges will be laid at once and cables connected as in sub.para (i)(c) above.

    (h) Where bombs are more than 50 yards apart or their combined weight of main fillings exceeds 1,000 lb, double charges will be laid, individual cables brought to the firing point.

(ii) <u>Where demolition in situ is not acceptable</u>

    (a) Except in the case of Priority bombs the time limitations during which bombs may be approached as given in para. 2 sub. para.(i) are to be strictly observed.

    (b) The tail unit if present, is to be removed immediately on arrival at the site and the pistol inspected to ascertain the condition of the ampoule.

    (c) The arming screw is to be removed and the inside of the pistol and threads carefully examined.

    N.B.: Before removing the arming screw check which way the vanes would turn it and turn the <u>opposite</u> way. The Mk.III Pistol has a L.H. thread and the Mk.IV Pistol a right hand thread. The latter will be most common.

    (d) If the ampoule is broken there will be a strong smell of acetone, the cup of the pistol and/or the threads of the arming screw may be stained and/or it may be possible to see the

broken ..

47c

broken edges of the ampoule. The acetone is coloured red or, in the case of shortest delay, blue.

(e) <u>If the ampoule is broken</u> one of the following alternatives is to be adopted :-

<u>First Alternative</u>. Employ the Mk.IV Extractor in the prescribed manner, i.e., removing the pocket, NOT unscrewing the pistol.

<u>Second Alternative</u>. If the Mk.IV Extractor is not available flush out the pistol by carefully directing a jet of water from the stirrup pump into the arming screw cavity for at least three minutes; obtain an Extractor from the nearest B.S.O. with one available. Full safety precautions are meanwhile to be observed.

NOTE: If the washing out process is done properly there should be no smell of acetone left.

<u>Third Alternative</u>. Flush out the pistol as above and tow the bomb from a safe distance to a prepared pit where demolition is acceptable.

(f) <u>If the ampoule is not broken</u> one of the following alternatives is to be adopted.

<u>First Alternative</u>. Employ the Mk.IV Extractor in the prescribed manner (as in (e) above).

<u>Second Alternative</u>. Transport the bomb carefully to the nearest suitable site for immediate demolition.

SECTION 5.—H.E. BOMBS—OVERSEAS

1. B.S.O.s may be called upon to deal with British bombs under these conditions.

2. The procedure is as laid down in Sections 1–4, but the general tendency will be to demolish in position whenever possible rather than to extract pistols or fuzes.

5   C.A.F.O. P.575/4

Add new page 47d.

47d

SECTION 4.O. No. 873 Nose Fuze :—

1. (*a*) If the safety cap is present and undamaged the fuze may be removed by hand after inserting a safety pin.

(*b*) In all other cases the bomb must be demolished, *in situ* if possible.

(*c*) If detonation of the bomb *in situ* is impossible, the fuze should be extracted by remote control (Mark IV Extractor) and the fuze taken carefully to the nearest suitable demolition site. Demolish by firing a 2 oz. cartridge of P.B.G. against the magazine.

Page 47*d.* *After* Section 4O *add* following Sections 4P to 4U :—

SECTION 4P.—TAIL FUZE, Nos. 880, 881, 882 (8-LB. F. BOMB)

1. These fuzes will be difficult to distinguish from one another.

2. No. bomb containing them (*i.e.* 8-lb. F. bombs) should be approached for 12 hours (24 hours under cold conditions); then any U.X.B.s will be demolished in position without disturbing them in any way.

3. The general principles of approach, reconnaissance, etc., used for the German S.D.2 bombs should be applied also to these bombs.

SECTION 4.Q.—No. 895A, MARK I FUZE
(Used in the A.S. 100-lb. Mark I Bomb.)

1. Provided the bomb containing the fuze has not been immersed in water of greater depth than 12 ft., the fuze is to be removed and destroyed by means of a 2-oz. cartridge of P.B.G. tamped across the magazine. Safety distance, 50 yards.

2. When the bomb has been immersed in water deeper than 12 ft. it should be demolished *in situ*.

SECTION 4R.—No. 47 LONG DELAY SIDE PISTOL
Disposal

1. Since the 47 pistol is not fitted with an anti-withdrawal device there is no reason why the pistol should not be unscrewed. As the striker might be embedded in the cap, it is recommended that the pistol should only be unscrewed by remote control.

2. Should the pistol be so damaged that it cannot be distinguished from a damaged 37 pistol, disposal should be as for the 37 pistol (D.B.D. Tech. Inst. 218A).

SECTION 4S.—No. 53 AND No. 53a LONG DELAY TAIL FUZE

1. Bombs containing these pistols should not be approached until three hours have elapsed from the time of impact.

2. Whenever possible the bombs should be demolished *in situ*.

3. In no circumstance will the pistols be removed other than by remote control.

4. Damaged pistols which cannot be identified as No. 53 or No. 53a are, where necessary, to be withdrawn in accordance with the method used for a No. 37 pistol.

SECTION 4T.—No. 54 MARK I TAIL PISTOL

Great care is to be exercised when handling bombs fuzed with this pistol due to the "all-ways" action of the pistol.

2. The probe may be used during excavation providing care is observed.

3. The pistol must be considered armed if the head of the arming fork protrudes more than $\frac{1}{4}$-in. above the top of the body.

4. Even if a pistol appears unarmed there is the possibility that the arming fork spindle may have been fractured below the retaining plate by the force of impact.

5. In no circumstances may this pistol be removed from the bomb other than by remote control.

SECTION 4U.—No. 885 TAIL FUZE

As for No. 860 tail fuze.

(*T.* 06720/44.—*C.A.F.O. P.*6/45.)

SECTION 6.—H.E. BOMBS—ON BOARD SHIP

1. Bombs on board ship will have to be rendered safe or removed from the ship in all cases.

2. The general procedure is laid down in N.M.E.R. Article 250 *et seq.* and A.F.O. 5948/42. Where applicable, the procedure laid down in Part II, Chapter I, Sections 1–4 of these notes should be followed.

CONFIDENTIAL

C.B. 3126 - Amendment No. 1

(PART II Chap. 1)

Section 7

(a) <u>AIRCRAFT BOMB, INFANTRY TRAINING 6 LB. MARK I</u>

    1. It will usually be possible to demolish this bomb in situ.

    2. If (1) is impossible deal with the No. 34 Nose Pistol as laid down in Part II, Chap. 1, Section 4 H.

(b) <u>250 LB. 'B' BOMB</u>

    1. If the bomb is undamaged and has never been in water, it is safe to transport it with care for demolition at a convenient site.

    2. If damaged, the bomb should be demolished in situ.

    3. If the bomb has been submerged in water, it should be treated as dangerous even if the contact disc chains are not tight. Demolish in situ.

    4. If the position of the bomb is such that demolition in situ cannot be allowed, the bomb should be towed from a safe distance to a convenient site for demolition.

Page 49a. Section 7. *After* (b) *add* new paragraph (c) :—
- (c) *60-lb. Training Bomb, Mark I*
    1. After removal of pistol and detonator the bomb may be moved and demolished.
    2. Where defuzing is not practicable demolish the bomb *in situ.*

Note.—Safety distance 100 yards under cover.

CHAPTER II

INCENDIARIES AND PYROTECHNICS

Section	Page
1A.—4-lb. Incendiaries	51
1B.—25-lb. Incendiary Bomb	51
1C.—30-lb. Incendiary Bomb	51
1D.—45-lb. Incendiary Bomb	52
1E.—250-lb. Incendiary Bomb	53
1F.—30 lb. 'J' Type Incendiary Bomb	53
2A.—4-lb. Smoke Bomb	54
2B.—100-lb. Smoke Bomb	54
2C.—120-lb. Smoke Bomb	54
3.—Practice Bombs. 10-lb. and 11½-lb. Smoke and Flash Bombs and 8½-lb. Break-up Bomb.	55
4A.—Smoke Float, Aircraft No. 1, Mark IV	56
4B.—Smoke Float No. 2, Marks I and II	56
4C.—Smoke Float No. 3, Mark I	56
5.—Smoke Generators	57
6A.—Flame Floats, Mark II, and No. 4, Mark I, and Flame Float, Message Carrying, Mark I.	58
6B.—Flame Float No. 3, Mark I, and Marker, Marine, Marks I and II	58
6C.—Marker, Marine, Mark III	58
7.—Sea Markers	59
8.—Flares	60
9A.—4·5-in. Photographic Flashes, Marks I and II	61
9B.—Heavy Photographic Flash, 6·5 in.	61
10.—Bomb, Aircraft Target Illuminating, 250 lbs.	62
11.—Fuzes and Pistols used in Flares, Photographic Flashes and Bombs (*see* Sections 8–10).	63
12.—Miscellaneous. (*a*) Calibrator, Altimeter Flash, Mark I	64
13.—Incendiaries and Pyrotechnics on Board Ship	65

SECTION 1A.—4-LB. INCENDIARY BOMBS

1. If markings are difficult to ascertain, all 4-lb. incendiaries must be treated as Type X.

2. **4-lb. Incendiary Bombs** (Non-explosive)—These should be disposed of by burning. They should be burned in a pit at least 4 ft. deep, not more than forty at a time. All inflammable material should be removed for a radius of 20 yards round the pit.

3. To initiate the burning, two of the bombs should have the cork inserts removed and safety fuze then be placed in the holes. After lighting the fuze, all personnel should retire to a distance of 50 yards. The pit should not be approached until one hour after burning has ceased.

4. **4-lb. Incendiary Bombs, Type E.**—These should be dealt with in the same way as the ordinary 4-lb. incendiary bombs, but they should be disposed of not more than ten at a time. The safety distance should be 100 yards and the time allowed after burning has ceased should be 30 minutes.

5. **4-lb. Incendiary Bombs, Type X.**—Type X I.B.s are to be disposed of two at a time in a pit 3 ft. deep. They should both be initiated by safety fuze placed in the holes left after removing the cork inserts. The length of safety fuze should be sufficient to allow personnel to retire to a safety distance of 200 yards. Even at this distance personnel should be under cover. Bombs of similar delays (*i.e.*, 2 minutes or 4 minutes) should be disposed of together. If there is any failure to detonate, the bombs should not be approached for half an hour after the burning has finished. If partially burned, then a 2-oz. cartridge of Polar blasting gelatine should be used to detonate the C.E. charge *in situ*. Before fitting the charge the bombs must be allowed to cool.

SECTION 1B.—25-LB. INCENDIARY

1. If the safety rod is present it is safe, or if an unopened parachute is present it is safe; otherwise fire the bomb by placing it horizontally in a pit 4 ft. deep and blowing a cartridge of P.B.G. against the junction of the tail unit and the bomb body.

2. A safety distance of 100 yards should be observed.

SECTION 1C.—30-LB. INCENDIARY BOMBS, MARKS I, II, IIM, III, IIIM

1. (*a*) **No. 38 Fuze, Marks I and II.**—(i) The fuze is first to be rendered safe by slackening the locknut, screwing out the striker to its full extent and then tightening the lock nut against the top surface of the cap.

(ii) The fuze is next to be unscrewed from the bomb, having first removed the circlip and nose fairing.

(iii) Demolish the fuze by tamping a length of cordtex securely across the magazine. Adequate safety precautions are to be observed.

(iv) The remains of the fuze are to be collected and reduced to salvage, after ensuring that the detonator in the inertia cap holder has been destroyed.

(v) Should the detonator not be fired, which is most unlikely, it is to be demolished as in paragraph (iii) above.

(*b*) **No. 846, Mark I.**—When bombs fitted with a No. 846, Mark I, fuze, jettisoned or otherwise, become detached from aircraft the fuze is always in a live condition.

Handling and Disposal.—(i) Whenever possible the No. 846 fuze is to be removed from the bomb. During handling prior to and whilst removing the fuze, the bomb is always to be kept in a horizontal or nose-up position and care is to be exercised to ensure that the fuze does not function due to rough handling or any other reason.

(ii) To remove the fuze from the bomb, the nose plug is first to be carefully unscrewed and the pins disengaged from the blind housings in the head of the fuze.

(iii) Before transporting the fuze a transit safety pin is to be inserted in the safety pin channel.

Note.—To insert the transit safety pin hold the fuze horizontally with the safety pin channel uppermost.

(iv) If the magazine ring can be removed easily, the magazine is to be unscrewed and demolished separately at the nearest suitable site, using a length of safety fuze and observing adequate safety precautions. The inertia cap holder is to be demolished at the same time, and the brass fuze body returned for salvage.

(v) If the magazine cannot be removed the fuze is to be demolished at the nearest suitable site by laying a length of cordtex flat across the magazine, securing with insulating tape and detonating. The usual safety precautions are to be observed. It will usually be found that the fuze body, which is thrown several yards by the detonation, can be reduced to salvage.

(c) *Disposal of Bombs.*—(i) 30-lb. incendiary bombs are usually carried on aircraft in 250-lb. small bomb containers, each container holding eight bombs.

(ii) Usually the S.B.C.s are severely damaged on impact and when jettisoned at a low altitude the bombs are generally found scattered about on the surface.

(iii) Occasionally the S.B.C. will be found buried to a depth of 4–5 ft. with the sides of the container crushed in, wedging the bombs firmly inside the wreckage of the container, when the precautions outlined below are to be rigidly observed.

(iv) When all S.B.C.s, reported as having been jettisoned, are accounted for, search for bombs is to be continued until the number found gives the full load of eight per case.

(d) *Precautions During Recovery.*—(i) Personnel handling bombs are to wear damped rubber gloves and rubber boots.

(ii) If jettisoned from a low altitude on soft ground the bombs may sustain only superficial damage to nose fairing and/or tail, and may be fit for return for re-use. A *careful examination* is to be made of each individual bomb before this decision is reached, to ensure that the bomb body has sustained no damage, however slight, which may result in the contents leaking or being exposed to the atmosphere.

(iii) Bombs unfit for return are to be handled with great care since :—
   (a) The bombs are fully armed, ; and
   (b) The filling will ignite spontaneously after a short exposure to air.

(iv) Where digging has to be carried out to uncover damaged containers, rubber boots are to be worn as a protection against contact with pockets of incendiary filling. Such small accumulations of filling, where encountered, are to be covered with earth to prevent their ignition on drying out.

(e) *Handling and Disposal.*—(i) Wherever possible damaged bombs are to be de-fuzed and disposed of *in situ*, the fuzes being dealt with in accordance with the above instructions. Should it be necessary to transport the bomb prior to defuzing and/or disposal, it is to be carried horizontally or nose uppermost.

(ii) If the filling plug at the rear of the bombs can be unscrewed, the bombs are to be emptied into a pit at least 4 ft. deep and the empty bodies also placed in the pit. Not more than eight bombs are to be dealt with at a time.

(iii) The filling is then to be burned under precautions, the fire being initiated by means of a train of paraffin-soaked rag leading into the filling.

(iv) Where it has not been possible to remove any of the filling plugs, burning is to be initiated by means of 2-oz. of P.B.G. inserted in the fuze pocket of one of the bombs. A danger area of 100 yards radius is to be cleared.

(v) Where it has not been possible to remove the fuze from a bomb each bomb is to be demolished separately by means of a 2-oz. of P.B.G. primer, tamped securely against the nose of the bomb, and initiated under precautions, observing a safety distance of at least 100 yards.

(vi) When burning is complete the empty cases are to be removed, the excavation filled in and the surrounding ground examined for any small accumulations of unburned contents ; these, if found, should be collected and burnt.

(vii) It is important that before the empty bomb cases are returned for salvage, all traces of filling be removed, since even after burning small quantities of the contents have been known to remain in the crevices of the bomb case. They are to be allowed to weather in the open for at least 24 hours before removal, providing no damage can result from spontaneous ignition of small particles of phosphorus and finally to be subjected to a steam jet for at least 10 minutes and allowed to weather in the open for at least another 24 hours.

(viii) Where demolition of *damaged bombs* cannot be carried out *in situ* arrangements are to be made for them to be transported, completely immersed in water, to the nearest suitable site.

SECTION 1D.—45-LB. INCENDIARY BOMB, MARK I

1. Small bomb containers will carry three of these bombs.

2. Disposal should be as for the 30-lb. incendiary bomb after it has been defuzed.

N.B.—The filling is spontaneously inflammable, more so than the 30-lb. bomb.

Part II, Chapter II

SECTION 1E.—250-LB. INCENDIARY BOMB, MARK I

1. (i) The No. 36, Mark II, N.D. fuze should first have the safety pillar returned to the correct hole and the vanes taped so that they cannot move. The fuze and ejector charge should then be removed.

(ii) Demolish the fuze and ejector charge, using a length of cordtex taped across the magazine of the fuze. Take full safety precautions.

(iii) Empty the bomb through the filling hole in the base and burn as in the case of the 30-lb. incendiary bomb.

(iv) If the fuze cannot be removed, then a 2-oz. charge of P.B.G. should be fired against the side of the fuze. A safety distance of 100 yards should be observed.

Page 53.
 Section 1E. *After* (iv) *add* "(v) If no safety pin is available and the red groove is not visible, rotate the vanes in an anti-clockwise direction until the red groove is visible and then remove the fuze by hand.

"(vi) Damaged fuzes should be removed by Mark IV extractor, or the bomb demolished as in (iv) above. The fuze should then be demolished as in (ii) above.

"*N.B.*—R.A.F. Implement Ammunition No. 89 fits the locking ring (*see* Appendix to Part II)."
(*U.B. 294/43.—C.A.F.O. P.575/44.*)

...should be taken to prevent the striking of sparks in the vicinity of the bomb, e.g. by the use of metal tools.

2. Disposal usually consists of functioning the bomb

Section 1F. *Before* paragraph 1 *insert* "If clusters containing these bombs disintegrate, then all the bombs in the cluster must be demolished."
(*U.B. 294/43.—C.A.F.O. P.575/44.*)

(*Amendment No. 1.—C.A.F.O. P.464/44.*)

...from the base ...ly 1 minute. ...removed by unscrewing the six retaining screws to facilitate inspection of the position of the safety plunger. The bomb is to be placed on its side during this operation.

4. Where disposal 'in situ' is acceptable, the bomb is to be placed nose down in a pit at least 4 ft. deep with the safety plunger retained in the 'safe' position.

5. Where disposal 'in situ' is not acceptable the safety plunger is to be securely fixed in position either using tape or by means of the retaining ring, before being transported carefully to the nearest suitable site for disposal, and the procedure as outlined in para. 4 above is then to be followed.

6. Each bomb is to be initiated by means of cordtex taped securely across the head of its striker. The safety plunger which is to be retained in the 'safe' position whilst taping the cordtex, is now to be freed.

7. Not more than seven bombs are to be dealt with simultaneously and all detonators are to be wired in series. A safety distance of at least 100 yds, with all personnel 'up wind', is to be observed.

8. Where bombs which cannot be disposed of 'in situ' are found to be leaking from small cracks, the cracks are to be plugged with suitable material (e.g. luting or plasticine) and taped with adhesive tape before transporting them to the nearest suitable site for disposal.

SECTION 1G.—500-lb., MARK I, INCENDIARY BOMB

1. *General.*—(i) The Bomb Incendiary Aircraft, 500 lb., Mark I, containing a special liquid phosphorus filling is described in A.M.I. No. 697.

(ii) Owing to the very high incendiary content of this bomb it will not often be found practicable to demolish it *in situ*.

(iii) Disposal is not to be undertaken within 4 hours of blackout.

(iv) Personnel engaged in the recovery and/or disposal of this bomb are to wear rubber boots and gloves which are to be kept damped. These and any implements which may have come in contact with the phosphorus filling or with impregnated spoil are to be washed thoroughly immediately after use. For this purpose an ample supply of water is to be available throughout disposal operations.

(v) When there is risk of fire to crops or buildings during disposal, arrangements are to be made for the N.F.S. to be in attendance.

2. *Disposal of Surface Bombs.*—(i) Bombs which are apparently intact and undamaged are to be defuzed and returned to await inspection.

Note.—After removal of the pistol, *the bomb must be plugged.*

(ii) If a bomb is too badly damaged for re-use but is not leaking, it is to be defuzed, the detonator removed and the bomb placed in a pit at least 5-ft. deep. It is to be demolished by cordtex placed in the burster charge.

Note.—The excavation is to be backfilled without any attempt being made to salvage the case.

(iii) The demolition site is to be free from inflammable material for a radius of at least 100 yards and a safety distance of at least 200 yards upwind is to be observed with all personnel under and behind adequate cover.

(iv) Due regard is to be paid when arranging for the demolition of this bomb, to the fact that a considerable smoke screen is emitted for at least two hours, its density increasing with the humidity of the atmosphere.

(v) When a surface bomb is found to have *small* leaks, it is to be washed thoroughly with water and the leaks stopped with mud or plasticine and covered with insulating tape before any attempt is made to remove the bomb.

(vi) In exceptional circumstances where the site is completely free from vegetation over a radius of at least 300 yards, the bomb may be demolished on the surface. For such demolition the safety distance is to be increased to 300 yards upwind.

(vii) When it is impossible to defuze a damaged bomb, demolition is to be effected by means of 1 lb. of P.B.G., protected from contact with the surface of the bomb by means of wet paper, wet cloth or similar material.

(viii) If demolition *in situ* is not possible, the bomb, if leaking, is to be transported in the manner described in paragraph 4 below.

3. *Disposal of Buried Bombs.*—(i) Extreme care is to be taken when dealing with a buried 500-lb. incendiary bomb, since, should the case have broken up on impact, liquid phosphorus (which is spontaneously inflammable in contact with air) will have been released.

(ii) Evidence of fracture of the bomb case will be given by the presence of white fumes rising from the shaft and from the smell of phosphorus.

... of the bomb may be carried out under the

9. After all burning has ceased and the bombs are sufficiently cool to be handled, the central tube of the bomb is to be inspected to ensure that all its incendiary filling has burnt.

10. The casing will then be opened either with cordtex of a 2 oz. P.B.G. under normal demolition precautions, the remaining contents poured out, and, where necessary, burnt under precautions

11. The cases are to be allowed to weather for 24 hours before reducing them to salvage.

SECTION 1E.—250-LB. INCENDIARY BOMB, MARK I

1. (i) The No. 36, Mark II, N.D. fuze should first have the safety pillar returned to the correct hole and the vanes taped so that they cannot move. The fuze and ejector charge should then be removed.

(ii) Demolish the fuze and ejector charge, using a length of cordtex taped across the magazine of the fuze. Take full safety precautions.

(iii) Empty the bomb through the filling hole in the base and burn as in the case of the 30-lb. incendiary bomb.

(iv) If the fuze cannot be removed, then a 2-oz. charge of P.B.G. should be fired against the side of the fuze. A safety distance of 100 yards should be observed.

Section 1.F - 30 LB. 'J' TYPE INCENDIARY BOMB

1. The 'J' Incendiary bomb contains a highly volatile, inflammable liquid filling under pressure and fire risk exists therefore over a large area surrounding damaged bombs. Smoking or the presence of naked lights, therefore, is not permitted within 200 yds of the site. In addition, precautions should be taken to prevent the striking of sparks in the vicinity of the bomb, e.g. by the use of metal tools.

2. Disposal usually consists of functioning the bomb normally, when, after a short interval, it emits from the base an intensely hot flame 15 ft. long for approximately 1 minute.

3. The parasheet container, if present, is to be removed by unscrewing the six retaining screws to facilitate inspection of the position of the safety plunger. The bomb is to be placed on its side during this operation.

4. Where disposal 'in situ' is acceptable, the bomb is to be placed nose down in a pit at least 4 ft. deep with the safety plunger retained in the 'safe' position.

5. Where disposal 'in situ' is not acceptable the safety plunger is to be securely fixed in position either using tape or by means of the retaining ring, before being transported carefully to the nearest suitable site for disposal, and the procedure as outlined in para. 4 above is then to be followed.

6. Each bomb is to be initiated by means of cordtex taped securely across the head of its striker. The safety plunger which is to be retained in the 'safe' position whilst taping the cordtex, is now to be freed.

7. Not more than seven bombs are to be dealt with simultaneously and all detonators are to be wired in series. A safety distance of at least 100 yds, with all personnel 'up wind', is to be observed.

8. Where bombs which cannot be disposed of 'in situ' are found to be leaking from small cracks, the cracks are to be plugged with suitable material (e.g. luting or plasticine) and taped with adhesive tape before transporting them to the nearest suitable site for disposal.

SECTION 1G.—500-lb., MARK I, INCENDIARY BOMB

1. *General.*—(i) The Bomb Incendiary Aircraft, 500 lb., Mark I, containing a special liquid phosphorus filling is described in A.M.I. No. 697.

(ii) Owing to the very high incendiary content of this bomb it will not often be found practicable to demolish it *in situ*.

(iii) Disposal is not to be undertaken within 4 hours of blackout.

(iv) Personnel engaged in the recovery and/or disposal of this bomb are to wear rubber boots and gloves which are to be kept damped. These and any implements which may have come in contact with the phosphorus filling or with impregnated spoil are to be washed thoroughly immediately after use. For this purpose an ample supply of water is to be available throughout disposal operations.

(v) When there is risk of fire to crops or buildings during disposal, arrangements are to be made for the N.F.S. to be in attendance.

2. *Disposal of Surface Bombs.*—(i) Bombs which are apparently intact and undamaged are to be defuzed and returned to await inspection.

Note.—After removal of the pistol, *the bomb must be plugged*.

(ii) If a bomb is too badly damaged for re-use but is not leaking, it is to be defuzed, the detonator removed and the bomb placed in a pit at least 5-ft. deep. It is to be demolished by cordtex placed in the burster charge.

Note.—The excavation is to be backfilled without any attempt being made to salvage the case.

(iii) The demolition site is to be free from inflammable material for a radius of at least 100 yards and a safety distance of at least 200 yards upwind is to be observed with all personnel under and behind adequate cover.

(iv) Due regard is to be paid when arranging for the demolition of this bomb, to the fact that a considerable smoke screen is emitted for at least two hours, its density increasing with the humidity of the atmosphere.

(v) When a surface bomb is found to have *small* leaks, it is to be washed thoroughly with water and the leaks stopped with mud or plasticine and covered with insulating tape before any attempt is made to remove the bomb.

(vi) In exceptional circumstances where the site is completely free from vegetation over a radius of at least 300 yards, the bomb may be demolished on the surface. For such demolition the safety distance is to be increased to 300 yards upwind.

(vii) When it is impossible to defuze a damaged bomb, demolition is to be effected by means of 1 lb. of P.B.G., protected from contact with the surface of the bomb by means of wet paper, wet cloth or similar material.

(viii) If demolition *in situ* is not possible, the bomb, if leaking, is to be transported in the manner described in paragraph 4 below.

3. *Disposal of Buried Bombs.*—(i) Extreme care is to be taken when dealing with a buried 500-lb. incendiary bomb, since, should the case have broken up on impact, liquid phosphorus (which is spontaneously inflammable in contact with air) will have been released.

(ii) Evidence of fracture of the bomb case will be given by the presence of white fumes rising from the shaft and from the smell of phosphorus.

(iii) Excavation to within 2 ft. of the bomb may be carried out under the following precautions :—

  (a) The ground is to be kept well drenched with water.
  (b) Personnel engaged in digging are to wear eye-shields, rubber boots and gloves.

(iv) If there is reason to suppose the case has been cracked on impact, the digging is then to be continued by one man only, who is to be equipped with a lifeline.

(v) Further digging is to continue solely with the object of exposing sufficient of the bomb to enable a demolition charge to be placed.

53b

(vi) Having exposed a portion of the surface of the bomb, the P.B.G. is to be placed in position as described in paragraph 2, sub-paragraph (vii) above and the bomb detonated *in situ* electrically.

(vii) When during excavation the ground is found to be impregnated with liquid phosphorus to such an extent as to suggest that the case is badly fractured rather than leaking, the qualified officer is to be guided in his course of action by local conditions.

(viii) If burning *in situ* is permissible four 4-lb. incendiary bombs are to be burned on the floor of the excavation and above the bomb, burning being initiated electrically by means of a low tension igniter placed in one of the vent holes. This will normally have the effect of igniting the phosphorus filling and detonating the burster charge.

Note.—The incendiary bombs are to be bundled together, the low tension igniter inserted and the whole lowered down the shaft.

(ix) No approach is to be made to the excavation until an hour after all signs of burning have ceased, when an inspection is to be carried out.

(x) If detonation of the burster charge has taken place and the filling burnt, the excavation is to be backfilled and no attempt made to salvage the case.

(xi) If detonation has not taken place, further operations are to be postponed for 24 hours, when more spoil is to be carefully removed, work stopping instantly if any considerable fuming begins, and a further waiting time of 24 hours observed. The procedure outlined in sub-paragraph (viii) above will then be repeated.

(xii) If, on the other hand, conditions do not permit this course of action, then the attendance of the N.F.S. on the site is to be arranged before any further steps are taken.

(xiii) Further action will be taken in conjunction with the N.F.S. officer, who is to be made aware of the existence of an explosive charge ($1\frac{1}{2}$ to 2 lb. C.E.T.N.T.) among the remains.

4. *Transport of Damaged Bombs.*—(i) Where damaged bombs have to be transported, the bomb is first to be defuzed and plugged.

(ii) It is then to be transported to the nearest demolition site *completely immersed in water* and protected against rolling.

(iii) A small portable N.F.S. dam affords an excellent medium, if no other facility exists.

(iv) Throughout the loading and unloading involved, the personnel engaged are to wear anti-gas suits in addition to rubber gloves and boots. If contamination is suspected all the above articles are to be kept moist with water until they can be thoroughly washed in hot water to which a small quantity of washing soda has been added.

(*T. 06720/44.—C.A.F.O. P.6/45.*)

SECTION 2A.—4-LB. SMOKE BOMB

If all safety devices present, it can be moved, otherwise demolish *in situ* with a 2-oz. P.B.G. charge on the Safety distance 50 yards.

SECTION 2B.—100-LB. SMOKE BOMB

Disposal as for the 4-lb. bomb. Safety distance 100 yards.

SECTION 2C.—120-LB. SMOKE BOMB

(*a*) **No. 864 Nose Fuze.**—(i) First render the fuze safe by slackening the locknut, screwing out the striker to its full extent and then tightening the locknut against the top surface of the fuzecap.

(ii) Next unscrew and remove the fuze from the bomb.

(iii) Demolish the fuze by tamping a length of cordtex securely across the magazine.

(iv) Should the detonator not be fired, it should be demolished as in (iii) above.

(*b*) **The Bomb.**—(i) After removal of the fuze the bomb should be placed horizontally in a pit 4 ft. deep. A 2-oz. cartridge of P.B.G. should be placed in the fuze pocket and fired. Safety distance at least 150 yards. Allow the smoke emission to finish before approaching the bomb.

(ii) If the fuze cannot be removed the procedure in (*b*) (i) should be followed except that the charge of P.B.G. should be placed against the side of the fuze and tamped.

(iii) If the inner smoke container is found by itself, it should be initiated by firing a 2-oz. cartridge of P.B.G. across the nose of the container. Safety distance should be 50 yards.

SECTION 2D.—500-LB. SMOKE BOMB

Treat No. 30 tail pistol as indicated in Part II, Chapter I. The bomb should be demolished in a pit with safety distance of 200 yards. Make sure that the smoke will not cause trouble before proceeding.

(*T. 06720/44.—C.A.F.O. P.6/45.*)

SECTION 3.—SMOKE AND FLASH 10-lb. AND 11½-lb., 8½-lb. BREAK-UP SMOKE BOMB

1. If undamaged and all safety devices are present, the bomb may be moved.

2. *Disposal.*—Where a damaged bomb is recovered with all its safety devices present, it is to be disposed of in the following manner :—
   (a) The grub screw securing the nose to the body is to be removed and the nose section unscrewed, holding the bomb horizontal throughout.
   (b) The bomb is then to be carefully placed in a pit 3 ft. deep and the 28 detonator burster demolished, using a Briska detonator taped across its head.

3. Where the bomb is recovered with the safety devices missing and/or the bomb is badly damaged, it is normally to be destroyed *in situ*.
   (a) A 2-oz. P.B.G. cartridge is to be tamped securely on the bomb body approximately 3 in. to the rear of the suspension lug and detonated by means of cordtex.

4. If it is impracticable to destroy the bomb *in situ* it may be carried carefully in a horizontal position to the nearest available site and destroyed as in 3 (a) above.

5. In all cases a safety distance of 50 yards is to be observed with all personnel under and behind adequate protection.

6. Where the practice flash is to be disposed of, the safety distance is to be increased to 100 yards.

SECTION 4A.—SMOKE FLOATS, AIRCRAFT, No. 1, MARK IV

1. If the store appears to be undamaged and intact, it should be retained for A.I.D. inspection. If, however, its condition is such that it is not considered capable of re-use, the procedure outlined below is to be followed:—

Disposal.—(i) Remove the grub screw and take out the pistol.

(ii) Place the store nose downwards in a shallow pit and demolish with a Briska detonator placed in the aperture left by the removal of the pistol.

(iii) A safety distance of at least 50 yards is to be observed.

(iv) The pit is not to be approached for 20 minutes after smoke has ceased to be emitted.

(v) The store is to be reduced to salvage.

Note 1.—The pistol, if undamaged, is to be handed to the R.A.F. or F.A.A.

Note 2.—Should the pistol not be present, the brass sealing disc is to be removed and the procedure outlined in paragraph 2, sub-paragraph (ii), (iii), (iv) and (v) above is to be followed.

SECTION 4B.—SMOKE FLOAT No. 2, MARKS I AND II

1. Before disposing of these floats make sure that the smoke produced will not inconvenience. Remember that the smoke produced will give a smoke cloud 1,000 yards long by 200 ft. square. Time of emission is 8–10 minutes.

2. *Disposal.*—(i) Remove the fuze or pistol and take to a convenient site.

(ii) Place an electric igniter down the fuze cavity on to the primer and fire it.

SECTION 4C.—SMOKE FLOAT No. 3, MARK I

These should be fired as in the instructions for use, taking care that the smoke produced will not cause inconvenience.

SECTION 5.—SMOKE GENERATORS

These should be fired as in the instructions for use, with the exception of No. 6, Mark II, which is fired by removing the safety pin, if present, and tapping the striker head, which protrudes from the base of the generator, with a hammer.

SECTION 6A.—FLAME FLOATS, MARK II, AND No. 4, MARK I, AND FLAME FLOAT, MESSAGE CARRYING, MARK I

1. Sever wires securing the body to the inner container and remove inner container from the body.

2. Pierce the sealing cup in the rear of the float, using the punch attached to the tail unit.

3. Punch a hole in the side of the container below the buoyancy chamber, *i.e.*, so as to give direct access to the calcium phosphide.

4. Place the float in a pail full of water and allow to burn out at a safe distance.

Note.—Though the stipulated burning time is 6 minutes, this store continues to emit flames for at least $2\frac{1}{4}$ hours. Disposal of the store should not normally be commenced, therefore, unless at least 3 hours daylight remains before " black-out " time.

SECTION 6B.—FLAME FLOAT No. 3, MARK I, AND MARKER MARINE, AIRCRAFT, MARK I AND MARK II

1. Remove sealing discs and place in water sufficient to allow them to float. In the case of the No. 3, Mark I, the rupture disc should be broken by pulling the ring or pushing the pillar sideways.

2. Leave to burn out at a safe distance.

3. When the flame is extinguished leave to weather in the open for 24 hours.

N.B.—Allow four times the normal burning time when disposing.

SECTION 6C.—MARKER MARINE, MARK III, 21-LB.

1. Unscrew the screw-on cover on the nose and remove the clockwork delay mechanism.

2. Remove the press cap at the tail end.

3. Proceed as in Section 6B.

N.B.—If undamaged, the store may be returned to nearest R.A.F. or F.A.A. station.

SECTION 7.—SEA MARKERS

1. *Marks I and V.*—Place in a pit and burst. Fill in the pit, saturating the ground with water.

2. *Mark III.*—Treat as a practice bomb, except that if safety devices are not present the 2-oz. P.B.G. charge should be placed against the striker head.

SECTION 8.—FLARES

1. It is of the utmost importance that the difference in appearance between flares and flashes should be clearly understood. These stores are similar in external appearance, but the flash explodes violently and can be a source of considerable danger.

2. The flash can be distinguished from the flare externally by the word "FLASH" stencilled on the body near the nose and on late issues by the bright red tail end of the body.

3. The flash contains no parachute and, in the absence of external distinguishing marks and if any doubt exists, the closing dome should be removed and the inside examined. If there is neither parachute *NOR shackle* and the press cap and overseal are visible the suspected store is a flash.

4. If a shackle and candle are visible it is a flare from which the parachute has become detached.

"Flare, Aircraft, Skymarker, 25 lb. Mark I White Drip"

5. *Disposal.*—Flares, aircraft reconnaissance, target and training.

   (a) Whenever possible the parachutes attached to the flares are to be salvaged intact and returned to service.

   Note.—In the case of the 4-in. training flares, the suspension ropes are on no account to be pulled away from the flare as this will actuate the striker and cause ignition.

   (b) DO NOT remove fuze.

   (c) Place the flare in a pit at least 3 ft. deep.

   (d) Ignite by means of a 2-oz. P.B.G. charge placed against nose.

   (e) Observe full safety precautions.

Part II, Chapter II

SECTION 9A.—PHOTOGRAPHIC FLASH, MARKS I AND II

(*Read* Section 8 on flares which gives the distinguishing features.)

1. *Disposal.*—As for flares, but the safety precautions must be more carefully observed. Where possible, demolish *in situ* and always keep at a safety distance of 100 yards under cover when disposing of these bombs. Only in cases of vital importance should these bombs be moved.

SECTION 9B.—HEAVY FLASH, PHOTOGRAPHIC, 6·5 IN.

1. If the safety devices of the Fuze, M. 111, are present the fuze may be unscrewed by hand after putting tape round the safety segments.

2. If any safety devices are missing the flash should be demolished *in situ* or, if essential to prevent an explosion, the fuze may be removed by remote control, using the Mark IV extractor.

C.A.F.O. P.6/45

Add new page 62 :—

SECTION 10.—BOMB, AIRCRAFT, T.I., 250 LB.

1. Where possible, the damaged bomb is to be defuzed and the fuze destroyed by firing cordtex across the magazine.

(ii) The tail unit is to be removed and the bomb placed in a narrow pit 4 ft. deep and at least 6 ft. long, with the nose of the bomb close to one end of the pit.

(iii) A 1-oz. primer is to be placed in the fuze pocket in contact with the burster charge and initiated by means of a No. 27 or No. 33 detonator. A safety distance of 150 yards with all personnel under and behind adequate cover is to be observed.

(iv) No approach is to be made to the site until 30 minutes after all signs of burning have ceased.

(v) Should any unburnt filling remain after the above disposal it is to be collected and placed in a separate pit and burnt remotely.

(vi) Initiation will be effected by means of a 1¼-lb. incendiary bomb across the top of which is a No. 27 detonator (to which a foot length of safety fuze is attached) has been securely taped.

Note.—This will not apply to contents for which disposal instructions have been issued separately.

(vii) Where it is impossible to remove a fuze, demolition is to be effected by means of a 1-oz. primer carefully tamped against the fuze and the procedure outlined in sub-paragraphs (ii) to (vi) above, is to be followed.

2. *Tracer.*—(i) Consequent upon the introduction of this store it is essential when dealing with bombs, aircraft, T.I., that a thorough search is made for the tail unit to check the presence of the tracer.

(ii) Normally the tracer will be found still attached to the tail unit, in which case it is to be disposed of without being removed from the tail unit.

(iii) With the tail unit securely anchored, the tracer is to be functioned remotely by means of a length of cord (about 10 yards) attached to the drill plate of the ball cage.

(iv) Where the tracer is badly damaged and it is impossible to function it in the manner described in sub-paragraph (ii) above, it is to be initiated by means of a 1¼-lb. incendiary placed in contact with the damaged igniter.

(v) A safety distance of 20 yards is to be observed immediately after initiation.

SECTION 10.—BOMB, AIRCRAFT, T.I., 250 LB.—HANDLING AND DISPOSAL

1. (i) Where it is possible to empty the bomb, the fuze is to be removed first and dealt with in accordance with paragraph 2 of this section. The burster charge is to be extracted and demolished separately by inserting a length of safety fuze into the bag.

(ii) The shear rivets holding the tail plate in position are next to be removed, the tail plate taken off, and the candles and primed cambric disc removed and burnt.

(iii) Where the No. 1 or No. 2 bomb " White " is involved, the " X " type incendiaries are to be demolished separately and the other incendiaries dealt with as the 4 lb. incendiary bomb.

(iv) For the other series of this store the explosive candles are to be segregated from the non-explosive type and burnt two at a time, using a Briska detonator secured to the primed cambric strip and millboard washer of one of the candles. A safety distance of at least 50 yards is to be observed, and all personnel are to be under adequate cover. Non-explosive candles are to be burnt, using a 1¼-lb. incendiary as initiator. When in doubt all candles must be treated as explosive.

(v) Where the bomb body is so damaged that it is not possible to remove the candles, the fuze is to be carefully removed and the bomb placed *horizontally* in a suitable pit at least 4 ft. deep, with the nose of the bomb towards the firing point.

(vi) A 2-oz. P.B.G. charge is to be securely tamped inside the burster container in contact with the burster charge and detonated using Cordtex.

WARNING.—A safety distance of at least 100 yards is to be observed, and the site is to be free from inflammable material over that distance. All personnel are to be under adequate cover.

(vii) Where the fuze cannot be removed demolition is to be effected by means of a 2-oz. P.B.G. charge securely tamped against the fuze.

(viii) The bomb case is to be reduced to salvage.

2. The 860 fuze, which is used in this bomb, should be dealt with as folllows :—

   (i) Wherever practicable, the 860 fuze is to be unscrewed from the bomb by hand. No spanners or other implements are to be used.

   (ii) If the fuze is undamaged, the arming vane cover still in position, and the waterproof disc over the base of the magazine intact, the fuze is to be returned for A.I.D. inspection.

   (iii) Before returning for inspection, the screw in the safety pin hole is to be replaced by the appropriate pin, if available, or by wire of suitable diameter as a temporary safety precaution.

   (iv) If the arming vane cover is missing, or the waterproof disc broken, or, if the safety pin cannot easily be replaced, the fuze magazine and cap are to be demolished by firing a length of Cordtex taped in position against the disc of the magazine, observing adequate safety precautions.

   (v) The remainder of the fuze is to be reduced to salvage.

3. If any other fuze is used in this bomb, the fuze should not be removed and the bomb should be demolished *in situ*, using a 2-oz. P.B.G. charge tamped against the side of the fuze.

Part II, Chapter II

SECTION 11.—FUZES AND PISTOLS USED IN FLARES, PHOTOGRAPHIC FLASHES AND T.I. 250-LB. BOMB

(*See* Sections 8–10.)

SECTION 12.—MISCELLANEOUS

(*a*) **Calibrator, Altimeter Flash, Mark I.**—Unscrew the striker and put it in the safe positioning hole. The cartridges may then be removed.

(*b*)

SECTION 13.—INCENDIARIES AND PYROTECHNICS ON BOARD SHIP

1. These may in general be dealt with by lowering over the side and dumping in deep water. In the case of floats the buoyancy chambers should first be pierced.

2. The appropriate section of Sections 1–12 should be read to see whether danger is involved in moving the store, and any necessary precautions should then be observed. Also care should be taken to see that the disposal of smoke or flame floats or smoke bombs cannot be interpreted as a signal.

CHAPTER III

DEPTH CHARGES DROPPED FROM AIRCRAFT

1. Depth charges are safe to defuze if :—
   (a) They have never been submerged—pistol live or safe.
   (b) They have never been in any depth of water greater than 10 ft.—pistol live or safe.

2. In any depth of water greater than 10 ft. the depth charges cannot always be considered safe, even if they were dropped with the safety clip in position. *(Except for mk XX Pistol (Para 4))*
   The reasons for this are :—
   (a) Some safety clips jump off on impact with the water.
   (b) The Mark XIII pistols, which, although becoming obsolete, are still in use, depend upon keeping water out of a cavity. They cannot be relied upon to do this, because of possible distortion on impact.

3. If the pistol is visible, *e.g.*, if the depth charge is exposed at low water, then the presence or otherwise of the safety clip can be established and the type of pistol can be determined. If the clip is present and the pistol is *not* a Mark XIII, then the pistol may be removed, otherwise the depth charge should be demolished *in situ* or if detonation is undesirable, it may be towed to a suitable demolition site from a safe distance. If the latter procedure is adopted, it must be with the full knowledge that detonation may occur when the depth charge is moved.

   In defuzing :—

   Note.—No force is to be used in removing the pistol.

   (i) Remove the locking ring. Turn the bayonet joint washer and remove the pistol. The locking ring requires a 6161 or 6588 spanner, St. No., or a fuze key, Mark II (for German bomb) can be used. (*See* Appendix to Part II.)
      N.B.—Spanner, St. No. 6588, can be used with the depth charge tail in position.

   (ii) Remove grub screw and unscrew the detonator holder. (*See* Fig. 1, Chapter 3, Part I.)

   (iii) Remove the primer, using a spanner St. No. 5714 if available, otherwise tip the depth charge. (*See* Appendix to Part II.)

4. If the arming wire of the Mark II pistol can be seen and is present, the D.C. may be considered safe at any depth. It can be moved and the pistol removed.

(*Amendment No. 2.—C.A.F.O. P.575/44.*)

CHAPTER IV

AIRCRAFT LAID MINES

The responsibility for rendering safe British aircraft mines which have been jettisoned or have otherwise become detached from aircraft or are present in crashed aircraft, rests with the Land Incident Section of the Admiralty (D.T.M.).

Until instructions are issued in these notes, in cases of extreme emergency, B.S.O.s who are called upon to deal with these mines should refer to C.B. 4105 for the detailed instructions or, if it is available, the more recent C.B. 3115(1) of 1943.

CHAPTER V

SECTION 1.—ROCKET SHELL

DISPOSAL OF ROCKET DEVICES

Section	Page
1.—Rocket Shell	
A.—H.E.	69
(i) " U " 5-in. Rocket Shell.	
(ii) 60-lb. S.A.P. Rocket Shell.	
(iii) 2-in. Rocket, Marks I, II and III.	
B.—Incendiary	69
C.—Smoke	69

SECTION 1A (i).—DISPOSAL OF ROCKET SHELLS

1. Whenever possible this is to be done by demolishing *in situ*.

   (a) *Blind Rounds on the Surface.*—If on inspection it is found that the striker pressure plate is flush with the top of the striker housing, then the striker has either failed to function, or it may have pierced the detonator and having failed to fire, returned to the " out " position under the influence of the striker spring. If, on the other hand, the striker pressure plate is " in " in the position shown in the diagram, then it is probable that the striker has pierced the detonator and having failed to fire, has become jammed in that position. In whichever position the fuze is found it must be regarded as extremely sensitive.

   (b) If it is not possible to demolish *in situ* then either :—
      (i) Remove the missile by dragging, or transporting it under full precaution, remembering that if it has to be lifted it should not be up-ended, should be kept horizontal and not subjected to jolts.
      (ii) Remove fuze, using the Mark IV extractor, under full precautions. The missile will probably have to be secured to a spar with a Spanish windlass to prevent turning.

   (c) *Blind Rounds Partially Buried.*—If not possible to uncover the shell partially and place detonating charge alongside it, an attempt to pull the missile clear (from under cover from a distance) with a rope round the tail of rocket can be tried. Then carry on as for a missile on the surface.

   (d) If only a hole is found and the shell or whole rocket has dug in, an attempt to open up the hole (under the usual precautions) with a 4-oz. charge placed down the hole can be tried.

Warning

2. When several unexploded 5-in. rocket shells are close together, either below the surface or on the surface, it must be remembered that the demolition of one might cause the fuse of another to fire.

SECTION 1A (ii).—60-LB. S.A.P. ROCKET SHELL

Disposal.—Should any blind rounds of this projectile be found, they are to be treated in the same way as any other blind H.E. shell, with an additional precaution that the shell should be given a jerk test under precaution, as this fuze has a long needle striker which, if already embedded in the cap, might fire on being shaken free; the shell would then detonate after the very short delay period.

SECTION 1A (iii).—DISPOSAL OF 2-IN. ROCKET, MARKS I, II AND III

1. *Ashore.*—If digging is necessary the greatest care must be taken not to allow any pressure to be exerted on the nose. Demolition must be *in situ* except in very exceptional circumstances, the charge being placed against the shell and not against the propellant portion.

If removal is absolutely necessary, carry the rocket in the horizontal position. When withdrawing it from the hole of entry, the arming cap must not be allowed to move in or out, nor must it be allowed to rotate.

2. *Afloat.*—Tape the arming vanes carefully in position without moving them in any way and carry as above and lower carefully over side, below water, before slipping.

SECTION 1B.—" U " 5-IN. INCENDIARY SHELL

Disposal.—This shell will be found under similar conditions to the " U " 5-in., 29-lb., H.E. shell, and should be disposed of in a similar manner.

SECTION 1C.—" U " 5-IN. SMOKE SHELL

Disposal.—As for " U " 5-in. rocket incendiary shell.

CHAPTER VI

DISPOSAL OF MISCELLANEOUS DEVICES

Section   *Page*

1.—Mortars for Use from Landing Craft   71
    (*a*) Hedgerow.
    (*b*) Unicorn.

SECTION 1 (a).—DISPOSAL OF "HEDGEROW"

1. Blind rounds of the "Hedgerow" can be caused in mainly three ways:—
    (a) Failure of spigot ejecting charge.
    (b) Fuze failure.
    (c) Round being deflected by detonation of near-by charge and not falling nose first.

2. In the case of (a) blind rounds are immediately dumped overboard and may wash ashore or be uncovered at low water.

3. In the case of (b) and (c) may mean that as the charge has not detonated live rounds can be expected in the immediate vicinity, and before approach is made it is well to check the pattern of the minefield, or better still, sweep with mine detector. When it is established that clear path exists, detonate round *in situ* by placing charge against side of nose where nose stick enters body of round.

4. Remember at all times that the fuze is very sensitive and if it must be carried away it should be done by carrying tail downwards or horizontally, taking great care not to touch red nose cap in any way.

SECTION 1 (b).—DISPOSAL OF 35-LB. UNICORN

As this weapon is used for anti-submarine warfare, it is unlikely that blind rounds will be washed ashore, but should such a round be found washed ashore, it should, if possible, be demolished *in situ*; but if it must be moved, it is quite practicable to remove the fuze with the Mark IV extractor, under suitable precautions, taking care not to touch the conical copper nose cap which covers the striker.

Care should be taken not to damage the charge case, as it is quite thin and a dent may result in the filling being pinched at the bottom edge of the Beehive cone which joins the main body at its widest part.

APPENDIX

SPANNER, KEYS, ETC.

(*See* Figs. 1 and 2.)

The diagrams are intended to give the general appearance of the keys and are not accurate in detail. All the keys have their numbers clearly stamped on them, so that rough recognition can be checked immediately by inspecting the key.

Implement Ammunition. No. 111 (Fig. 1).—Used for the No. 30 fuze locking ring in the S.A.P., Mark III, bombs.

Implement Ammunition. No. 134 (Fig. 1).—Used for the No. 30 fuze locking ring in the S.A.P., Mark IV, bombs. This key is similar to the No. 111.

Implement Ammunition. No. 106 (Fig. 1).—Used for the tail locking ring in the S.A.P., Mark III, bombs.

Implement Ammunition. No. 89 (Fig. 1).—Used for the locking ring in No. 32 fuze in the A.S., Mark III, bombs.

Implement Ammunition. No. 129 (Fig. 1).—Used for the No. 37 fuze locking ring in the A.P. 2,000-lb. bomb.

Implement Ammunition. No. 104 (Fig. 1).—Used for holding the body of a No. 32 fuze. Also used for No. 845 fuze.

Implement Ammunition. No. 126 (Fig. 1).—Used for setting the delay in the No. 32 fuze.

R.A.F. Implement Ammunition. No. 208 and 209 (Fig. 2).—Used for the No. 862 fuze in the A.S. 600-lb. bomb.

Admiralty Pattern No. S.T. 6161 (Fig. 2).—Used for the locking ring of the pistol in the depth-charges carried in aircraft.

Admiralty Pattern No. S.T. 6588 (figure forwarded later).—Used for the locking ring of the pistol in the depth-charges carried in aircraft.

Admiralty Pattern No. S.T. 5714 (Fig. 2).—Used for removing the primer from depth-charges.

R.A.F. Implement Ammunition. Detonator Extractor No. 2, Mark I (Fig. 2).—Used for removing the normal detonators used with pistols in H.E. bombs. The feet are fitted inside the head of the detonator and spring out under a ridge on the inside of the detonator head.

R.A.F. Implement Ammunition. Detonator Extractor No. 4, Mark I (Fig. 2).—The feet only are shown in the diagram. The rest of the extractor is like the No. 2, Mark I. Used for removing the D.38 detonator which is fitted when a No. 845 fuze is used. The thin head of detonator is held between the two turned-in strips of the feet.

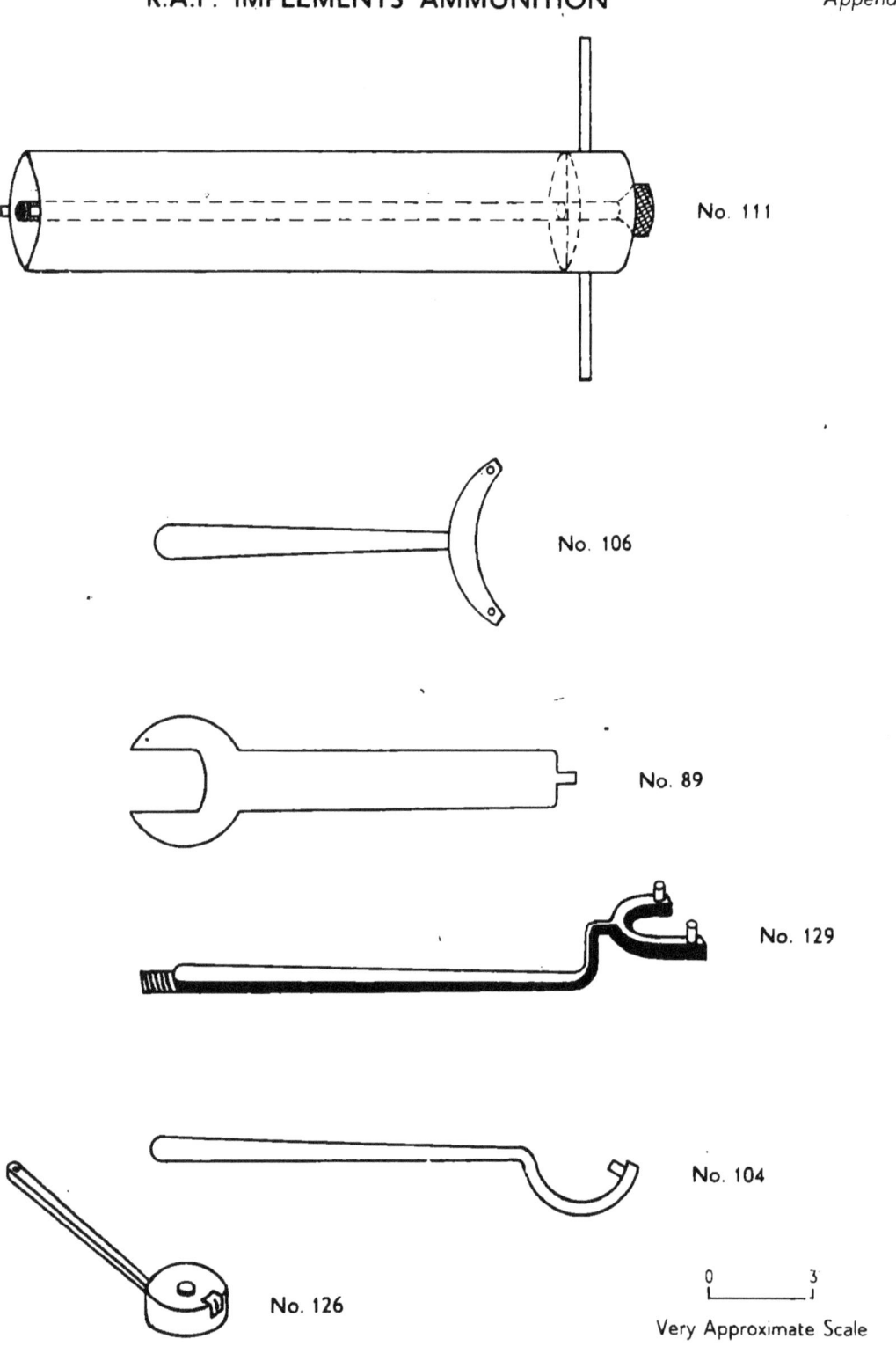

Fig. 1

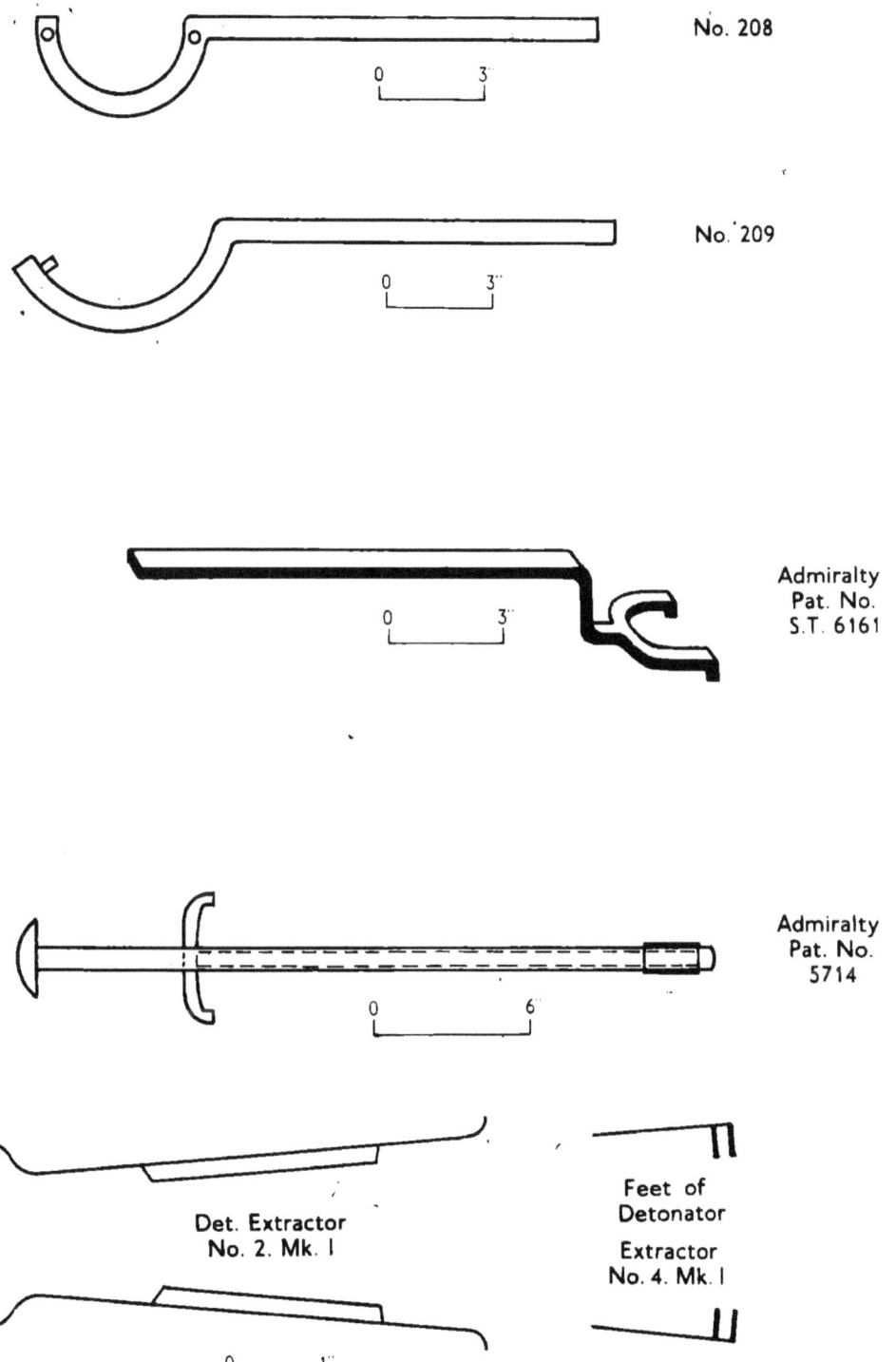

Fig. 2

www.ingramcontent.com/pod-product-compliance
Lightning Source LLC
Chambersburg PA
CBHW080806300426
44114CB00020B/2847